Refiguring Refiguring English Studies provides a forum for scholarship on English Studies as a discipline, a profession, and **ENGLISH** a vocation. To that end, the series publishes historical **STUDIES** work that considers the ways in which English Studies has constructed itself and its objects of study; investigations of the relationships among its constituent parts as conceived in both disciplinary and institutional terms; and examinations of the role the discipline has played or should play in the larger society and public policy. In addition, the series seeks to feature studies that, by their form or focus, challenge our notions about how the written "work" of English can or should be done and to feature writings that represent the professional lives of the discipline's members in both traditional and nontraditional settings. The series also includes scholarship that considers the discipline's possible futures or that draws upon work in other disciplines to shed light on developments in English Studies.

Volumes in the Series

David B. Downing, editor, *Changing Classroom Practices: Resources for Literary and Cultural Studies* (1994)

Jed Rasula, *The American Poetry Wax Museum: Reality Effects, 1940–1990* (1995)

James A. Berlin, *Rhetorics, Poetics, and Cultures: Refiguring College English Studies* (1996)

Robin Varnum, *Fencing with Words: A History of Writing Instruction at Amherst College during the Era of Theodore Baird, 1938–1966* (1996)

Jane Maher, *Mina P. Shaughnessy: Her Life and Work* (1997)

Michael Blitz and C. Mark Hurlbert, *Letters for the Living: Teaching Writing in a Violent Age* (1998)

Representing the "Other"

Basic Writers and the
Teaching of Basic Writing

Bruce Horner
Drake University

Min-Zhan Lu
Drake University

National Council of Teachers of English
1111 W. Kenyon Road, Urbana, Illinois 61801-1096

Staff Editor: Kurt Austin

Interior Design: Tom Kovacs for TGK Design

Cover Design and Illustration: Evelyn C. Shapiro

NCTE Stock Number: 41153-3050

It is the policy of NCTE in its journals and other publications to provide a forum for the open discussion of ideas concerning the content and the teaching of English and the language arts. Publicity accorded to any particular point of view does not imply endorsement by the Executive Committee, the Board of Directors, or the membership at large, except in announcements of policy, where such endorsement is clearly specified.

Library of Congress Cataloging-in-Publication Data

Horner, Bruce, 1957–
    Representing the "other": basic writers and the teaching of basic writing/Bruce Horner, Min-Zhan Lu.
        p.   cm.—(Refiguring English studies)
    Includes bibliographical references (p.   ) and index.
    ISBN 0-8141-4115-3 (pbk.)
    1. English language—Rhetoric—Study and teaching. 2. Basic writing (Remedial education) I. Lu, Min-Zhan, 1946–   II. Title. III. Series.
PE1404.H665 1999
808'.042'07—dc21   98-43798
                                                                                        CIP

*To Robert and Shirley Horner
and to the memory of P. K. and Daisy Loh*

Permissions

The following essays originally appeared in other publications. Grateful acknowledgment is made to the publishers for permission to reprint.

"The 'Birth' of 'Basic Writing'" is an expanded version of "Discoursing Basic Writing," originally published in *College Composition and Communication* 47 (1996), pages 199–222. Copyright©1996 by the National Council of Teachers of English.

"Conflict and Struggle: The Enemies or Preconditions of Basic Writing?" originally appeared in *College English* 54 (1992), pages 887–913. Copyright©1992 by the National Council of Teachers of English.

"Redefining the Legacy of Mina Shaughnessy: A Critique of the Politics of Linguistic Innocence" originally appeared in the *Journal of Basic Writing* 10.1 (Spring 1991), pages 26–40. Copyright©1991 by the *Journal of Basic Writing*, Instructional Resource Center, Office of Academic Affairs, The City University of New York. Reprinted by permission.

"Mapping Errors and Expectations for Basic Writing: From the 'Frontier Field' to 'Border Country'" originally appeared in *English Education* 26 (1994), pages 29–51. Copyright©1994 by the National Council of Teachers of English.

"Re-thinking the 'Sociality' of Error: Teaching Editing as Negotiation" originally appeared in *Rhetoric Review* 11 (1992): 172–99.

"Professing Multiculturalism: The Politics of Style in the Contact Zone" is an expanded version of an essay originally published in *College Composition and Communication* 45 (1994), pages 442–58. Copyright©1994 by the National Council of Teachers of English.

"Some Afterwords: Intersections and Divergences" presents some of the arguments originally published in "Students, Authorship, and the Work of Composition" in *College English* 59 (1997), pages 505–29. Copyright©1997 by the National Council of Teachers of English.

Contents

Acknowledgments

Work on this book was supported by grants from the Drake University Center for the Humanities, the Drake University Office of the Provost, and by the University of Iowa Center for Advanced Studies. We are grateful for the research assistance of Professor Paul Perkus of the City University of New York Central Office Library and Archives and Professor Barbara Dunlap, Chief of City College of New York Archives and Special Collections of the City University of New York. Thanks to Gesa Kirsch for suggesting we bring our book manuscript to Michael Greer at NCTE, and thanks to Michael for his expert guidance in seeing the book through to completion.

We received encouragement and thoughtful, helpful, generous readings of earlier versions of the work presented here from David Bartholomae, Patricia Bizzell, Gary Calpas, Bruce Campbell, David Foster, Thomas Fox, Joseph Harris, Anne Herrington, Glynda Hull, Joseph Lenz, Cynthia Lewis, Bruce Martin, Susan Miller, Elizabeth Robertson, Duane Roen, Mike Rose, James Seitz, Ira Shor, Mary Soliday, Nancy Sommers, Marilyn Sternglass, Patricia Lambert Stock, Thom Swiss, Susan Wall, and graduate students and faculty at the University of Washington. Thanks to all of them for showing us the best of what it can mean to read and write.

We want to thank our former colleagues at the University of Pittsburgh, especially David Bartholomae, for showing us the possibility and value of doing this work, and our colleagues at Drake University for giving us the support to attempt it.

Our thanks to all our students, past and present, for teaching us what matters in writing.

Finally, thanks to Yvonne for teaching us the meaning of schooling for others.

Introduction

Bruce Horner

Min-Zhan Lu

The essays collected in this volume participate in an ongoing debate over how best to represent basic writers and basic writing. Our essays perform cultural materialist readings of discursive practices in basic writing, foregrounding the specific sociopolitical and intellectual contexts of both the production and reception of a discourse dominating the field ("Basic Writing") and the social and political effects of its operation on a range of diverse research and teaching practices concerned with the education of students labeled "basic writers."[1] We map the central problematics, key terms, questions, and assumptions constituting the "foundation" of that discourse, operating to give the field unity and continuity by privileging some while marginalizing other practices. We consider the ways in which cultural materialist readings of basic writing might inform present and future research and teaching practices aimed at addressing the mediation of power relations in such practices.

In 1977, Mina Shaughnessy wrote, "Wherever the new students have arrived in substantial numbers English teachers have begun to realize that little in their background has prepared them to teach writing to someone who has not already learned how to do it" (*Errors and Expectations* 121). Understanding themselves to be in a "new" situation, teachers and researchers of writing have attempted to understand and address the specific needs of their students. They have investigated the characteristics of these students, developed pedagogies for them, and subjected these characterizations and pedagogies to ongoing critical review. Of a wealth of practices and projects addressing such concerns, some have emerged as dominant, constituting a canon of research methodology, pedagogies, and programs. Although critics have pointed out that the history of remedial education did not begin with the Open Admissions movements of the 1960s and 1970s, this discourse of Basic Writing has largely been treated as *new*, beginning with the founding of the

Journal of Basic Writing in 1975 and identified with work disseminated mostly in that journal and in NCTE publications and conferences. We map this hegemonic process to investigate the problematics of Basic Writing: how and why some questions and practices have come to seem central and others peripheral or irrelevant to Basic Writing.

In our essays, we trace Basic Writing's selection of certain terms as "key," certain questions to be pursued at the expense of others, certain pedagogies as "practical" or "effective," and we examine the political effects of such selections, showing how the New discourse denies the interrelationship of its discursive practice with the specific social and historical contexts of its production and reception. For this "New" discourse emerged in the context of a range of positions on the nature and goal of higher education during the 1960s and '70s taken by public officials, college faculty, university administrators, college students, parents of students and prospective students, figures in the public media, and established "writers" from minority ethnic or racial groups. We analyze the "birth" of Basic Writing in relation to the spectrum of political positions ranging from the far right to the far left, renewing, defending, or challenging prior positions on college admissions standards, "Bonehead English," and the role of higher education in society. The New discourse of Basic Writing thus represents one among many in a discursive *field*, emerging in response to what Robert Lyons, describing the genesis of Mina Shaughnessy's *Errors and Expectations,* has termed "the most contentious issue in higher education in New York, . . . at a college [City College] where feelings about this issue were particularly intense" ("Mina Shaughnessy and the Teaching of Writing" 6).

The New discourse speaks to the efforts and success of teachers dedicated to the education of "basic writers" to find a voice and establish authority for themselves through gaining legitimacy as an academic discipline. Positioned within a constellation of discourses constituting other fields within and without English Studies (literary studies, literacy studies, linguistics, sociology, educational psychology), it participates in the general disciplinary project of producing and regulating the movement of knowledge, the forms of language, and the training of minds. Specifically, it treats its statements as (purely) descriptive rather than (also) constitutive of the subject Basic Writing, focusing attention on the need to "get the job done," to understand the "meaning" of the writing produced by Basic Writers and to generate "new readings" of the students and their writing, thus drawing attention away from its role in defining the social and institutional position of Basic Writing. In seeming to try merely to discover, define, and understand the needs and problems of basic writers, it de-emphasizes the function of the teacher/researcher's choice of perspective, methods, and language in constructing those "needs" and "problems," in controlling the judgments and responses of students and teachers, and in aligning the teaching of Basic Writing with other power formations within English studies, American higher education, and society at large. However, the terms by which this discourse establishes itself, while ensuring it a specific kind of legitimacy and authority, simultaneously isolate it from the heterogeneity of positions and forms of power in the larger discursive field. In establishing itself as an "academic" discourse, it has risked becoming "merely academic"—participating in a tradition of separating the academic from the social and historical. We use recent challenges to the dominance of this "New" discourse in the field of basic writing to illustrate the need for those of us professing basic writing to attend to the ways in which social historical discursive constraints mediate our efforts to challenge the hegemonic position of Basic Writing within English Studies and American higher education and society. We should neither underestimate opposition nor overlook the full range of alliances which we might mobilize in our struggle to challenge the existing distribution of power, nor the often complex and contradictory pressures on our choice of alignments. By recognizing the heterogeneity of basic writing at any given time and place, teachers can draw on the full range of positions and forces—dominant, alternative, and oppositional as well as residual or emergent—with some of which we might align ourselves and with all of which we must contend.

Our analyses are built upon several assumptions about the relationship between language, power, and subjectivity: (1) a notion of discourse as a form of material practice operating through a grid of terms and questions to establish a body of knowledge, define a particular subject, and construct particular relationships between those participating in the discourse and various social institutions and systems of power; (2) the notion that individual subjectivity is nonessentialized, emerging out of a process of conflict and change each time a writer thinks, speaks, reads, or writes; (3) a view of "education" as constituted by the social, political, economic, and cultural structures of a given time as well as constitutive of these structures—contributing to the renewal and transformation of existing structures; (4) a concept of "hegemony" or "domination" that recognizes, on the one hand, the constraints which the dominant social and political forces of a given time and place exert on individual work, and, on the other, the range of alternative or directly oppositional politics and culture existing as significant elements in society at any given time: that is, the belief that the particular social conditions of a given time and place can exert pressures on an individual to act not only in

ways that maintain and renew existing ways of distributing and organizing social power but also to transform those ways; (5) a notion of
human agency as "overdetermined," working for social change but in
circumstances not of one's choosing.[2] These assumptions lead us repeatedly to call attention to issues of difference and power inscribed in ongoing debate on the meaning of such concepts as learning, resolution,
development, self-expression, community, frontier. We do so by drawing on images of negotiation, conflict, struggle, repositioning, and borders from the work of such feminist, post-colonial, and marginality critics as bell hooks, Gloria Anzaldúa, and Mary Louise Pratt. These latter
terms recur in our arguments, for to us they accentuate what has traditionally been denied, muffled, or displaced: the operation of power, society, and history on individuals, discourse, and institutions.

Two of the central aims of the essays collected here are to understand
all work in basic writing as social and historical, and thus to contest the
objectification of the researcher, research discourse, and the "object" of
research. It is therefore appropriate that an introduction to our own work,
represented by the writing collected here, locate that work in the conditions of its own production and reception. This is not, of course, to provide the defining narrative for or defense of that writing. Indeed, to do
so would be counter to our own understanding of writing/history as
constitutive rather than reflective. But we offer our account of the intellectual, historical, and institutional conditions of our work to invite in-
terrogation of the politics of our own representations of basic writing.

We see ourselves as part of a generation of compositionists trained in
the late 1980s whose experience of basic writing was shaped by the canonical reception of certain texts on basic writing in graduate programs
and professional journals. The gap between the official accounts of basic
writing and our day-to-day experience as writing teachers and students
resulted in a dissatisfaction with what we saw as the occlusion of attention from the social struggle and change involved in the teaching and
learning of basic writing, and representations of the "problems" of basic
writers and basic writing in ways that risked perpetuating their marginal position in higher education. This furthered our interest in and
desire to contribute to an emerging position in composition and literary
and cultural studies which relocated writing and the teaching of writing in society and history. By attempting to resituate texts as work performed in specific social and historical contexts, we have hoped to explore how the study and teaching of writing might proceed in the present
and future. For us, this has involved delineating the parameters setting
and set by the production and reception of canonized texts in Basic Writing—for example, investigating how and why and to what effect CUNY's

implementation of its SEEK and Open Admissions program during the 1960s and '70s has been constructed as the originating, authoritative center of Basic Writing, the site of its "birth."

We come to this project in part as a response to the "lived experiences" of family, friends, and ourselves negotiating cultural dissonance along lines of ethnicity, race, class, gender, and sex as this gets played out at the site of institutionalized education. Our interest in basic writing as an important site for our teaching and scholarship arises from our understanding of this experience and of the historical role of basic writing as the only space in English which seriously investigates the challenges of students whose writing is explicitly marked as "not belonging" to the academy. Simultaneously, this "lived experience" makes it difficult for us to accept representations of "basic writers" as the "other." It makes perspectives which foreground the politics of representation—acknowledging issues of power involved in the question of who is speaking for whom, about whom, when, where, and why—both relevant and necessary. This in turn makes more apparent the marginalization of such perspectives in dominant discourse on basic writing.

Our project is also a response to our experience of basic writing as already institutionalized, however problematically. In our own experience, we first confronted courses called "Basic Writing" not as "new" but as an established institutional fact, part of the undergraduate curriculum in courses called "Basic Writing" and "Basic Reading and Writing" in a wide range of colleges and universities across the nation. In graduate seminars, we encountered Basic Writing as an object of study and field of research, with its canonical texts and figures. The construction of Mina Shaughnessy as an authorizing figure in Basic Writing perhaps best illustrates the effects of this canonization. The dominant discourse of Basic Writing views critiques of the discourse with criticism of individuals' integrity and character: in the case of Shaughnessy's writings, with criticism of Shaughnessy. It approaches "history" by attempting to trace causal influences among events or the "evolution" of ideas whose "unity" and "origin" supposedly reside in the intentions and integrity of individual authors like Shaughnessy. In this discourse, Shaughnessy becomes the originating author of Basic Writing; critiques of texts associated with her thus become critiques of her. This has the effect of silencing critique and authorizing the individual figure and those who can then speak in that figure's name, having "known" her and, by implication, her "true" intentions.

Our project responds by historicizing the canonizing process that produces these effects. Rather than recovering originating intentions of an "author," we investigate the social and historical production, regulation, and effects of dominant discourse. While our project clearly arises from different theoretical assumptions, the difference in theoretical assumptions intersects with a difference in institutional and historical positions. First, it speaks to the historically changing currency of theoretical assumptions about discourse, identity, and meaning. It speaks as well, however, to different historical and institutional circumstances. Claims of access to authorial intentions have simply not been readily available to those of us studying, teaching, and writing in institutions such as the University of Pittsburgh and Drake University during the late 1980s and 1990s. Our relationship with Basic Writing is not populated by memories of having personal contact with the Basic Writing "trailblazers." Similarly, our perspective on the 1960s–1970s inception of basic writing programs speaks to our position as both institutional and historical "outsiders" to such movements. This is not to grant greater "authority" to those who might claim to have "been there," nor greater "objectivity" for those "outside." Radical differences in the stories told by those who might make such claims negate the attribution of any such authority to any such individuals.[3] But our "distance" from those movements makes it possible for us to engage in discursive analysis of those movements in a manner less readily available to those writers who were "part of" them. Simply put, we respond to a different set of interests and pressures by virtue of the specific social and historical locations of our work. This is perhaps most evident in our concern with the resurgence of New Right attempts at retrenchment and attacks on "political correctness," a concern obviously not available to earlier writers but which motivates our interest in the strategies of Open Admissions and the academic retrenchment of the later 1970s.

We started our careers at institutions interested in exploring the implications of poststructural theory and cultural materialism for the structure and work of English departments. We have been encouraged in our work both at the graduate level and as English faculty to challenge distinctions traditionally maintained between English and other disciplines, theory and practice, research and teaching, composition, literature, criticism, and creative writing, and between "beginning" and "advanced" performance. That institutional setting encouraged us to challenge the distinction between "beginning" and "advanced" writing, aligning us with the conclusions drawn by teachers in open admissions programs as they confronted the limitations such distinctions placed on their work as teachers, as researchers, and as administrators.[4] We are the beneficiaries of such conclusions, which we encountered not as tentative formulations but as established assumptions informing the programs, theories, and teaching to which we were introduced.

Finally, our work is made possible by other, very specific material circumstances. We speak here not just of matters of time and money in the form of grants for course release and research support, important and necessary as these are and as important as we believe it is to acknowledge these bases for intellectual work. We mean as well the freedom given us to work with a variety of students and to design our own courses with appropriate enrollments that make certain kinds of work with students possible. We mean, also, conditions in which our work in "composition" receives institutional encouragement and is accorded status at least equal to work in other areas of English, while not being viewed as separate from those areas. In short, our work is made possible and thus indebted to the institutionalization of basic writing as an academic field, which we problematize.

The writing of the essays collected here did not follow any simple, linear narrative of research and report. Rather, while all emerge out of the assumptions described above, each adopts a somewhat different angle and focus toward thinking through the problematics of representing basic writing. We have therefore not arranged these in the chronological order in which they were either written or first appeared. Instead, we present them in two clusters. The first five essays—"The 'Birth' of 'Basic Writing'," "Conflict and Struggle," "Importing Science," "Redefining the Legacy of Mina Shaughnessy," and "Mapping Errors and Expectations"—situate Basic Writing in various discursive fields and historic moments to examine the complex material conditions mediating its production and reception. The first of these situates the emergence of the discourse of Basic Writing in the context of political and institutional struggles surrounding the adoption and implementation of CUNY's Open Admissions policy in the late 1960s and early 1970s. It approaches some of the key terms dominating Basic Writing's representations of itself as "new" and on the "frontier," and of students as "new," apolitical beginners hoping to join mainstream American life, as active responses to the discourse on open admissions opposing "academic excellence" to "political activism" and social concerns, and linking academic unpreparedness with minority identity and political interests.

"Conflict and Struggle" further locates dominant discourse on Basic Writing among competing ways of representing and addressing the "needs" of student writers to negotiate with cultural dissonance. It examines the hegemony of two views of education as acculturation or accommodation in culturally authorized narratives of the experience of "minority" students. It argues that these operate to dissolve rather than make productive use of conflict and struggle in the teaching and learning of writing. Just as "Conflict and Struggle" shows Basic Writing discourse to participate in ongoing debates on education, "Importing Science: Neutralizing Basic Writing" shows how research in that dominant discourse actively participates in an "expressive realism" pervasive across mainstream composition, literary criticism, education, linguistics, and various other social sciences during the 1970s. It approaches Basic Writing's success in establishing itself as a legitimate academic field in terms of its ability to use "science" to promote the "objectivity" of teaching, research, and writing at an historical period and in classrooms where the dominant found issues of diversity and power most difficult to contain.

"Redefining the Legacy of Mina Shaughnessy: A Critique of the Politics of Linguistic Innocence" shows how such alignments operate in Shaughnessy's reading of error to occlude attention to issues of power and subject positioning in the process of learning to master "correct" English. "Mapping Errors and Expectations for Basic Writing" identifies the conceptual dilemmas in which Basic Writing discourse has been trapped through its attempts to understand and justify the teaching of basic writing by imagining basic writers either as beginners growing cognitively or as aliens becoming initiated into a specific discourse community.

In one way or another, all these work to locate basic writing in history: a response to, produced and sustained by, and altering specific social and historical conditions and thus as never fixed but always provisional and strategic, continually involving individuals in renegotiating their positions and their work. The remaining pair of essays—"Rethinking the 'Sociality' of Error: Teaching Editing as Negotiation" and "Professing Multiculturalism"—apply this understanding to the classroom, specifically to the question of how to present and address "error," the issue that, perhaps more than any other, has defined basic writing for many. Uniting both is an understanding of the work of writing—including deviations from conventions of "correct" English—as not an "object" to be consumed but as a practice, with the material writing understood as notations part of a larger process of production and reception and thus liable to changing forms of social relationship (see Raymond Williams, *Problems in Materialism and Culture* 46–47). In this understanding, "error" represents not a phenomenon located on the page but a negotiated social power relationship between specific readers and writers. Contrasting this view with theories that explain error as evidence of writers' cognitive development or discourse habits, "Rethinking" argues for a pedagogy highlighting the negotiating process between readers and writers that produces work as either in "error" or not.

"Professing Multiculturalism" describes a pedagogy that problematizes the distinction traditionally maintained between "error" and "style" in approaches to the writing of "student" and established authors. It demonstrates how error—traditionally the province of basic writing alone and proof that it deserves its "low status"—represents a zone for the reconfiguring of discursive practices traditionally compartmentalized by definitions of low and high ranking literature, literary criticism, creative writing, "advanced composition," and "basic writing."

"Some Afterwords" offers our sense of ongoing debates now dominant in discourse on basic writing and in composition studies generally: the possibility of eliminating basic writing through "mainstreaming" or other strategies; the relevance of contact zone pedagogies to basic writing; intersections between basic writers and other writers; the continuing distinction between matters of "style" and matters of "content"; feminist and post-colonial critiques of composition work; and the perduring textual bias of research in composition. By delineating what we see as intersections and divergences between our work and such debates, we hope both to further the location of the work that we have begun in this Introduction and to suggest directions we and others might take to address the specific gaps and strengths we identify in the struggles now confronting us all.

The pieces in this book are all separately authored, with Min-Zhan Lu writing chapters 2, 3, 4, and 7, and Bruce Horner chapters 1, 5, 6, and "Some Afterwords." Rather than reworking these into a unified voice, in the form of the "we" speaking here, we have chosen to retain the differences between and among the multiple "I's" appearing in the chapters. We hope to use these disjunctions in the speaking voices to acknowledge two aspects of this collaborative project. First, it is a project spanning nine years of extensive discussion between the two authors over the texts each of us was reading and writing. Drafts and revisions of each chapter were composed by one of us in response to questions raised by the other. Moreover, the inception of many of these chapters has arisen from questions provoked in one of us by reading the other's work. For example, Horner's critique of an earlier version of Lu's essay on "Professing Multiculturalism" led Lu toward a further exploration of the intersection as well as differences between the "contact zone" approach to error she describes and pedagogies described earlier by Epes, Tricomi, and Lees. Horner responded to Lu's "Redefining the Legacy of Mina Shaughnessy" by contextualizing the construction of basic writing as an academic field in "The 'Birth' of 'Basic Writing.'" Similarly, in "Professing Multiculturalism," Lu places the approach to teaching editing Horner presents in "Rethinking the 'Sociality' of Error" in the context of multicultural approaches to style in both literature and composition classrooms.

The second aspect of this collaborative project we would highlight is the fact of differences in the personal, social, and academic conditions each of us has brought to the project at different moments through the years. The direction of the project bears traces of the different trajectories in which the teaching and scholarship of each of us has developed. This is perhaps most obvious in Horner's use of historical studies of literacy practices and Lu's use of feminist, post-colonial, and Marxist criticism. Shifts in the "I" appearing in the chapters by each of us also bear traces of changes in the vocabularies used and questions raised in dominant discourse on composition studies and traces of our specific, varied experiences in teaching. The book thus presents the changing ways in which we have engaged and re-engaged the issues of the teaching of writing, as the conditions, pressures, and possibilities of our respective academic careers and teaching experiences shift. For example, Chapter 4, originally a part of Lu's 1989 dissertation, aims at applying theories of language to a canonical text in the field, while Chapter 7 revisits the field (in 1994) and her dissertation from the perspective of her experience attempting to develop a "multicultural" pedagogy for teaching both composition and literature. In "Some Afterwords," written in 1996, Horner revisits issues of the politics of pedagogy first addressed in 1992 in relation to the teaching of editing (Chapter 6) from the perspectives afforded by subsequent work on authorship and contact zone pedagogies.

We have found these disjunctions in our work and between our concerns and interests a constructive resource. We hope that by leaving these visible, our project might invite different ways of imagining how we might follow, respond to, and intervene productively in one another's work. And we hope the presence of these differences will enable readers working in a range of sites and conditions to pursue the intersections of their work with Basic Writing.

I Discoursing Basic Writing

1 The "Birth" of "Basic Writing"

Bruce Horner

The teaching of basic writing occupies a peculiar position in composition studies. It is the specialty of some of the leading figures in composition studies and, simultaneously, the province of teachers and students placed at the bottom of the academic institutional hierarchy. The emergence of basic writing as an academic field in the early 1970s has been cited as crucial historically in the development of composition. John Trimbur, noting that "[m]any of the teaching and research projects we [composition teachers] now take for granted began in the wake of open admissions and educational opportunity programs in the late sixties and early seventies," attributes "a number of remarkable innovations in the study and teaching of writing" to basic writing ("Cultural Studies" 14). James Slevin identifies the period as the time of Composition's "rise," a "writing movement" addressing "broad questions about the aims of education and the shape of various educational institutions" and having as its focus "the revitalizing of the teaching of writing" (12). Ira Shor likewise describes this time as one when teachers faced "a creative and exciting frontier of cultural democracy" (*Critical Teaching* 269).

Trimbur, Slevin, and Shor all identify the lessons and insights of teaching from this period in political terms: a "movement" for "cultural democracy" that explicitly called into question the social and political role of educational institutions and the politics of representing students, or prospective students, and their writing in particular ways, e.g., as "literate" or "illiterate," "college material" or "remedial," "skilled" or "unskilled." It is significant, however, that all three writers identify such lessons and insights as at risk of being lost or forgotten. We need, Trimbur notes, to "relearn" the insights of open admissions ("Cultural Studies" 14–15). Slevin worries that the training of writing teachers typically does not include investigation of the history of writing instruction and its role in socializing those new student populations historically called "remedial" (14). Shor offers his own account of teaching in Open Admissions "as a means to *resist* the erasure of memory" (*Critical Teaching* 269, my emphasis).

In what follows, I explore why and how such insights of basic writing got lost to such an extent that they now need to be "relearned," in order that they not be "re-lost." I analyze a dominant discourse on basic writing whose meanings and forms are central to such works as Mina Shaughnessy's *Errors and Expectations*, the *Journal of Basic Writing*, the 1987 *Sourcebook for Basic Writing Teachers* and various bibliographies on basic writing. I refer to this discourse as Basic Writing to highlight both its institutional power and its selective representation of the wealth of practices and projects in teaching basic writing.[1] I argue that Basic Writing represents a response to another, powerful public discourse on higher education and students deemed underprepared for college. I map the formation of that discourse by analyzing the key terms and assumptions operating in a range of public debate on open admissions in general and Open Admissions at City University of New York (CUNY) in particular, the institution most closely associated with texts shaping much of Basic Writing discourse. I argue that public discourse on higher education and Open Admissions perpetuates the hegemonic denial of the location of the academy in material, political, social, and historical contexts. The success of Basic Writing in legitimizing the institutional place of basic writing courses and students cannot be separated from the ways in which it works within the framework of public discourse on higher education and Open Admissions, particularly its silence about the concrete material, political, institutional, social, and historical realities confronting basic writing teachers, students, and courses. The costs of such a strategy, however, have been the erasure of the sort of critical insights that first propelled practices and projects in basic writing and the near permanent institutional marginalization of basic writing courses, teachers, and students.

This exploration should interest not just basic writing teachers but all those involved in the teaching of college writing. Not only has the emergence of Basic Writing contributed significantly to the field of Composition; basic writing students, teachers, and courses represent Composition's problems of academic institutional status "writ large." Like college composition generally, basic writing has long been perceived as marginal at best: expendable, temporary, properly the responsibility of the high schools and therefore a "drain" on English departments specifically and colleges and universities in general. Basic Writing's efforts to work within and against public discourse on higher education dramatically highlight the ideological and material constraints with which all teaching of "entry-level" students has had to contend. Examining the strategic value and limitations of Basic Writing's response to these constraints suggests how and why college composition as a whole has, as Susan Miller puts it, "formed a continuing special circumstance" (81).

Addressing two possible objections to my focus may help clarify my project. It can be and has been argued that the teaching of basic writing (and the practice of open admissions) long pre-dates the *term* Basic Writing, discourse associated with that term, and CUNY's late-1960s–1970s Open Admissions policy. While this is true, my interest is in exploring how and why Basic Writing discourse has effectively eclipsed that other extensive, fluid, and heterogeneous work. My aim is to contest such a displacement by highlighting the conditions leading to it. Second, and relatedly, some may object that restricting my focus to dominant Basic Writing discourse as I have defined it perpetuates the silencing of alternative discourses and practices that transgress institutional boundaries of the discipline of basic writing, or any composition, teaching, whether by those involved in basic writing or by others, at CUNY or elsewhere. Patricia Laurence, for example, argues that exclusive attention to Mina Shaughnessy's published writings ignores what once had to be "submerged," noting that "in reading *Errors and Expectations,* we are reading only part of a conversation in an urban educational institution at a certain historical moment" and we need to read it with such "historical specificity" in mind, as one of a plurality of voices ("Vanishing Site" 22, 27). While I would echo Laurence's subsequent call for the emergence of stories once submerged, her criticism begs the question of how and why some stories have been kept "submerged" while others have been elevated. We need to know how and why this has happened, and with what consequences for teachers' understanding and practice as "professionals" in their work as teachers, scholars, administrators. Examining this process thus should serve not to repress other stories but to make their emergence more likely, to provoke, if you will, their recovery, circulation, and application.

Many of the texts constituting Basic Writing discourse were produced in response to a dominant public discourse on open admissions programs, and particularly Open Admissions at CUNY. On July 9, 1969, the New York City Board of Higher Education adopted a policy of open admissions for the senior and community colleges making up the City University of New York system. Noting in its statement the significant attention given the "Five Demands" made by the Black and Puerto Rican Student Community of City College (originally known as the Committee of Ten), the Board charged the chancellor of CUNY with producing the plan for open admissions by October 1969, four months later (Board of Higher Education). In adopting this policy, the Board shortened by five years a "Master Plan" it had adopted in 1964. That Master plan had called for implementing a policy by 1975 that would grant admission to CUNY to all New York City high school graduates.

Participants in the heated debate that followed read the Board's decision as a response to specific political, budgetary, and labor pressures. For example, links were made between the decision and the violent confrontations that accompanied various stages of the negotiations of the "Five Demands," including the burning of one of the City College buildings and the closing of the College, the most senior and arguably the most illustrious college of the CUNY system (see "CUNY Opening Doors," Hamalian and Hatch). These events at City College were likened by some to student takeovers at nearby Columbia University and to other campus disturbances to reinforce a sense that the Open Admissions policy represented an appeasement of student militants, black and Puerto Rican students, and political agendas of the student Left (see Heller 12, 24; Wagner, chapter 3). The Board's decision was also linked to city politics. For example, Mayor Lindsay's endorsement of the policy during that year's New York City mayoral election was widely seen as an attempt to buy votes (see "New Era for CUNY").

The fact that the Board in its statement did not address in explicit terms the budgetary demands implied by its policy decision also led to the view that the policy was an indirect means of applying pressure on both New York City and New York State to increase CUNY's budget allocation (see *Right* 16). It was estimated that implementing the Open Admissions policy would cost a minimum increase the first year of $35.5 million ("Record Budget"). And it was unclear how CUNY was to find the additional space and faculty to meet the needs of the estimated fourteen thousand additional students ("City U. Gets Braced," "City U. in a Crusher"), especially how it was to find them within a year. Yet at the time of the Board's statement, the state allocation for the CUNY budget was in doubt. Albert Bowker, then Chancellor of CUNY, had gone so far as to threaten that there would be no 1969 freshman class at CUNY because of budget restrictions (*Right* 11).

The Board's decision also brought back the contention between the CUNY administration and the faculty union over increased workloads and strains on the physical plant, expected to be exacerbated by implementation of open admissions (see Barasch 15). During a heated union election a year prior to the Board's policy, the CUNY chancellor, in urging faculty not to vote for union representation, had identified the movement toward collective bargaining with resistance to "flexibility, both for the buildup of the institution with many new programs and for the rapid expansion of the enrollment of disadvantaged minorities" (quoted in Polishook 379–80). Faculty interests were thus pitted against not the administration per se but such programs, suggesting that those interests would be in competition with such programs for limited resources.

Debate on CUNY's Open Admissions policy was decidedly not confined to educational administrators or those in city or state government, nor did the debate cease after 1970, when open admissions was put into place. Not only faculty but college and high school students, parents, civic organizations, and the media were active participants. In addition, because of CUNY's reputation, media coverage of the student unrest preceding the policy, and the sheer size of the CUNY system (the third largest system in the United States), the policy attracted national attention. Further, the association of the policy with campus violence, and the magnitude of the demands which the implementation of the policy made on existing faculty and facilities, had the effect of polarizing the debate on open admissions so that certain issues and terms became codes for one's position on Open Admissions (see Quinn and Kriegel 413, 414; Kaplan 219; Lyons 1980, 6–7; Resnik 4–5). For example, because those opposed to Open Admissions frequently raised questions about the material demands of implementing the policy—who was going to pay, how much, where would the many new classes be held, who would teach them—any mention of such questions came to be recognized as signalling opposition to Open Admissions and was dismissed out of hand by those favoring the policy. For such questions called attention to what the policy denied or attempted to silence.

This polarization of debate on Open Admissions operated on a series of binaries that was part of a dominant discourse on education. We can see in that discourse a binary opposing student activism to academic excellence, identifying the former with lack of academic preparation and the latter with political disinterestedness. This is most evident in the charges against Open Admissions, but it also pervades the discourse as a whole. In the debate, it was charged that the policy rewarded student violence and politicized the curriculum, and that the policy would displace intellectually deserving students with the undeserving. Operating from the assumption of both limited resources and CUNY's educational integrity prior to Open Admissions, it was charged that the policy was a "quota" system discriminating against students not black or Puerto Rican by depriving the former of the limited commodity of higher education. On the assumption that the new students could only take from, rather than contribute to, CUNY's academic excellence, it was also charged that as a "quota" system, Open Admissions would dilute standards by letting in all those "unqualified" blacks and Puerto Ricans and so undermine the value of the college degree. Finally, it was charged that the policy made unrealistic demands on CUNY's budget and physical and staff resources.

The discourse in which such charges participate posits two types of students set in opposition to one another: the open admissions students, associated with politics and minority activism, and the ideal college students, assumed to be interested in and capable of pursuing academic excellence because they were not distracted by political interests (see also Chapter 5). This binary made invisible to most commentators those students who crossed the division between political activism and academic excellence: those students who had met traditional admissions requirements but who were politically active. Indeed, public images of student activists regularly neglected the strong correlation of campus activism with highly selective admission standards (Keniston 120). Instead, student activism was regularly equated with illiteracy, as when Lewis Mayhew claimed that

> [d]issenting youth . . . all too frequently seem unable to say or write a simple English sentence. Their concerns are expressed . . . in a . . . flow of words possessing neither syntax nor grammatical effectiveness. . . . So pronounced are these linguistic failures that I have begun to wonder whether or not they might represent a pathology worthy of some further study. (92–93)

In a widely publicized speech, Vice President Agnew went so far as to claim that the intrusion into universities of "those unqualified for the traditional [university] curriculum" was "a major cause of campus . . . unrest" (110). Such lumping of student activism with lack of academic preparation is further exemplified by frequent references to such students as the "new barbarians," a phrase which links difference in language (as in "barbarism") with a threat to (the speaker's own) civilization.

A second, related myth marked open admissions students not only as being activists but as belonging to ethnic minorities. For example, all evidence showed that the majority of CUNY Open Admissions students were whites of working-class background ("Report Card" 27; "'Open Enrollment' Results Told"; "CUNY Open-Admissions Plan Found Benefiting Whites Most"; "Open Admission Found of Benefit to Whites, Too"). Yet the myth persisted in popular media discourse that all or most Open Admissions students at CUNY were black or Puerto Rican (Healy, "New Problems"; Kaplan 220; Stoerker 1014; "Open Admissions," WNBC-TV). Unimaginable within the framework of the binary were the so-called "white ethnics": working-class whites, many of them at

CUNY of Italian or Irish Catholic background, and many of them conservative in their political views. While the invisibility of white working-class ethnics speaks most obviously to the pervasive blindness of
Americans to social class and the persistence of racism, it speaks also
and more specifically to the constitutive power within and outside the
academy of the public discourse linking minority students, political activism, and academic underpreparedness, a power which made invisible students who might lack both academic preparation and interest in
political activism.

These myths pervaded the general debate on open admissions from
both the left and right. For example, a statement of 18 June 1969 by what
came to be known as the "Weathermen" splinter of the SDS asserted,
"any kind of more open admissions means . . . there are more militant
blacks and browns making more and more fundamental demands on
the schools" ("You Don't Need" 282). A *Washington Post* editorial by conservatives Rowland Evans and Robert Novak critiquing open admissions as the "Wrecking of a College" identifies open admissions students strictly as Negro or Puerto Rican youth. William F. Buckley Jr.,
drawing heavily on writings from City College English professor
Geoffrey Wagner, seconded the Weathermen's perception that the bulk
of the CUNY Open Admissions students were militant, describing them
as an "ignorant and disruptive" contingent ("Among the Illiterate"). This
association of Open Admissions with the student New Left extended to
teachers of Open Admission students. Wagner himself described teachers favoring open admissions as "the balding, bearded guerrillas with
tenure" (136), and he accused Basic Writing teachers of "teaching more
about the injustices of society outside the classroom than the use of punctuation within it" (143).

The binary opposing academic pursuits to the pursuit of social goals
was maintained not only by those who opposed Open Admissions but
those making the case for it. For example, a 1973 editorial in *Change*
magazine presenting "The Case for Open Admissions" asserts that the
American university "was once more thoroughly dedicated than it can
be now to the academic pursuit of knowledge. The challenge of open
admissions . . . is to find an equivalent more suitable to the needs of its
students and of the city of New York" ("Case" 10). The editorial thus
maintains the distinction between "academic" and other pursuits even
as it argues for the others toward which it claims open admissions works.
The more general debate over the "politicization" of the university en-
capsulated this distinction. Conservatives warned against the increasing politicization of the university. As Miro Todorovich put it in explaining actions of the faculty group University Centers for Rational Alterna-

tives, "All available energies had to be mobilized in support of . . . the survival of a nonpoliticized, free, and open-minded university" defended against the "forcible incursions of the 'barbarians of virtue' into the academy" (xiv–xv). Those on the left retorted that the university had already been politicized, albeit with the politics of liberalism. For example, in a 1966 SDS position paper explaining the purpose of working toward university reform, Carl Davidson, like Todorovich, warns of an invasion—not of "barbarians"—but of "corporate liberalism," whose "penetration into the campus community is awesome" (42). In either case, however, at least in the more common arguments, any politicization was viewed as a taint to be avoided or washed out rather than something inherent in university activity of which one ought to be aware.

Arguments for open admissions claimed to resolve these opposed goals by accommodating all. That is, they claimed to maintain the role of the university in preserving and reproducing "academic excellence" but to add to that a different role for the university accommodating a different kind of student. Such arguments thus maintained the terms of the binary while offering a narrative of resolution. The New York City Board of Higher Education's July 9, 1969, policy statement on Open Admissions itself enunciates the key terms dominating discourse on Open Admissions:

> The issues with which the Board was confronted transcended the immediate concerns of City College, and in fact the University itself. They are the basic issues of our City and of our society. In dealing with these issues, the Board was faced with the necessity of reexamining our programs and structures so as to meet legitimate needs and aspirations of all the City's youth, while at the same time preserving the educational integrity of the University, without which we would be perpetrating a cruel hoax upon all those who desire and deserve a higher education of true excellence. We believe that the actions we are directing meet both of these requirements. . . .
>
> (a) [The plan] shall offer admission to some University program to all high school graduates of the City.
> (b) It shall provide for remedial and other supportive services for all students requiring them.
> (c) It shall maintain and enhance the standards of academic excellence of the colleges of the University.
> (d) It shall result in the ethnic integration of the colleges.
> (e) It shall provide for mobility for students between various programs and units of the University.
> (f) It shall assure that all students who would have been admitted to specific community or senior colleges under the admissions criteria which we [the Board] have used in the past shall still be so admitted. In increasing educational opportunity for all, at-

tention shall also be paid to retaining the opportunities for students now eligible under present Board policies and practices.
(3–4)

Most remarkable is how the Board's statement either explicitly or implicitly opposes ethnic integration to academic excellence, the academi-
cally prepared and those needing remediation (presumed to be students
hitherto restricted from CUNY), the sociopolitical interests of the "City
and society" and academic interests (represented, for example, by the
reference to "the immediate concerns of City College"). In the Board
statement, the goal of "preserving the educational integrity of the University" is set off as distinct from and in competition with the goals of
meeting "the legitimate needs and aspirations of all the City's youth"
and achieving "the ethnic integration of the colleges." The issues with
which the Board has wrestled are described not as those of the University but ones which "transcend" it. If only by implication, Open Admissions is assumed to threaten the educational integrity of the University,
whether or not such a risk is justified by political exigencies.

This set of assumed oppositions becomes more evident if we imagine
alternative ways the Board could have framed the issues. For example,
the Board could have justified re-examining its programs and structures
and admitting the new students as a means by which to *achieve* "educational integrity" rather than presenting the admission of the new students as something threatening that integrity. That the University should
"provide for remedial and other supportive services for all students requiring them," as the Board advises in its statement on Open Admissions, could be taken as a policy directive appropriate to any school re-
gardless of its admissions policy rather than one made necessary strictly
by a policy of open admissions, and it could be described as one integral
to rather than distinct from maintaining and enhancing academic excellence. Issues of social justice could be presented as co-terminous with
rather than as distinct from and potentially a threat to the academy and
its "educational integrity." But the Board statement instead works to
represent prior practices and students admitted under earlier admissions policies as normal, possessing educational integrity and academic
excellence, and to represent those students to be newly admitted as a
threat to these. The university would add to its roles that of "change
agent," but the change was to be enacted on neither the definition of the
university's integrity as it had existed in the past nor on society but on
the new students.

In keeping with this argument, students to be admitted were cast in
the role of those desiring not to overthrow society but to join and be-

come more productive members of it. In CUNY Chancellor Robert Kibbee's 1971 testimony to the New York State joint legislative committee on higher education, Kibbee distinguished even protesters at CUNY in this way. Observing that in 1969 on some American campuses the "prime target may have been the war, racism, the system," he claimed, "Here at City University, the focal point of protest was admission *to* the system" (4, my emphasis). As a *Change* editorial put it, the purpose of open admissions was "to give the poor and working-class people of New York City a chance to get into the mainstream of the city's economic life. It is to qualify them for jobs that are more than marginal to the vitality of the city—to give them some purchase on what is called the American dream" ("Case" 9). Then vice-chancellor Timothy Healy put the case more negatively. Noting the steady decrease in the number of manufacturing jobs in the city, he predicted a vast increase in the number of poor "without a significant increase in our pools of educated men and women" ("Will Everyman"). But CUNY's Open Admissions, he argued, can serve "as poverty interrupter for New York," and in so doing "short circuit the terrible rhythm of disappointment and rage . . . [of] inner-city youth . . . that can create a new race of barbarians" ("Will Everyman"). That is, Open Admissions, by training people for service industry jobs, was represented as a measure preventing the poor from *becoming* barbarians rather than an appeasement of already existing barbarians. But in either case, the social change was to be enacted not on the "mainstream of the city's economic life," possibly the source of city residents' "terrible rhythm of disappointment and rage," but on the residents themselves.

In keeping with the emphasis on higher education as a means of changing students into more "productive" workers, stories promoting the "success" of Open Admissions took the form of "before-after" portraits, usually of students whose education at CUNY promised to help them secure employment in service sector work. CUNY press releases of 18 September 1970 highlighted the stories of new students whose high school experience hadn't marked them as "college" material but who had enrolled at CUNY under Open Admissions and aspired to careers in business and civil service ("News: Open Admissions"). Subsequent press releases on CUNY graduates who had entered CUNY under Open Admissions compared the students' high school grade records with their college grade point averages, showing significant change in their academic performance from high school to college. As a result of their college education, the releases emphasized, the students were now prepared for work in teaching, medical records administration, and "such diverse fields as accounting, data processing, physical therapy, psychiatric social work, social welfare and speech pathology" ("News from

Hunter College"; "Brooklyn College Graduates," 6 June 1974; "Open Admissions," WNBC-TV). In place of the image of Open Admissions students as militant activists, the students were portrayed as well-adjusted and well-placed citizens, modern day Horatio Algers, in such stories as "Hard Work Pays Off" and "Lad Finds Open Way to Degree." CUNY's identification of the goal of social "service" as one additional to its goal of preserving academic excellence maintained a hierarchy between the goals that privileged the latter while placing it in opposition to but not in competition with the former. Such arguments rendered Open Admissions vulnerable to attack from conservatives like Evans and Novak, who acknowledged that Open Admissions might be effective in "taking slum youth off the street" but doubted that this result merited the financial cost and the "high price of drastically lowered academic standards." In short, the strategy of accommodation rendered Open Admissions vulnerable by representing it as additional to and a potential drain on programs assumed to be integral to the university and its "standards." Those adopting this strategy were thus necessarily circumspect regarding financial costs of open admissions programs, conflicts among and between those programs and students and other programs and students, and any political interests motivating such programs, their students, and their teachers.

[I]t is not . . . political stances which determine people's stances on things academic, but their positions in the academic field which inform the stances that they adopt on political issues in general as well as on academic problems.
            —Pierre Bourdieu, *Homo Academicus* xvii–xviii.

The writings of CUNY basic writing teachers and of Mina Shaughnessy in particular have been perceived as crucial in constituting Basic Writing discourse. Shaughnessy is credited with christening the field with the term "Basic Writing" and with founding its flagship academic publication, the *Journal of Basic Writing* (Gray; Kasden 4; Moran and Jacobi 2; Bartholomae, "Writing" n. 3). Her book *Errors and Expectations* has been described without irony as the "gospel" of basic writing (Horning) and as having "almost on its own established basic writing as an important subfield within composition" (Faigley, *Fragments* 61). If one's position in the academic field informs the stances one adopts on political issues in general as well as on academic problems, as Bourdieu suggests, then these teachers' representations of basic writing students, programs, and pedagogies need to be understood in part by the knowledge that the positions they occupied were institutionally marginal and highly vulnerable: their academic status and political motives were in question, many lacked job security, and they taught students whose own political leanings were also questioned, whose worthiness for college admission was constantly challenged, and whose demands on institutional resources were constantly lamented and scrutinized. That positioning both required that they contend, and shaped how they contended, with terms of the public discourse prevailing in debate on the educational rights and capacities of their students.

As I've shown above, the larger public discourse on open admissions most commonly described open admissions students as "barbarians": outsiders by virtue of their racial and/or ethnic identity and illiteracy who threatened the university—Western civilization's palace of rationality—whether by their mere physical presence and demands, with "politicization," and/or simply by virtue of lacking the qualifications for university work. In response, while Basic Writing discourse accepted the identification of basic writers as "outsiders," it characterized them as nonthreatening, apolitical, would-be immigrants. Specifically, it represented them as beginners and/or foreigners seeking and able to join the American mainstream. For example, Sarah D'Eloia, in defending "Teaching Standard Written English," the first essay appearing in the first issue of the *Journal of Basic Writing,* argues that the decision of "most students, including those at City College . . . to enter college and their perseverance in pursuing their degrees indicate a desire to participate in mainstream American culture" (9). Shaughnessy describes Basic Writing students at CUNY in similar terms, claiming these students "were in college now for one reason: that their lives might be better than their parents', that the lives of their children might be better than theirs so far had been," and explaining that "BW students write the way they do, not because they are slow or non-verbal, indifferent to or incapable of academic excellence, but because they are beginners and must, like all beginners, learn by making mistakes" (*Errors* 3, 5). Such images argued for allowing these students in college by emphasizing their educability, defining both them and their difficulties with writing as not fixed but *in process,* and aligning them with the mainstream and its standards in their aspirations if not their current status (Horner, "Mapping" 31–32). It thus "naturalized" them both in a cognitive developmental and a civic sense, locating them at a particular stage in a natural sequence of learning and attributing to them the aspiration to join with rather than disrupt mainstream American society.

At the same time, these images consolidated the dominance of the binary of political activism and academic excellence by sidestepping the specific circumstances in which the students found themselves: most obviously, the historical circumstances leading to their arrival in schools—the disruptions and negotiations leading to CUNY Open Admissions in the first place—and more generally, the economic, social, political, and technological pressures in the United States making college education a requirement for social, economic, and political survival. Moreover, they left unchallenged particular notions of "academic excellence" and how the achievement of such excellence by basic writing students and their teachers was ultimately to be measured.

A City College English Department memorandum by Shaughnessy illustrates the institutional pressures confronting teachers concerned to defend the education of such students:

> There is . . . a kind of pressure . . . to do a quick job of producing correct writing since the ability to manage Standard English is often unconsciously accepted as proof of educability, and this kind of proof is sought after by most critics and some well-wishers of open admissions.
>
> Yet our sense of our students and of the skill we are trying to teach suggests that our priorities ought to be different from those pressed upon us by the exigencies of open admissions. . . . Students and teachers both feel the urgency, but they are caught in a kind of Catch-22 dilemma—a student can use up so much energy mastering the mechanics of English that he misses the chance of learning how to write, but if he doesn't master the mechanics he may not have a chance to write. . . .
>
> I am not of course suggesting that it is debasing education to help a student gain control of Standard English and the mechanics of formal writing but only that the effort to do this quickly can lead to doing it exclusively, which means almost inevitably the neglect, at a crucial point, of the deeper and ultimately more important resources our students bring to the classroom.
>
> I see no immediate solution to this problem of conflicting goals. . . . Meanwhile . . . it seems to me we must try to develop more efficient and challenging ways of teaching grammar and mechanics so that we have some time left over to do something else. ("Basic Writing and Open Admissions" 3–4, 5)

The memo highlights a tension between the "conflicting goals" of what teachers perceive as ideal for their students and what the institution demands. While it rejects the idea that "the ability to manage Standard English" constitutes "proof of educability" and stresses "the deeper and ultimately more important resources our students bring to the classroom," it accepts that, at the moment, the goal of meeting such debased "proof" must take precedence over the goal of attending to those other resources, or else the students will lose any chance of learning how to write—they will no longer be admitted to class.

The devotion of the first issue of the *Journal of Basic Writing* to the subject of "Error" speaks to the effect of these pressures on Shaughnessy and the contributors to that issue, all of them, significantly, Shaughnessy's colleagues at City College. In that and subsequent work, the conflict between the demand to "develop more efficient and challenging ways of teaching grammar and mechanics" and to acknowledge and draw on the resources students bring to the classroom is resolved by exploring how those same "resources" can inform the mastering of standard English. The power of *Errors and Expectations* can be attributed to just such a resolution: showing how students' errors in many ways result from those resources and thus speak not to their illiteracy but their educability. At the same time, the strategy of such a resolution operates within the dominant conceptual framework on education positing the ability to be educated as a cognitive rather than political matter, and it accepts, in however qualified a manner, traditional definitions of that educability. The focus resulting from such a strategy is on pedagogical technique, the designing of "more efficient and challenging ways of teaching grammar and mechanics" rather than on questioning the legitimacy of such measures of educability or the possibility of political resistance to their imposition. The Catch-22 within which such a strategy participates is that those measures continue unabated, and thus, as Shaughnessy predicts in her memo, "the effort to [teach students to produce 'correct' writing] quickly" not only can but does in fact all too often "lead to doing it exclusively." A 1986 survey of Basic Writing courses cites a teacher complaint that largely echoes Shaughnessy's quoted above:

> The problem . . . is that surface amenities are given far more attention than the actual writing process. For example, the departmental syllabus is directed towards the error count for comma splices, misuse of semicolons, and the like. (quoted in Gould and Heyda 18)

Just as Basic Writing discourse defined basic writers as beginners, it defined the enterprise of teaching basic writing as new, "frontier territory," "unmapped" (*Errors and Expectations* 4) and the teachers as "pioneers" of a "new profession." Such definitions helped legitimize Basic Writing in several ways. First, the enterprise of Basic Writing was aligned with a depoliticized conception of educational practices and goals. The frontier imagery invoked was utopian, a purely intellectual rather than political space. In contrast to the American frontier experience, on this frontier no natives were displaced or herded into special reservations, no territory was conquered from others, and people's appearance on the scene was compelled by no obvious social, political, economic, or historical force (see Horner, "Mapping"). Rather, teachers ventured into uninhabited territory as so many pedagogical Eves and Adams, pursuing a mysterious, divinely ordained destiny. Introducing a list of "Suggested Readings" for teachers, Shaughnessy claimed in *Errors and Expectations* that each title "offers a place to begin in a field where almost everything remains to be done" (298). The introduction to the first issue of the *Journal of Basic Writing* (1975) characterized the aims of the journal as beginning a "new discussion about teaching writing," a discussion which the journal's editors hoped would enlarge the experience of what it labeled "a new profession" (Shaughnessy, Introduction 3, 4). The purported "newness" of the dominant discourse, its subject, and its practitioners had the further advantage of defining both the teachers and the *problems* they addressed as "new." For, cast as frontier pioneers, Basic Writing teachers could be granted both credibility as "professionals" and leeway to experiment with what practices might "work" and even with those that might not "work" while exploring a "pedagogical West" that, as new, poached on no one's turf. In so doing, teachers aligned themselves to CUNY administration arguments which emphasized the magnitude of the numbers of "new" students Open Admissions promised to bring into the mainstream to explain away particular blunders. Regarding CUNY's Open Admissions program as a whole, for example, CUNY Vice Chancellor Healy had announced, "We're going to get more and bigger results and make more and bigger mistakes—because we're moving faster and farther than anyone else" (quoted in "Open Admissions: American Dream or Disaster?" 66).

While defining the field of basic writing as a "new frontier" has had, as I have argued, strategic uses, it is nonetheless worth recalling warnings about frontiers. Shor accepts designating college as the site of a "new frontier" but reminds us that a frontier "gets developed by settlers who use tools and ideas from old sectors of society. Their material and ideological resources create the character of what emerges. . . . The same forces which propel development also limit it" (*Critical Teaching* 14). Shaughnessy similarly warns teachers heading to the "pedagogical West" that they "are certain to be carrying many things . . . that will clog their journey as they get further on" (*Errors* 4). These warnings point to several related blind spots consequent on conceptualizing basic writing, or indeed any work on the teaching of writing, as new, "frontier" territory: blindness to history; blindness to the politics of such imagery; blindness to the politics of the "new" tools that seem closest at hand. Most obviously, constructing Basic Writing as a "pedagogical West" has prevented teachers and administrators of basic writing programs from learning from past endeavors. As critics have begun to point out, the history of remedial writing instruction, though not labeled "basic writing," began long before the 1970s (Connors; Lunsford, "Politics"; Rose, "Language").

Acknowledging the history of remedial writing instruction would not only enable teachers "not to make the same old mistakes over and over again" (Lunsford, "Politics" 252); it would enable them to counter damaging representations of their own work and of their students as temporary, marginal, and therefore easily expendable. The divorce of Basic Writing from the history of "remedial" writing instruction effected by its claims to "newness" has prevented teachers from arguing for the historical centrality of their teaching of writing. "New" programs tend to be viewed as experimental, responses to "crises" by definition "temporary" and so worthy of only temporary, and limited, funding. And as "new," they are automatically defined as non-central, add-ons to what is imagined to be an already integrated system. Defenders of CUNY's Open Admissions frequently complained that the "experiment" had not yet been given a chance to succeed. But their language allowed critics to demand constant evaluation of the program, defined as an "experiment," and to challenge its funding to an extent that would be unimaginable for programs conceived of as "central" or "traditional." In fact, however, there is a long tradition of "remedial" college writing instruction in America, however problematic the methods and aims employed, to which teachers might point in refuting attempts to exclude basic writing from the academy, to remove its "credit," or to place or keep it on the periphery. Miller has observed of college composition instruction in the United States that,

> defined as the field around a freshman course, [it] began in a political moment that was embedded in ambivalence about how to assimilate unentitled, newly admitted students in the late nineteenth-century "new university," which was in turn formed to address its era's social, economic, and political changes. (79)

By substituting the term "nineteenth-century" with "twentieth-century," one could easily say the same of Basic Writing. But talk of Basic Writing as a "new" field or "frontier" and of students as themselves "new," "beginners," or "foreigners," ignores this tradition. And while such talk may have secured a place for Basic Writing in the academy, it has also insured that place securely on the academy's margins, and with a lease that, if perennial, is also perennially short-term.

More damaging, naturalizing basic writing and basic writing students by positing them as "new" and "beginning" erases the ties of both to history and society. Bourdieu, writing of the discourse of geopolitical borders, notes that

> Regionalist discourse is a *performative* discourse which aims to impose as legitimate a new definition of the frontiers. . . . The act of categorization, when it manages to achieve recognition or when it

is exercised by a recognized authority, exercises by itself a certain power: 'ethnic' or 'regional' categories . . . institute a reality by using the power of *revelation* and *construction* exercised by *objectification in discourse.* (*Language* 223)

It is thus that, as he puts it earlier, "The frontier . . . produces cultural difference as much as it is produced by it" (*Language* 222). Defining Basic Writing as frontier territory effectively constructs the differences between those students labeled Basic Writers and those not, establishing the legitimacy of the distinction. As Bartholomae has described the situation,

> As a profession, we have defined basic writing . . . by looking at the writing that emerges in basic writing courses. We begin, that is, with what we have been given, and our definition is predetermined by a prior distinction, by a reflex action to sort students into two groups (groups that look "natural" or "right"). . . . We know who basic writers are, in other words, because they are the students in classes we label "Basic Writing." ("Writing on the Margins" 67)

Such categorizing, stripped of its politics, ends up instituting "Basic Writing" as an objective reality rather than a set of social practices. Rather than describing basic writers and basic writing in historical, social, and political terms, the binary of academic/political is maintained, so that statements about basic writing are presented as objective, scientific truths descriptive of facts about who the Basic Writers—this new breed of student—are, what they need, what works for them and what doesn't. As the dominated members of the dominant, teachers can use such representations to negotiate their own interests and those of their students, as I have shown above, establishing by traditional measures of academic worth a legitimized place for basic writing and basic writers in the academy. But this "objectification" of basic writing also masks the role of basic writing instruction in the larger ongoing social, economic, and political drama of history. Though in one sense that drama can seem sufficiently removed from the immediate demands of the classroom to be safely ignored, in fact its force inevitably mediates the values, beliefs, and actions of students and teachers in the classroom, the location and conditions of that classroom, and the aims and performance of all concerned with the course, day by day, year by year. Recovering the "practical" operation of that force in our teaching would be a start toward theorizing our practice and practicing our theory, locating both in society and history.

Such a recovery would counter the alliance of much Basic Writing discourse with the ideology of equal opportunity, an ideology behind Open Admissions itself. That ideology has long been subject to dispute

(Karabel 42–43; Shor, *Critical Teaching* xxii–xxiii, 2; Stuckey; Fox, "Standards" 41–43). But less obviously, that ideology has tended to equate the work of basic writing, like the work of composition teaching generally, with the provision of skills (to ensure equal opportunity). The seeming innocuousness of that equation stems from its denial of social and political oppression, substituting the provision of politically innocent "skills" for political means of fighting such oppression and thus renaming oppression as cognitive lack. Though such a substitution may render composition teaching more politically palatable to some, it has also contributed significantly to the marginal position of composition in the academy and so to the material impoverishment of composition programs. Mike Rose has shown how the identification of the teaching of "remedial" writing with skills acquisition has led to its marginalization in the academy. But ignoring the ideology and the social and political forces underlying that marginalization has prevented teachers from doing more than decrying it, as in Barbara Kaplan's lament, in a 1972 critique of CUNY's implementation of Open Admissions, that, "skill development work has not been treated with the respect it deserves" (217).

Aligned to the depiction of the work of basic writing as provision of "skills" is the "practical" bent of much Basic Writing discourse. The *Journal of Basic Writing* has for a number of years included a warning in its "Call for Articles" that the editors "seek manuscripts that are . . . clearly related to practice." Shaughnessy has described the literature in basic writing as "a miscellany of articles on what has been working, or appears to the teacher to have been working, in a variety of places with a variety of teachers and pedagogies" ("Basic Writing" 147). Shor has noted that in response to the "pedagogical confusion" resulting from "the permanence of mass higher education," there has appeared "a prodigious number of publications . . . spew[ing] forth no end of tonics and cure-alls for bewildered teachers" (*Critical Teaching* 19).

What makes this "practical" bent problematic is what it excludes or discourages from consideration in pursuit of its "practical" results. Raymond Williams, writing on the term "realistic," observes that it often

> shares the implicit impatience of one sense of *practical*. 'Let's be realistic' probably more often means 'let us accept the limits of this situation' (*limits* meaning *hard facts*, often of power or money in their existing and established forms). (*Keywords* 217–18)

The "practical" bent in much Basic Writing discourse accepts the "limits of this situation" in two ways. First, and this seems to have earned it the most criticism, is its neglect of the whys and wherefores of work in basic writing. Stephen North observes that Practitioner inquiry is fundamentally "reactive: The Practitioner needs to decide what to do as a means to an end determined by someone or something else . . . imposed from outside, beyond the bounds of [teachers'] immediate relationship with the students" (37). Like the articles Shaughnessy describes as concentrating on "what works," practitioners and their lore are "concerned with what has worked, is working, or might work in teaching, doing, or learning writing" (North 23). However,

> Practitioners need to know *what* to do, not necessarily—other than "It works"—*why*. This bedrock pragmatism is habit-forming. Practitioners tend to become habitually impatient with complicated causal analyses, which in turn makes them relatively cavalier about such analyses even for the purposes of inquiry. (North 40)

Errors and Expectations fits North's model in documenting Shaughnessy's need, as North puts it, "to come to grips with this radically new situation [of Open Admissions at CUNY], and to invent new ways to deal with it, as well" (North 34). The book does not investigate the policy itself or how it has been implemented but simply finds ways to deal with the conditions to which that policy has led. As Shor observes of Shaughnessy's work, Shaughnessy, while taking a "sympathetic and inside view" of students' writing, "did not investigate the question of critical literacy, or writing for what?" (*Culture Wars* 98). Instead, the presence of the students and the need for them to work on their writing to meet conventional expectations of it are taken largely as givens. While this can serve to secure the place of both basic writing students and teachers in the university, as Shaughnessy argues in the report cited above, it also accepts a particularly marginal position for both to occupy there and a limited notion of the work they are to carry out. That is, while historically the enterprise of basic writing can be seen as foregrounding the politics of how and why one teaches, such a potential is suppressed by the quest for the practical/realistic, which occludes attention to the political through its focus on "skills."

Second, and less noticed, this "practicality" tends to accept as "givens" the material constraints on the work of basic writing. I refer here to such seemingly mundane but nonetheless crucial matters—especially at the time of Open Admissions, but also at present—as salaries, job security, teaching loads, class size, classroom facilities, office space, and secretarial support; also to the conditions giving rise to the problems many basic writing students bring with them to college, such as health problems, lack of child care, inadequate financial aid, and a history of inadequate schooling; and finally to the immediate historical circumstances leading to the presence of these students in college and the ongoing family, economic, and social pressures on those students. No one teaching basic writing, at the time of Open Admissions or since, can be unaware of the power those constraints exert on the work both students and teachers produce, yet Basic Writing discourse gives little space to addressing such issues as intrinsic to teaching and learning. In her report cited above, for example, Shaughnessy acknowledges political pressures on basic writing teachers and students, doubts their legitimacy, and yet turns her attention in the (long) "meanwhile" to accommodating those pressures, calling for the development of more efficient methods of teaching grammar and mechanics. When references to material and institutional constraints do appear in the literature, they generally do so as asides, presented as seemingly unalterable facts about which one might joke, curse, or grieve but not as the subject of analysis.

For example, in a 1977 address in which she considers why most English professors fail to take an interest in teaching writing, Shaughnessy includes among her reasons the fact that

> as writing instruction is presently organized, the teacher who wishes to give his best energies to the instruction of ill-prepared freshmen must be ready to forego many of the rewards and privileges of his profession. He must be resigned to being an altruistic teacher. . . . [though] the fact remains that systems do not function efficiently on altruism, and the educational system must offer the same sorts of prizes and incentives that energize people in other systems—money, time, security, and working conditions that encourage excellence— if the teaching of writing is to advance beyond its present state. ("English Professor's Malady" 95)

This has the makings of a manifesto on working conditions, and what follows at least suggests why writing instruction is "presently organized" as it is in spite of public outcries about the "literacy crisis" (96–97). But the general effect of the argument is to warn teachers of the conditions they should expect for the foreseeable future: such teachers "must be resigned" to working altruistically. It thus echoes a similar call for altruism, mixed jarringly with appeals for better working conditions, sounded in the conclusion to a 1970 essay by Howard Weiner on "The Instructor and Open Admissions":

> While funds, temporary buildings, counselors, technology, tutors, and grand plans are essential, the fate of open admissions, perhaps, will be determined most by the amount of motivation, sensitivity, and hard work the instructor can muster and the presence of plausibly small classes. (293)

Shaughnessy seems to have had just such ideal instructors in mind when she refers to her discovery of "the number of [CUNY] teachers who, without fanfare or remissions and with heavy class loads, have been at work developing imaginative new materials for our students" ("Miserable Truth" 114). Shaughnessy says teachers have been "pedagogically radicalized" by the experience, through teaching CUNY Open Admissions students, of "what it means to be an outsider in academia," by which she seems to mean that teachers have come to reject the "traditional meritocratic model of a college" ("Miserable Truth" 114). But that "radicalization" does not seem to have affected a basic position of accommodation to the conditions about which Shaughnessy complains in "The Miserable Truth," the conditions of retrenchment at CUNY in the mid-1970s. Instead, as Shor has noted of this period, "Low-cost basics made students and teachers settle for less at the very moment they were in schools running on austerity budgets" (*Culture Wars* 94).

Such "settling" is pervasive in the literature, from Weiner's 1970 complaint, cited above, to the present. "Survival of the Fittest," an unusual description of a university writing program from 1976 to 1987 by six successive directors, illustrates the constancy of that settling (Roskelly). The essay is a series of mini-histories by each of the program's directors during a ten-year span, who tell tales of cockroaches, flooding, tiny and precarious budgets, and budget staffing requiring constant attempts to economize. Though the program undergoes several changes as directors attempt to implement different theories about writing instruction, the "basic," basement conditions under which the program operates (in an actual basement) prevail throughout the ten years. Hephzibah Roskelly, one of the directors, notes that one of the difficulties for the program lay in the fact that all of the directors were graduate students, requiring them to assume "a strangely subordinate-but-equal role in administrative politics" (14). But the practice of hiring graduate students as directors itself both speaks to and ensures the continuing subordinate status of the program. In sometimes humorous fashion, the directors recount heroic efforts to secure paychecks due them, acquire a mimeograph machine, and fight floodwaters. But those efforts operate within delimitations that virtually guarantee the ongoing necessity of similar efforts to "survive." The Orwellian "subordinate-but-equal" position of the graduate student/directors, as one of the "conditioning" delimitations, makes any challenge to those limitations unlikely, since such a challenge would put the individual director's own position at risk. Moreover, those conditions define the "fittest" sort of graduate student/teacher/administrator precisely as someone who can learn to endure under such conditions: someone who "fits."

Those conditions are not restricted to ten years at one university. Nor are such discursive moves unusual for basic writing teachers and administrators. For example, "The COMP-LAB Project," one of the essays appearing in the 1979 issue of the *Journal of Basic Writing* devoted to "Programs," describes an experimental Basic Writing program at CUNY's York College that combines particular classroom activities with the use of autotutorial lab work, the latter focusing mostly on editing problems. This program, the authors argue, is both "a better way to solve the most serious writing problems of nontraditional students at CUNY and elsewhere" and "a cheaper way to do that in face of shrinking budgets for remedial courses" (Epes et al. 19). Under a section entitled "Cost-Savings," they suggest that their course "can save instructional dollars for our college" and also cut indirect institutional costs by providing "considerable administrative and staffing flexibility, and higher student retention and pass rates" (35, 36). And they end with the hope that through their program "at least the basics of this skill [of writing in standard English] may be acquired by many students in one semester, and within current budgetary restrictions on remedial education" (37).

It's clear from other statements the authors make that one of their purposes in developing the program has been to protect basic writing students from unjust derision and, more generally, to argue for the educability of such students against those who confound "illiteracy with stupidity" in rejecting the admission of basic writing students into colleges (36–37). They thus can be seen as participating in what Shaughnessy describes as teachers' efforts to "develop more efficient and challenging ways of teaching grammar and mechanics so that we have some time left over to do something else" in order that basic writing students can stay in college (Shaughnessy, "Basic Writing and Open Admissions" 5, 3–4). In short, they are driven by unquestionable and impressive devotion to their students. As their essay also makes clear, they are motivated as well by particular understandings of writing and how it is learned. In other words, not good intentions alone but also careful thought informs the program. But they appear to have been placed in a position whereby their laudable desire to serve students and their professional attention to the problems of learning to write are channeled in a way that effectively reinforces instead of challenging the legitimacy of the conditions of "shrinking budgets" under which they work. The technical solution that the program offers to accomplishing work under those conditions, to the extent that it is "successful," might well be used to justify the size of those budgets and the shrinking of budgets in excess of those. Indeed, it seems likely that from some viewpoints the program's success would be defined only in terms of its cheapness rather than what it enables teachers to teach and students to learn. In other words, the required foregrounding of the "practical"—what "works" or might work—under particular budgetary restrictions pushes into the background any challenging of those restrictions. "Practicality," while eminently understandable and valuable, enables such conditions to remain as unalterable "givens" that will require continued "practicality." This "channeling," it is worth emphasizing again, speaks not to the intentions or the expertise of the authors but to the delimitations of the field of basic writing within which they and others work, the effect a form of discursive positioning of teachers in that field can have in shaping the kind of statements possible and impossible for them to make. Within dominant discourse on Basic Writing, to challenge budgetary conditions would require, in effect, re-imagining and recreating one's position as a teacher of basic writing, and to attempt to do so would be to risk losing one's position—in all senses—as a "teacher of basic writing" and thus to be silenced altogether.[2] For CUNY teachers facing retrenchment, to challenge such conditions would be to give additional fodder to critics of Open Admissions who decried its expense and so to anger administrators ostensibly "supportive" of Basic Writing. Such teachers could thus be "successful" only to the extent that they could accommodate the demands of both those who sought results and those who tabulated the budget.

Material constraints thus come to constitute mere "background" in Basic Writing. Given the combined oppressiveness and pervasiveness of such conditions, it might seem surprising how few references to them one finds in the texts instrumental in establishing Basic Writing as an academic field. However, given the vulnerability of the teachers' position and the dominance of a discourse that defines academic work in opposition to material and political considerations, their rarity is not surprising, nor is the fact that, when such references do appear, their presence is often muffled, set off in conditionals, asides. Indeed, "The COMP-LAB Project" and "Survival of the Fittest," though they present such matters primarily as "background," are unlike most essays describing basic writing programs in mentioning them at all. This tendency dominates even descriptions of those programs that have enjoyed substantial institutional support. David Bartholomae and Anthony Petrosky's description of their program in *Facts, Artifacts, and Counterfacts*, for example, mentions the considerable institutional support given their program only in the Preface.

Though Shaughnessy herself and others speak more critically of such matters in unpublished work, even in these unpublished documents they are presented as "background," and a similar acquiescence to them appears in place of the questioning one might expect. For example, in a January 1972 intradepartmental report on Open Admissions,

Shaughnessy, after speculating on the social and economic pressures affecting basic writing students, concludes:

> But for whatever the reasons, here [the students] are . . . and [City College] is assuming, or learning to assume, their educability at the college level and moving on to the question of what, given harsh limits on time, space, and money, can be done to make Open Admission succeed. ("A Second Report" 6)

Though the "question" she alludes to might suggest an interest in challenging the "harsh limits on time, space, and money," the possible challenges are represented as unrealistic:

> An experiment that proves, for example, that ten students working with two exceptional teachers four hours a day can make impressive gains in writing is of no use to us. It tells us what we know but can't afford. We are working, in Basic Writing, with about 3500 students a semester, and our innovations must be feasible on that scale. (6)

Thus, while the report mentions a variety of conditions imposed by and on Open Admissions and basic writing, this passage has the effect of closing discussion of those conditions with its mock suggestion and its series of assertions of "givens," and it aligns teachers with current institutional policies: "here they are . . . City College has chosen. . . . given harsh limits on time, space, and money. . . . We are working." Later in the report, Shaughnessy warns, "Certainly the greatest peril we face at City [College] is the limitations not of our students but of our budget," but she then ends on this note: "In three semesters, under grotesquely inadequate conditions, we have begun to see how Open Admissions might be made to work. The decision of whether it will be allowed to work now rests with those who have the power to set public priorities" (7, 8). We can see Shaughnessy walking a kind of tightrope here, arguing for the effectiveness of the work done by her and her colleagues, aligning herself with the institution while simultaneously pleading for better treatment from it. Unfortunately, her note can serve not only as a call to improve conditions but also as a reminder of what it is possible to accomplish "under grotesquely inadequate conditions," and its acceptance of a crucial distinction between teachers and "those who have the power to set public priorities" reinforces the position of teachers as powerless altruists who work to achieve under grotesque conditions. As a consequence, the note has the force less of a demand for improvement of those conditions but more of a plea for sympathy (which comes much cheaper). That it had such an effect is suggested by evidence that the complaint was one of many preceding and following it which went unheeded. In December 1971 the department as a whole wrote a letter to City College Dean Chavarria-Aguilar protesting appalling classroom facilities and increased class size for sections of Basic Writing (Faculty). In October 1975, roughly four years later, Theodore Gross, then himself Dean of the City College Humanities Division, in a letter to City College Provost Egon Brenner, complained, "Our real attempt to be helpful, to take on a task of huge proportions . . . has not been supported even minimally by the central administration" (Letter, 3 October 1975). Accompanying Gross's letter is a letter from then English department chair Edward Quinn to Gross, in which Quinn himself complained, "the lack of cooperation in regard to the large basic writing sections is really galling. . . . The sense we are developing here is that teaching writing has the lowest priority of any instructional activity at the College. Morale is sinking fast and along with it our hope for success" (Quinn, Letter). Later letters to Brenner from Gross corroborate this sense of low priority and morale: "Language instruction at the City College, especially under the conditions of a continuing fiscal crisis, is a critical problem" (16 October 1975); "[members of the English department] feel that any cooperation on their part will be taken out of their hides" (27 October 1975). But the 1971 letter of protest from the department had already marked English faculty for such exploitation in a Catch-22. That letter ends with the faculty refusing to take the responsibility "for diluting the Basic Writing program," but they also avow, "We will do our job—more than our job—because we believe in the concept of Open Admissions" (Faculty).

Unfortunately, pedagogies labeled "effective" at producing results within the constraints of degrading material conditions work in tandem with such reports and protests to legitimize those conditions—conditions of "crisis" that seem somehow never to be relieved. Silence about such conditions in much Basic Writing discourse further legitimizes such conditions by its lack of protest or guidance. Teachers of basic writing seeking advice on improving their marginal institutional positions will find nothing on such matters in Shaughnessy's *Errors and Expectations*, despite her noted administrative expertise, nor in much of the other Basic Writing literature. The denigration of basic writing teachers and students which those material conditions both speak to and maintain position the "subject" of Basic Writing as tied to those conditions. Teachers are cast into the position of being hard-working servants doing service, devoted and underpaid to the point of being altruistic volunteers; students are expected to be grateful for their chance to get ahead, being presumably in *no* position to complain. Paradoxically, defining the "practice" of Basic Writing in "academic"—i.e., nonmaterial, nonpolitical—terms, is eminently impractical, leaving undeterred the ways in which

material constraints, rather than academic theories, come to determine
the how and what as well as the why of teaching.

———————

Educational historian Michael Katz has warned that while educational
institutions and structures represent choices that "reflected circumstances
at the time of their origin and the priorities of their founders. . . . the
reification of these historical products has become one of the great obstacles to change. For it casts them as inexorable, transcending history,
even natural, and, as a result, it limits the terms of the debate" (*Reconstructing* 1). The construction of Basic Writing provides an exemplary
instance of compositionists' need to heed Katz's warning. Indeed, in an
eerie echo of Katz, Bartholomae has recently expressed concern that the
"provisional position" which the term "Basic Writing" once represented
has become "fixed, naturalized," suspecting that calling certain courses
and the students in them "Basic Writing" no longer has "strategic value"
("Tidy House" 21). Of course, the "success" of Basic Writing discourse
in becoming "fixed" speaks to its "strategic value," especially during
the early years of Open Admissions. The price of that success, however,
has been the loss of what some teachers now identify as the crucial lessons of Open Admissions.

Bartholomae argues that, at best, basic writing should "continue to
mark an area of contest, of struggle, including a struggle against its stability or inevitability," a "contested area in the university community, a
contact zone, a place of competing positions and interests" ("Tidy House"
8, 21). For this to happen will involve giving voice to different, and suppressed, stories, finding and sharing in our specific experiences and those
of our students as yet untold tales of struggle, defeats, victories, and
resistance, thereby teaching and learning from strategies of resistance
and outright opposition. But to engage in *that* sort of "frontier" work,
we will have to abandon the naturalization and fixing of basic writers,
or any writers, on a developmental scale, and we will have to acknowledge, in our teaching, administering, and our professional discourse,
the place of teaching writing in immediate, ongoing history, part of a
larger education not only of students but of teachers and institutions
about the place, purpose, and practice of higher education in the life of
society.

Shaughnessy has noted that "[r]estricted notions of what writing is
for" caused by the lack of understanding of the history of "what has
gone on in the name of freshman composition over the past hundred
years or so" "encourage us to accept current ways of organizing and
assessing writing instruction . . . lock[ing] us into convictions about what

is most important to learn, who should learn what, or who should teach whom at a point when the uses of literacy in this society need to be re-examined" ("English Professor's Malady" 93). Slevin has argued that to be fully prepared for their profession, teachers of writing ought to know not just "how to teach writing, but the history of writing instruction" (14). The literacy historian Harvey Graff has promised that "the proper study of the historical experience of literacy . . . has much to tell us that is . . . relevant to policy analysis and policy making in the world in which we live today" (77). But until discourse on the teaching of writing recovers the specific historical, material, institutional, and political context of that teaching and that discourse, it will be difficult for us to hear what study of the historical experience of literacy has to say, including the historical experience of basic writing, forcing us to re-learn what that history should have taught us long ago.

2 Conflict and Struggle: The Enemies or Preconditions of Basic Writing?

Min-Zhan Lu

Harlem taught me that light skin Black people was better look, the best to suceed, the best off fanicially etc this whole that I trying to say, that I was brainwashed and people aliked.

I couldn't understand why people (Black and white) couldn't get alone. So as time went along I began learned more about myself and the establishment.

—Sample student paper, *Errors and Expectations*

. . . Szasz was throwing her. She couldn't get through the twelve-and-a-half pages of introduction. . . .

One powerful reason Lucia had decided to major in psychology was that she wanted to help people like her brother, who had a psychotic break in his teens and had been in and out of hospitals since. She had lived with mental illness, had seen that look in her brother's eyes. . . . The assertion that there was no such thing as mental illness, that it was a myth, seemed incomprehensible to her. She had trouble even entertaining it as a hypothesis. . . . Szasz's bold claim was a bone sticking in her assumptive craw.

—Mike Rose, *Lives on the Boundary*

In perceiving conflicting information and points of view, she is subjected to a swamping of her psychological borders.

—Gloria Anzaldúa, *Borderlands/La Frontera: The New Mestiza*

In the Preface to *Borderlands*, Gloria Anzaldúa uses her own struggle "living on borders and in margins" to discuss the trials and triumphs in the lives of "border residents." The image of "border residents" captures the conflict and struggle of students like those appearing in the epigraphs. In perceiving conflicting information and points of view, a writer like Anzaldúa is "subjected to a swamping of her psychological borders" (79). But attempts to cope with conflicts also bring "compensation," "joys," and "exhilaration" (Anzaldúa, Preface). The border resident develops a tolerance for contradiction and ambivalence. She learns to sustain contradiction and turn ambivalence into a new consciousness—"a *third* element which is *greater* than the sum of its *severed parts*":

"a mestiza consciousness" (79–80; emphasis mine). Experience taught Anzaldúa that this developing consciousness is a source of intense pain. For development involves struggle which is "inner" and is played out in the outer terrains (87). But this new consciousness draws energy from the "continual creative motion that keeps breaking down the unitary aspect of each new paradigm" (80). It enables a border resident to act on rather than merely react to the conditions of her or his life, turning awareness of the situation into "inner changes" which in turn bring about "changes in society" (87).

Education as Repositioning

Anzaldúa's account gathers some of the issues on which a whole range of recent composition research focuses, research on how readers and writers necessarily struggle with conflicting information and points of view as they reposition themselves in the process of reading and writing. This research recognizes that reading and writing take place at sites of political as well as linguistic conflict. It acknowledges that such a process of conflict and struggle is a source of pain but constructive as well: a new consciousness emerges from the creative motion of breaking down the rigid boundaries of social and linguistic paradigms.

Compositionists are becoming increasingly aware of the need to tell and listen to stories of life in the borderlands. The CCCC Best Book Award given Mike Rose's *Lives on the Boundary* and the two Braddock Awards given to Glynda Hull and Mike Rose ("This Wooden Shack Place") for their research on students like Lucia attest to this increasing awareness. *College Composition and Communication* recently devoted a whole issue (February 1992) to essays which use images of "boundary," "margin," or "voice" to re-view the experience of reading and writing and teaching reading and writing within the academy (see also Lu, "From Silence to Words"; Bartholomae, "Writing on the Margins"; and Mellix). These publications and their reception indicate that the field is taking seriously two notions of writing underlying these narratives: the sense that the writer writes at a site of conflict rather than "comfortably inside or powerlessly outside the academy" (Lu, "Writing as Repositioning" 20) and a definition of "innovative writing" as cutting across rather than confining itself within boundaries of race, class, gender, and disciplinary differences.

In articulating the issues explored by these narratives from the borderlands, compositionists have found two assumptions underlying various feminist, Marxist, and poststructuralist theories of language useful: first, that learning a new discourse has an effect on the re-forming of individual consciousness; and second, that individual consciousness is necessarily heterogeneous, contradictory, and in process (Bizzell, "Beyond"; Flynn, "Composing"; Harris, "The Idea"; Lunsford, Moglen and Slevin; Trimbur, "Beyond"). The need to reposition oneself and the positive use of conflict and struggle are also explored in a range of research devoted to the learning difficulties of Basic Writers (Bartholomae, "Inventing"; Fox, "Basic Writing"; Horner,"Rethinking"; Hull and Rose, "This Wooden Shack Place"; Lu, "Redefining"; Ritchie; Spellmeyer; Stanley). Nevertheless, such research has had limited influence on Basic Writing instruction, which continues to emphasize skills (Gould and Heyda) and to view conflict as the enemy (Schilb, Brown). I believe that this view of conflict can be traced in the work of three pioneers in Basic Writing: Kenneth Bruffee, Thomas Farrell, and Mina Shaughnessy. In what follows, I examine why this view of conflict had rhetorical power in the historical context in which these pioneers worked and in relation to two popular views of education: education as acculturation and education as accommodation. I also explore how and why this view persists among Basic Writing teachers in the 1990s.

Although Bruffee, Farrell, and Shaughnessy hold different views on the goal of education, they all treat the students' fear of acculturation and the accompanying sense of contradiction and ambiguity as a *deficit.* Even though stories of the borderlands like Anzaldúa's suggest that teachers can and should draw upon students' perception of conflict as a constructive resource, these three pioneers of Basic Writing view evidence of conflict and struggle as something to be dissolved and so propose "cures" aimed at *releasing* students from their fear of acculturation. Bruffee and Farrell present students' acculturation as inevitable and beneficial. Shaughnessy promises them that learning academic discourse will not result in acculturation. Teachers influenced by the work of these pioneers tend to view all signs of conflict and struggle as the *enemy* of Basic Writing instruction. In perpetuating this view, these teachers also tend to adopt two assumptions about language: (1) an "essentialist" view of language holding that the essence of meaning precedes and is independent of language (see Lu, "Redefining" 26); (2) a view of "discourse communities" as "discursive utopias," in each of which a single, unified, and stable voice directly and completely determines the writings of all community members (see Harris, "The Idea" 12).

In the 1970s, the era of open admissions at CUNY, heated debate over the "educability" of Basic Writers gave these views of language and of conflict exceptional rhetorical power. The new field of Basic Writing was struggling to establish the legitimacy of its knowledge and expertise, and it was doing so in the context of arguments made by a group of writers—including Lionel Trilling, Irving Howe, and W. E. B. Du Bois—who could be viewed as exemplary because of their ethnic or racial backgrounds, their academic success, and the popular view that all Basic Writers entering CUNY through the open admissions movement were "minority" students. The writings of Bruffee, Farrell, and Trilling concur that the goal of education is to acculturate students to the kind of academic "community" they posit. Shaughnessy, on the other hand, attempts to eliminate students' conflicting feelings toward academic discourse by reassuring them that her teaching will only "accommodate" but not weaken their existing relationship with their home cultures. Shaughnessy's approach is aligned with the arguments of Irving Howe and W. E. B. Du Bois, who urge teachers to honor students' resistance to deracination. Acculturation and accommodation were the dominant models of open admissions education for teachers who recognized teaching academic discourse as a way of empowering students, and in both models conflict and struggle were seen as the enemies of Basic Writing instruction.

This belief persists in several recent works by a new generation of compositionists and "minority" writers. I will read these writings from the point of view of the border resident and through a view of education as a process of repositioning. In doing so, I will also map out some directions for further demystifying conflict and struggle in Basic Writing instruction and for seeing them as the preconditions of all discursive acts.

Education as Acculturation

In *Errors and Expectations,* Mina Shaughnessy offers us one way of imagining the social and historical contexts of her work: she calls herself a trailblazer trying to survive in a "pedagogical West" (4). This metaphor captures the peripheral position of Basic Writing in English. To other members of the profession, Shaughnessy notes, Basic Writing is not one of their "'real' subjects"; nor are books on Basic Writing "important enough" either to be reviewed or to argue about ("English Professor's Malady" 92). Kenneth Bruffee also testifies to feeling peripheral. Recalling the "collaborative learning" which took place among the directors of CUNY writing programs—a group which included Bruffee himself, Donald McQuade, Mina Shaughnessy, and Harvey Wiener—he points out that the group was brought together not only by their "difficult new task" but also by their sense of having more in common with one another than with many of their "colleagues on [their] own campuses" ("On Not Listening" 4–5).

These frontier images speak powerfully of a sense of being *in* but not *of* the English profession. The questionable academic status of not only their students (seen as "ill-prepared") but also themselves (Basic Writing was mostly assigned to beginning teachers, graduate students, women, minorities, and the underemployed but tenured members of other departments) would pressure teachers like Shaughnessy and Bruffee to find legitimacy for their subject. At the same time, they had to do so by persuading both college administrators who felt "hesitation and discomfort" toward open admissions policies and "senior and tenured professorial staff" who either resisted or did not share their commitment (Lyons 1985, 175). Directly or indirectly, these pioneers had to respond to, argue with, and persuade the "gatekeepers" and "converters" Shaughnessy describes in "Diving In." It is in the context of such challenges that we must understand the key terms the pioneers use and the questions they consider—and overlook—in establishing the problematics of Basic Writing.

One of the most vehement gatekeepers at CUNY during the initial period of open admissions was Geoffrey Wagner (Professor of English at City College). In *The End of Education,* Wagner posits a kind of "university" in which everyone supposedly pursues learning for its own sake, free of all "worldly"—social, economic, and political—interests. To Wagner, open admissions students are the inhabitants of the "world" outside the sort of scholarly "community" which he claims existed at Oxford and City College. They are dunces (43), misfits (129), hostile mental children (247), and the most sluggish of animals (163). He describes a group of Panamanian "girls" taking a Basic Writing course as "abusive, stupid, and hostile" (128). Another student is described as sitting "in a half-lotus pose in back of class with a transistor strapped to his Afro, and nodding off every two minutes" (134). Wagner calls Basic Writing courses offered at City a form of political psychotherapy (145), a welfare agency, and an entertainment center (173). And he calls Shaughnessy "the Circe of CCNY's remedial English program" (129). To Wagner, Basic Writers would cause "the end of education" because they have intellects comparable to those of beasts, the retarded, the psychotic or children; and because they are consumed by non-"academic"— i.e., racial, economic, and political—interests and are indifferent to "learning."

Unlike the "gatekeepers," Louis Heller (Classics professor, City College) represents educators who seemed willing to shoulder the burden of converting the heathens but disapproved of the ways in which CUNY was handling the conversion. Nonetheless, in *The Death of the American University,* Heller approaches the "problems" of open admissions students in ways similar to Wagner's. He contrasts the attitudes of open admissions students and of old Jewish City College students like himself:

> In those days ["decades ago"] there was genuine hunger, and deprivation, and discrimination too, but when a child received failing marks no militant parent group assailed the teacher. Instead parent and child agonized over the subject, placing the responsibility squarely on the child who was given to know that *he* had to measure up to par, not that he was the victim of society, a wicked school system, teachers who didn't understand him, or any of the other pseudosociological nonsense now handed out. (138)

According to Heller, the parents of open admissions students are too "militant." As a result, the students' minds are stuffed with "pseudosociological nonsense" about their victimization by the educational system. The "problem" of open admissions students, Heller suggests, is their militant attitude, which keeps them from trying to "agonize over the subject" and "measure up to par."

Wagner predicts the "end of education" because of the "*arrival* in urban academe of *large,* indeed *overwhelming, numbers* of *hostile* mental children" (247; emphasis mine). As the titles of Heller's chapters suggest, Heller too believes that a "death of the American University" would inevitably result from the "Administrative Failure of Nerve" or "Capitulation Under Force" to "Violence on Campus," which he claims to have taken place at City College. The images of education's end or death suggest that both Wagner and Heller assume that the goal of education is the acculturation of students into an "educated community." They question the "educability" of open admissions students because they *fear* that these students would not only be hostile to the education they promote but also take it over—that is, change it. The apocalyptic tone of their book titles suggests their *fear* that the students' "hostile" or "militant" feelings toward the existing educational system would weaken the ability of the "American University" to realize its primary goal—to acculturate. Their writings show that their view of the "problems" of open admissions students and their view of the goal of education sustain one another.

This view of education as a process of acculturation is shared by Lionel Trilling, another authority often cited as an exemplary minority student (see, for example, Howe, "Living" 108). In a paper titled "The Uncertain Future of the Humanistic Educational Ideal" delivered in 1974, Trilling claims that the view of higher education "as the process of initiation into membership" in a "new, larger, and more complex community" is "surely" not a "mistaken conception" (*The Last Decade* 170). The word "initiation," Trilling points out, designates the "ritually prescribed stages by which a person is brought into a community" (170–71). "Initiation" requires "submission," demanding that one "shape" and "limit" one-self to "*a* self, *a* life" and "preclude any other kind of selfhood remaining available" to one (171, 175; emphasis mine). Trilling doubts that contemporary American culture will find "congenial" the kind of "initiation" required by the "humanistic educational ideal" (171). For contemporary "American culture" too often encourages one to resist any doctrine that does not sustain "a multiplicity of options" (175). And Trilling admits to feeling "saddened" by the unlikelihood that "an ideal of education closely and positively related to the humanistic educational traditions of the past" will be called into being in contemporary America (161).

The trials of "initiation" are the subject of Trilling's short story "Notes on a Departure." The main character, a young college professor about to leave a university town, is portrayed as being forced to wrestle with an apparition which he sometimes refers to as the "angel of Jewish solitude" and, by the end of the story, as "a red-haired comedian" whose "face remained blank and idiot" (*Of This Time* 53, 55). The apparition hounds the professor, often reminding him of the question "'What for?' Jews did not do such things" (54). Toward the end of the story, the professor succeeds in freeing himself from the apparition. Arriving at a state of "readiness," he realizes that he would soon have to "find his *own* weapon, his *own* adversary, his *own* things to do"—findings in which "this red-haired figure . . . would have *no* part" (55; emphasis mine).

This story suggests—particularly in view of Trilling's concern for the "uncertain future" of the "humanistic educational ideal" in the 1970s—that contemporary Americans, especially those from minority cultural groups, face a dilemma: the need to combat voices which remind them of the "multiplicity of options." The professor needs to "wrestle with" two options of "selfhood." First, he must free himself from the authority of the "angel"/"comedian." Then, as the title "Notes on a Departure" emphasizes, he must free himself from the "town." Trilling's representation of the professor's need to "depart" from the voice of his "race" and of the "town" indirectly converges with the belief held by Wagner and Heller that the attitudes "parents" and "society" hand out to open admissions students would pull them away from the "university" and hinder their full initiation—acculturation—into the "educated" community.

Read in the 1990s, these intersecting approaches to the "problems" of "minority" students might seem less imposing, since except perhaps for Trilling, the academic prestige of these writers has largely receded. Yet, we should not underestimate the authority these writers had within the academy. As both the publisher and the author of *The End of Education* (1976) remind us within the first few pages of the book, Wagner is not only a graduate of Oxford but a full professor at City College and author of a total of twenty-nine books of poetry, fiction, literary criticism, and sociology. Heller's *The Death of the American University* (1973) indicates that he has ten years' work at the doctoral or postdoctoral level in three fields, a long list of publications, and years of experience as both a full professor of classics and an administrator at City College (12). Furthermore, their fear of militancy accorded with prevalent reactions to the often violent conflict in American cities and college campuses during the 1960s and '70s. It was in the context of such powerful discourse that composition teachers argued for not only the "educability" of open admissions students but also the ability of the "pioneer" educators to "educate" them. Bruffee's and Farrell's eventual success in establishing the legitimacy of their knowledge and expertise as Basic Writing teachers, I believe, comes in part from a conjuncture in the arguments of the two Basic Writing pioneers and those of Wagner, Heller, and Trilling.

For example, Thomas Farrell presents the primary goal of Basic Writing instruction as acculturation—a move from "orality" to "literacy." He treats open admissions students as existing in a "residual orality": "literate patterns of thought have not been interiorized, have not displaced oral patterns, in them" ("Open Admissions" 248). Referring to Piaget, Ong, and Bernstein, he offers environmental rather than biological reasons for Basic Writers' "orality"—their membership in "communities" where "orality" is the dominant mode of communication. To Farrell, the emigration from "orality" to "literacy" is unequivocally beneficial for everyone, since it mirrors the progression of history. At the same time, Farrell recognizes that such a move will inevitably be accompanied by "anxiety": "The *psychic strain* entailed in moving from a highly oral frame of mind to a more literate frame of mind is *too great* to allow rapid movement" (252; emphasis mine). Accordingly, he promotes teaching strategies aimed at "reducing anxiety" and establishing "a supportive environment." For example, he urges teachers to use the kind of "collaborative learning" Bruffee proposes so that they can use "oral discourse to improve written discourse" ("Open Admissions" 252–53; "Literacy" 40–41). He reminds teachers that "highly oral students" won't engage in the "literate" modes of reasoning "unless they are shown how and reminded to do so often," and even then will do so only "gradually" ("Literacy" 40).

Kenneth Bruffee also defines the goal of Basic Writing in terms of the students' acculturation into a new "community." According to Bruffee,

Basic Writers have already been acculturated within "local communities" which have prepared them for only "the narrowest and most limited" political and economic relations ("On Not Listening" 7). The purpose of education is to "reacculturate" the students—to help them "gain
membership in another such community" by learning its "language,
mores, and values" (8). However, Bruffee believes that the "trials of
changing allegiance from one cultural community to another" demand
that teachers use "collaborative learning" in small peer groups. This
method will "create a *temporary transition* or 'support' group that [one]
can join *on the way*" (8; emphasis mine). This "transition group," he maintains, will offer Basic Writers an arena for sharing their "trials," such as
the "uncertain, nebulous, and protean thinking that occurs in the process of change" and the "painful process" of gaining new awareness
("On Not Listening" 11; "Collaborative Learning: Some Practical Models" 640).

Two points bind Bruffee's argument to Farrell's and enhance the rhetorical power of their arguments for the Wagners, Hellers, and Trillings.
First, both arguments assume that the goal of education is acculturation
into a "literate" community. The image of students who are "changing
allegiance from one cultural community to another" (Bruffee), like the
image of students "moving" from "orality" to "literacy" (Farrell), posits
that "discourse communities" are discrete and autonomous entities
rather than interactive cultural forces. When discussing the differences
between "orality" and "literacy," Farrell tends to treat these "discourses"
as creating coherent but distinct modes of thinking: "speaking" vs. "reading," "cliches" vs. "explained and supported generalizations," "addi-
tive" vs. "inductive or deductive" reasoning. Bruffee likewise sets "*coherent* but *entirely* local communities" against a community which is
"broader, highly diverse, *integrated*" ("On Not Listening" 7; emphasis
mine). Both Farrell and Bruffee use existing analyses of "discourse communities" to set up a seemingly nonpolitical hierarchy between academic
and nonacademic "communities." They then use the hierarchy to justify
implicitly the students' need to be acculturated by the more advanced
or broader "community." Thus, they can be construed as promising "effective" ways of appeasing the kind of "hostility" or "militancy" feared
in open admissions students. The appeal of this line of thinking is that it
protects the autonomy of the "literate community" while also professing a solution to the "threat" the open admissions students seem to pose
to the university. They provide methods aimed at keeping students like
Anzaldúa, Lucia, and the writer of Shaughnessy's sample paper from
moving the points of view and discursive forms they have developed in
their home "communities" into the "literate community" and also at
persuading such students to willingly "move" into that "literate community."

Second, both Bruffee and Farrell explicitly look for teaching methods aimed at reducing the feelings of "anxiety" or "psychic strain" accompanying the process of acculturation. They thus present these feelings as signs of the students' still being "on the way" from one community to another, i.e., as signs of their failure to complete their acculturation or education. They suggest that the students are experiencing these trials only because they are still in "transition," bearing ties to both the old and new communities but not fully "departed" from one nor comfortably "inside" the other. They also suggest that these experiences, like the transition or support groups, are "temporary" (Bruffee, "On Not Listening" 8). In short, they sustain the impression that these experiences ought to and will disappear once the students get comfortably settled in the new community and sever or diminish their ties with the old. Any sign of heterogeneity, uncertainty, or instability is viewed as problematic; hence conflict and struggle are the enemies of Basic Writing instruction.

This linkage between students' painful conflicts and the teacher's effort to assuage them had rhetorical power in America during the 1970s because it could be perceived as accepting rather than challenging the gatekeepers' and converters' arguments that the pull of non-"academic" forces—"society" (Wagner), "militant parents" (Heller), and minority "race" or "American culture" at large (Trilling)—would render the open admissions students less "educable" and so create a "problem" in their education. It feeds the fear that the pulls of conflicting "options," "selfhoods," or "lives" promoted by antagonistic "communities" would threaten the university's ability to acculturate the Basic Writers. At the same time, this linkage also offers a "support system" aimed at releasing the gatekeepers and converters from their fear. For example, the teaching strategies Farrell promotes, which explicitly aim to support students through their "psychic strain," are also aimed at gradually easing them into "interiorizing" modes of thinking privileged by the "literate community," such as "inductive or deductive" reasoning or "detached, analytic forms of thinking" ("Literacy" 39, 40). Such strategies thus provide a support system for not only the students but also the kind of discursive utopia posited by Trilling's description of the "humanistic educational ideal," Heller's "American University," and Wagner's "education." Directly and indirectly, the pedagogies aimed at "moving" students from one culture to another support and are supported by gatekeepers' and converters' positions toward open admissions students.

The pedagogies of Bruffee and Farrell recognize the "psychic strain" or the "trials" experienced by those reading and writing at sites of contradiction, experiences which are depicted by writers like Trilling ("Notes on a Departure"), Anzaldúa, and Rose and witnessed by teachers in their encounters with students like Lucia and the writer of Shaughnessy's sample paper. Yet, for two reasons, the approaches of Bruffee and Farrell are unlikely to help such students cope with the conflicts "swamping" their "psychological borders." First, these approaches suggest that the students' primary task is to change allegiance, to "learn" and "master" the "language, mores, and values" of the academic community presented in the classroom by passively internalizing them and actively rejecting all points of view or information which run counter to them (Bruffee, "On Not Listening" 8). For the author of Shaughnessy's sample student paper, this could mean learning to identify completely with the point of view of authorities like the Heller of *The Death of the American University* and thus to reject "militant" thoughts about the "establishment" in order to "agonize over the subject." For Lucia, this could mean learning to identify with the Trilling of "Notes on a Departure," viewing her ability to forget the look in her brother's eyes as a precondition of becoming a psychologist like Szasz. Yet students like Lucia might resist what the classroom seems to indicate they must do in order to achieve academic "success." As Rose reminds us, one of the reasons Lucia decided to major in psychology was to help people like her brother. Students like these are likely to get very little help or guidance from teachers like Bruffee or Farrell.

Second, though Bruffee and Farrell suggest that the need to cope with conflicts is a temporary experience for students unfamiliar with and lacking mastery of dominant academic values and forms, Rose's account of his own education indicates that similar experiences of "confusion, anger, and fear" are not at all temporary (*Lives* 235–36). During Rose's high school years, his teacher Jack MacFarland had successfully helped him cope with his "sense of linguistic exclusion" complicated by "various cultural differences" by engaging him in a sustained examination of "points of conflict and points of possible convergence" between home and academic canons (193). Nevertheless, during Rose's first year at Loyola and then during his graduate school days, he continued to experience similar feelings when encountering texts and settings which reminded him of the conflict between home and school. If students like Rose, Lucia, or the writer of Shaughnessy's sample paper learn to view experiences of conflict—exclusion, confusion, uncertainty, psychic pain or strain—as "temporary," they are also likely to view the recurrence of those experiences as a reason to discontinue their education. Rather than viewing their developing ability to sustain contradictions as heralding the sort of "new mestiza consciousness" Anzaldúa calls for (80), they may take it as signaling their failure to "enter" the academy, since they have been led to view the academy as a place free of contradictions.

Education as Accommodation

Whereas the gatekeepers and converters want students to be either barred from or acculturated into academic culture, Irving Howe (Distinguished Professor of English, Graduate Center of CUNY and Hunter College), another City graduate often cited by the public media as an authority on the education of open admissions students (see Fiske), takes a somewhat different approach. He believes that "the host culture, resting as it does on the English language and the literary traditions associated with it, has . . . every reason to be *sympathetic* to the *problems* of those who, from choice or necessity, may *live with* the *tension of biculturalism*" ("Living" 110; emphasis mine).

The best way to understand what Howe might mean by this statement and why he promotes such a position is to put it in the context of two types of educational stories Howe writes. The first type appears in his *World of Our Fathers,* in which he recounts the "cultural bleaching" required of Jewish immigrants attending classes at the Educational Alliance in New York City around the turn of this century. As Eugene Lyons, one immigrant whom Howe quotes, puts it, "We were 'Americanized' about as gently as horses are broken in." Students who went through this "crude" process, Lyons admits, often came to view their home traditions as "alien" and to "unconsciously resent and despise those traditions" (Howe, *World* 234). Howe points out that education in this type of "Americanization" exacted a price, leaving the students with a "nagging problem in self-perception, a crisis of identity" (*World* 642). Read in the context of Howe's statement on the open admissions students cited above, this type of story points to the kind of "problems" facing students who have to live with the tension between the "minority subcultures" in which they grow up and a "dominant" "Western" "host culture" with which they are trying to establish deep contact through education ("Living" 110). It also points to the limitations of an educational system which is not sympathetic to their problems.

The "Americanization" required of students like Eugene Lyons, Howe points out, often led Jewish students to seek either "a full return to religious faith or a complete abandonment of Jewish identification" (642). But Howe rejects both such choices. He offers instead an alternative story—the struggle of writers like himself to live with rather than escape from "the tension of biculturalism." In *A Margin of Hope,* he recounts his long journey in search of a way to "achieve some equilibrium with that earlier self which had started with childhood Yiddish, my language of naming, and then turned away in adolescent shame" (269). In

"Strangers," Howe praises Jewish writers like Saul Bellow and the contributors to *Partisan Review* for their attitudes toward their "partial
deracination" (*Selected Writings* 335). He argues that these writers demonstrated that being a "loose-fish" (with "roots loosened in Jewish soil
but still not torn out, roots lowered into American soil but still not fixed")
is "a badge" to be carried "with pride" (335). Doing so can open up a
whole "range of possibilities" (335), such as the "forced yoking of oppo-
sites: gutter vividness and university refinement, street energy and high-
culture rhetoric" Howe sees these writers achieving (338). This suggests
what Howe might mean by "*living with* the tension of biculturalism."
The story he tells of the struggle of these Jewish writers also proves that
several claims made in the academy of the earlier 1970s, as Howe points
out, are "true and urgent": (1) students who grow up in "subcultures"
can feel "pain and dislocation" when trying to "connect with the larger,
cosmopolitan culture"; (2) for these students, "there must always be some
sense of 'difference,' even alienation"; (3) this sense of difference can
"yield moral correction and emotional enrichment" ("Living" 110). The
story of these writers also suggests that when dealing with students from
"subcultures," the dominant culture and its educational system need,
as Howe argues, to be more "sympathetic to" the pain and alienation
indicated by the first two claims, and at the same time should value
more highly the "infusion of vitality and diversity from subcultures"
that the third claim suggests these students can bring (110).

Howe believes that the need for reform became especially urgent in
the context of the open admissions movement, when a large number of
"later immigrants, newer Americans" from racial as well as ethnic "subcultures" arrived at CUNY ("A Foot"). He also believes that, although
the dominant culture needs to be more "responsive" and "sympathetic"
toward this body of students, it would be "a dreadful form of intellectual condescension—and social cheating" for members of the "host culture" to dissuade students from establishing a "deep connection" with
it. The only possible and defensible "educational ideal" is one which
brings together commitments to "the widespread diffusion of learning"
and to the "preservation of the highest standards of learning" (109).

However, as Howe himself seems aware throughout his essay, he is
more convinced of the need to live up to this ideal than certain about
how to implement it in the day-to-day life of teaching, especially with
"the presence of large numbers of ill-prepared students in our classroom" ("Living" 110, 112). For example, the values of "traditionalism"
mean that teachers like Howe should try to "preserve" the "English language and the literary traditions" associated with "the dominant culture we call Western" (109, 110). Yet, when Howe tries to teach *Clarissa*

to his students, he finds out that he has to help students to "transpose" and "translate" Clarissa's belief in the sanctity of her virginity into their "terms." And he recognizes that the process of transposing would "necessarily distort and weaken" the original belief (112). This makes him realize that there is "reason to take seriously the claim" that "a qualitative transformation of Western culture threatens the survival of literature as we have known it" (112).

Although Howe promotes the images of "loose-fish" and "partial deracination" when discussing the work of Jewish writers, in his discussion of the education of "ill-prepared" students, he considers the possibility of change from only one end of the "tension of bi-culturalism"—that of "Western culture." His essay overlooks the possibility that the process of establishing a deep connection with "Western culture," such as teaching students to "transpose" their "subcultural" beliefs into the terms of "Western culture," might also "distort and weaken"—*transform*—the positions students take toward these beliefs, especially if these beliefs conflict with those privileged in "Western culture." In fact, teachers interested in actively honoring the students' decisions and needs to "live with the tension of bi-culturalism" must take this possibility seriously (see Lu, "Redefining" 33).

In helping students to establish deep connections with "Western culture," teachers who overlook the possibility of students' changing their identification with "sub-cultural" views are likely to turn education into an accommodation—or mere tolerance—of the students' choice or need to live with conflicts. This accommodation could hardly help students explore, formulate, reflect on, and enact strategies for coping actively with conflicts as the residents of borderlands do: developing a "tolerance for" and an ability to "sustain" contradictions and ambiguity (Anzaldúa 79). Even if teachers explicitly promote the image of "partial deracination," they are likely to be more successful in helping students unconsciously "lower" and "fix" their roots into "Western culture" than in also helping them keep their roots from being completely "torn out" of "subcultures."

Two recurring words in Howe's essay, "preserve" and "survival," suggest a further problematic, for they represent the students as "preservers" of conflicting but unitary paradigms—a canonical "literary tradition" and "subcultures" with "attractive elements that merit study and preservation" ("Living" 110). This view of their role might encourage students to envision themselves as living at a focal point where "severed or separated pieces merely come together" (Anzaldúa 79). Such perceptions might also lead students to focus their energy on "accommodating" their thoughts and actions to rigid boundaries rather than on actively engaging themselves in what to Anzaldúa is the resource of life in the borderlands: a "continual creative motion" which breaks entrenched habits and patterns of behavior (Anzaldúa 79). The residents of the borderlands act on rather than react to the "borders" cutting across society and their psyches, "borders" which become visible as they encounter conflicting ideas and actions. In perceiving these "borders," the mestizas refuse to let these seemingly rigid boundaries confine and compartmentalize their thoughts and actions. Rather, they use these "borders" to identify the unitary aspects of "official" paradigms which "set" and "separate" cultures and which they can then work to break down. That is, for the mestizas, "borders" serve to delineate aspects of their psyche and the world requiring change. Words such as "preserve" and "survival," in focusing the students' attention on accommodation rather than change, could not help students become active residents of the borderlands.

The problematics surfacing from Howe's writings—the kind of "claims" about students from "subcultures" that he considers "true and urgent," the kind of "problems" he associates with students living with the tension of conflicting cultural forces, and the questions he raises as well as those he overlooks when discussing his "educational ideal"—map the general conceptual framework of a group of educators to whose writings I now turn. The writings of Leonard Kriegel, another member of the CUNY English faculty, seem to address precisely the question of how a teacher might implement in the day-to-day teaching of "remedial" students at City College the educational ideal posited by Howe.

In *Working Through: A Teacher's Journey in the Urban University*, Kriegel bases his authority on his personal experience as first a City undergraduate and then a City professor before and during the open admissions movement. Kriegel describes himself as a "working-class Jewish youth"—part of a generation not only eager to "get past [its] backgrounds, to deodorize all smells out of existence, especially the smells of immigrant kitchens and beer-sloppy tables," but also anxious to emulate the "aggressive intellectualism" of City students (32, 123). Kriegel maintains that in his days as a student, there existed a mutual trust between teachers and students: "My teachers could assume a certain intelligence on my part; I, in turn, could assume a certain good will on theirs" (29).

When he was assigned to teach in the SEEK program, Kriegel's first impression was that such a mutual trust was no longer possible. For example, when he asked students to describe Canova's *Perseus Holding the Head of Medusa,* a student opened his paper, "When I see this statue it is of the white man and he is holding the head of the Negro" (176). Such papers led Kriegel to conclude that these students had not only "elementary" problems with writing but also a "racial consciousness [which] seemed to obscure everything else" (176). Yet working among the SEEK students gradually convinced Kriegel that the kind of mutual trust he had previously enjoyed with his teachers and students was not only possible but necessary. He discovered that his black and Puerto Rican students "weren't very different from their white peers": they did not lack opinions and they did want in to the American establishment (175, 178). They can and do trust the "good will" of the teacher who can honestly admit that he is a product of academic culture and believes in it, who rids himself of the "inevitable white guilt" and the fear of being accused of "cultural colonialism," and who permits the students to define their needs in relation to the culture rather than rejecting it for them (180). Kriegel thus urges teachers to "leave students alone" to make their own choices (182).

Kriegel's approach to his journey falls within the framework Howe establishes. The university ought to be "*responsive* to the needs and points of view of students who are of *two minds* about what Western culture offers them" ("Playing It Black" 11; emphasis mine). Yet, when summarizing the lessons he learned through SEEK, Kriegel implies that being "responsive" does not require anything of the teacher other than "*permit[ting]* the student *freedom of choice,* to let him take what he felt he needed and let go of what was not important to him" (*Working Through* 207; emphasis mine). Kriegel ultimately finds himself "mak[ing] decisions based on old values" and "placing greater and greater reliance on the traditional cultural orientation to which [he] had been exposed as an undergraduate" (201–2). The question he does not consider throughout his book is the extent to which his reliance on "old values" and "traditional cultural orientation" might affect his promise to accommodate the students' freedom of choice, especially if they are of "two minds" about what Western culture offers them. That is, he never considers whether his teaching practice might implicitly disable his students' ability to exercise the "freedom" he explicitly "permits" them.

Kriegel's story suggests that business in the classroom could go on as usual so long as teachers openly promise students their "freedom of choice." His story implies that the kind of teaching traditionally used to disseminate the conventions of the "English language or literary tradition" is politically and culturally neutral. It takes a two-pronged approach to educational reform: (1) explicitly stating the teacher's willingness to accommodate—i.e., understand, sympathize with, accept, and respect—the students' choice or need to resist total acculturation; (2) implicitly dismissing the ways in which particular teaching practices "choose" for students—i.e., set pressures on the ways in which students formulate, modify, or even dismiss—their position toward conflicting cultures (for comparable positions by other City faculty, see Quinn, "We're Holding," and Volpe). This approach has rhetorical currency because it both aspires to and promises to deliver the kind of education envisioned by another group of minority writers with established authority in 1970s America, a group which included black intellectuals W. E. B. Du Bois and James Baldwin. Using personal and communal accounts, these writers also argue for educational systems which acknowledge students' resistance to cultural deracination. Yet, because their arguments for such an educational reform are seldom directly linked to discussion of specific pedagogical issues, teachers who share Kriegel's position could read Du Bois and Baldwin as authorizing accommodation.

For example, in *The Education of Black People,* Du Bois critiques the underlying principle of earlier educational models for black students, such as the "Hampton Idea" or the Fisk program, which do not help students deal with what he elsewhere calls their double-consciousness (12, 51). Instead, such models pressure students to "escape their cultural heritage and the body of experience which they themselves have built-up." As a result, these students may "meet *peculiar frustration* and in the end be unable to achieve success in the new environment or fit into the old" (144; emphasis mine).

Du Bois's portrayal of the "peculiar frustration" of black students, like Howe's account of the "problems" of Jewish students, speaks powerfully of the need to consider seriously Howe's list of the "claims" made during the open admissions movement ("Living" 110). It also supports Howe's argument that the dominant culture needs to be more "sympathetic" to the "problems" of students from black and other ethnic cultures. Du Bois's writings offer teachers a set of powerful narratives to counter the belief that students' interests in racial politics will impede their learning. In fact, Du Bois's life suggests that being knowledgeable of and concerned with racial politics is a precondition to one's eventual ability to "force" oneself "in" and to "share" the world with "the owners" (*Education* 77).

At the same time, Du Bois's autobiography can also be read as supporting the idea that once the teacher accepts the students' need to be interested in racial politics and becomes "sympathetic to"—acknowledges—their "peculiar frustration," business in the writing classroom can go on as usual. For example, when recalling his arrival at Harvard "in the midst of a violent controversy about poor English among students," Du Bois describes his experiences in a compulsory Freshman English class as follows:

> I was at the point in my intellectual development when the content rather than the form of my writing was to me of prime importance. Words and ideas surged in my mind and spilled out with disregard of exact accuracy in grammar, taste in word or restraint in style. I knew the Negro problem and this was more important to me than literary form. I knew grammar fairly well, and I had a pretty wide vocabulary; but I was bitter, angry and intemperate in my first thesis. . . . Senator Morgan of Alabama had just published a scathing attack on "niggers" in a leading magazine, when my first Harvard thesis was due. I let go at him with no holds barred. My long and blazing effort came back marked "E"—not passed. (*Autobiography* 144)

Consequently, Du Bois "went to work at" his English and raised the grade to a "C." Then, he "*elected* the best course on the campus for English composition," one which was taught by Barrett Wendell, "then the great pundit of Harvard English" (144–45; emphasis mine).

Du Bois depicts his teacher as "fair" in judging his writing "technically" but as having neither any idea of nor any interest in the ways in which racism "scratch[ed] [Du Bois] on the raw flesh" (144). Du Bois presents his own interest in the "Negro problem" as a positive force; enabling him to produce "solid content" and "worthy" thoughts. At the same time, he also presents his racial/political interest as making him "bitter, angry, and intemperate." The politics of style would suggest that his "disregard of exact accuracy in grammar, taste in word or restraint in style" when writing the thesis might have stemmed not only from his failure to recognize the importance of *form* but also from the particular constraints this "literary form" placed on his effort to "spill out" bitter and angry *contents* against the establishment. Regard for "*accuracy* in grammar, *taste* in words or *restraint* in style" would have constrained his effort to "let go at [Senator Morgan] with no holds barred" (emphasis mine). But statements such as "style is *subordinate* to content" but "*carries* a message further" suggest that Du Bois accepts wholeheartedly the view that the production of "something to say" takes place before and independent of the effort to "say it well" (144; emphasis mine). Nor does Du Bois fault his teachers for failing to help him recognize and then practice ways of dealing with the politics of a "style" which privileges "restraint." Rather, his account suggests only that writing teachers need to become more understanding of the students' racial/political interests and their tendency to view "the Negro problem" as more important than "literary form." Thus, his account allows teachers to read it as endorsing the idea that once the teachers learn to show more interest in what the students "have to say" about racism, they can continue to teach "literary form" in the way Du Bois's composition teachers did.

Neither do the writings of James Baldwin, whom Shaughnessy cites as the kind of "mature and gifted writer" her Basic Writers could aspire to become (*Errors* 197), provide much direct opposition to this two-pronged approach to reform. In "A Talk to Teachers" (originally published in the *Saturday Review,* 21 December 1963), Baldwin argues that "any Negro who is born in this country and undergoes the American educational system runs the risk of becoming schizophrenic" (*Price* 326; see also *Conversations* 183), thus providing powerful support for Howe's call for sympathy from the dominant culture. Baldwin does offer some very sharp and explicit critiques of the view of literary style as politically innocent. In "If Black English Isn't a Language, Then Tell Me, What Is?" Baldwin points out that "the rules of the language are dictated by what the language must convey" (*Price* 651). He later explains that standard English "was not designed to carry those spirits and patterns" he has observed in his relatives and among the people from the streets and churches of Harlem, so he "had to find a way to bend it [English]" when writing about them in his first book (*Conversations* 162). These descriptions suggest that Baldwin is aware of the ways in which the style of one particular discourse mediates one's effort to generate content or a point of view alien to that discourse. Yet, since he is referring to his writing experience *after* he has become what Shaughnessy calls a "mature and gifted writer" rather than to his experience as a student in a writing classroom, he does not directly challenge the problematics surfacing in discussions of educational reform aimed at accommodation without change.

The seeming resemblances between minority educators and Basic Writers—their "subculture" backgrounds, the "psychic woe" they experience as a result of the dissonance within or among cultures, their "ambivalence" toward cultural bleaching, and their interest in racial/class politics—make these educators powerful allies for composition teachers like Shaughnessy who are not only committed to the educational rights and capacity of Basic Writers but also determined to grant students the freedom of choosing their alignments among conflicting cultures. We should not underestimate the support these narratives could provide for the field of Basic Writing as it struggled in the 1970s to establish legitimacy for its knowledge and expertise. I call attention to this support because of the intersection I see between Shaughnessy's approach to the function of conflict and struggle in Basic Writing instruction and the problematics I have sketched out in discussing the writings of Howe, Kriegel, Du Bois, and Baldwin.

Like Howe and Du Bois, Shaughnessy tends to approach the problems of Basic Writers in terms of their ambivalence toward academic culture:

> College both beckons and threatens them, offering to teach them useful ways of thinking and talking about the world, promising even to improve the quality of their lives, but threatening at the same time to take from them their distinctive ways of interpreting the world, to assimilate them into the culture of academia without acknowledging their experience as outsiders. (*Errors* 292)

Again and again, Shaughnessy reminds us of her students' fear that mastery of a new discourse could wipe out, cancel, or take from them the points of view resulting from "their experience as outsiders." This fear, she argues, causes her students to mistrust and psychologically resist learning to write. And she reasons that "if students understand why they are being asked to learn something and if the reasons given *do not conflict* with deeper needs for self-respect and loyalty to their group (whether that be an economic, racial, or ethnic group), they *are disposed* to learn it" (*Errors* 125; emphasis mine).

Shaughnessy proposes some teaching methods toward that end. For example, when discussing her students' difficulty developing an "academic vocabulary," she suggests that students might resist associating a new meaning with a familiar word because accepting that association might seem like consenting to a "linguistic betrayal that threatens to wipe out not just a word but the reality that the word refers to" (*Errors* 212). She then goes on to suggest that "if we consider the formal (rather than the contextual) ways in which words can be made to shift meaning we are closer to the kind of practical information about words BW students need" (212). Shaughnessy's rationale seems to be that the "formal" approach (in this case teaching students to pay attention to prefixes and suffixes) is more "practical" because it will help students master the academic meaning of a word *without* reminding them that doing so might "wipe out" the familiar "reality"—the world, people, and meanings—previously associated with that word.

As I have argued elsewhere, the "formal" approach can be taken as "practical" only if teachers view the students' awareness of the conflict between the home meaning and the school meaning of a word as something to be "dissolved" at all costs because it will make them less "disposed to learn" academic discourse, as Shaughnessy seems to believe (Lu, "Redefining" 35). However, the experiences of Anzaldúa and Rose suggest that the best way to help students cope with the "pain," "strain," "guilt," "fear," or "confusions" resulting from this type of conflict is not to find ways of "releasing" the students from these experiences or to avoid situations which might activate them. Rather, the "contextual" approach would have been more "practical," since it could help students deal self-consciously with the threat of "betrayal," especially if they fear and want to resist it. The "formal approach" recommended by Shaughnessy is likely to be only a more "practical" way of preserving "academic vocabulary" and of speeding the students' internalization of it. But as Rose's experiences working with students like Lucia indicate, it is exactly because teachers like him took the "contextual" approach— "encouraging her to talk through opinions of her own that ran counter to these discussions" (Rose, *Lives* 184–85)—that Lucia was able to get beyond the first twelve pages of Szasz's text and learn the "academic" meaning of "mental illness" posited by Szasz, a meaning which literally threatens to wipe out the "reality" of her brother's illness and her feelings about it.

Shaughnessy's tendency to overlook the political dimensions of the linguistic choices students make when reading and writing also points to the ways in which her "essentialist" view of language and her view of conflict and struggle as the enemies of Basic Writing instruction feed on one another (see Lu, "Redefining" 26, 28–29). The supposed separation between language, thinking, and living reduces language into discrete and autonomous linguistic varieties or sets of conventions, rules, standards, and codes rather than treating language as a site of cultural conflict and struggle. From the former perspective, it is possible to believe, as Shaughnessy seems to suggest when opting for the "formal" approach to teaching vocabulary, that learning the rules of a new "language variety"—"the language of public transactions"—will give the student the "ultimate freedom of deciding how and when and where he will use which language" (*Errors* 11, 125). And it makes it possible for teachers like Shaughnessy to separate a "freedom" of choice in "linguistic variety" from one's social being—one's need to deliberate over and decide how to reposition oneself in relationship to conflicting cultures and powers. Thus, it might lead teachers to overlook the ways in which one's "freedom" of cultural alignment might impinge on one's freedom in choosing "linguistic variety."

Shaughnessy's approach to Basic Writing instruction has rhetorical power because of its seeming alignment with positions taken by "minority" writers. Her portrayal of the "ambivalent feelings" of Basic Writers matches the experiences of "wrestling" (Trilling) and "partial deracination" (Howe), "the distinctive frustration" (Du Bois), and "schizophrenia" (Baldwin) portrayed in the writings of the more established members of the academy. All thus lend validity to each other's understanding of the "problems" of students from minority cultures and

to their critiques of educational systems which mandate total acculturation. Shaughnessy's methods of teaching demonstrate acceptance of and
compassion toward students' experience of the kind of "dislocation,"
"alienation," or "difference" which minority writers like Howe, Du Bois,
and Baldwin argue will always accompany those trying by choice or
need to "live with" the tensions of conflicting cultures. Her methods of
teaching also demonstrate an effort to accommodate these feelings and
points of view. That is, because of her essentialist assumption that words
can express but will not change the essence of one's thoughts, her pedagogy promises to help students master academic discourse without forcing them to reposition themselves—i.e., to re-form their relation—toward conflicting cultural beliefs. In that sense, her teaching promises to
accommodate the students' need to establish deep contact with a "wider,"
more "public" culture by "releasing" them from their fear that learning
academic discourse will cancel out points of view meaningful to their
non-"academic" activities. At the same time, it also promises to accommodate their existing ambivalence toward and differences from academic
culture by assuming that "expressing" this ambivalence and these differences in academic "forms" will not change the "essence" of these
points of view. The lessons she learns from her journey in the "pedagogical West" thus converge with those of Kriegel, who dedicates his
book to "Mina Shaughnessy, who knows that nothing is learned simply." That is, when discussing her teaching methods, she too tends to
overlook the ways in which her methods of teaching "linguistic codes"
might weaken her concern to permit the students freedom of choice in
their points of view. Ultimately, as I have argued, the teaching of both
Shaughnessy and Kriegel might prove to be more successful in preserving the traditions of "English language and literature" than in helping
students reach a self-conscious choice on their position toward conflicting cultural values and forces.

Contesting the Residual Power of Viewing Conflict and Struggle as the Enemies of Basic Writing Instruction: Present and Future

The view that all signs of conflict and struggle are the enemies of Basic
Writing instruction emerged partly from a set of specific historical conditions surrounding the Open Admissions movement. Open Admissions
at CUNY was itself an attempt to deal with immediate, intense, sometimes violent social, political, and racial confrontations. Such a context
might have provided a "logic" for shifting students' attention *away* from
conflict and struggle and *toward* calm. However, the academic status
which pioneers like Bruffee, Farrell, and Shaughnessy have achieved

and the practical, effective *cures* their pedagogies seem to offer have combined to perpetuate the rhetorical power of such a view for Basic Writing instruction through the 1970s to the present. The consensus among the gatekeepers, converters, and accommodationists furnishes some Basic Writing teachers with a complacent sense that they already know all about the "problems" Basic Writers have with conflict and struggle. This complacency makes teachers hesitant to consider the possible uses of conflict and struggle, even when these possibilities are indicated by later developments in language theories and substantiated both by accounts of alternative educational experiences by writers like Anzaldúa and Rose and by research on the constructive use of conflict and struggle, such as the research discussed in the first section of this essay.

Such complacency is evident in the works of compositionists like Mary Epes and Ann Murphy. Epes's work suggests that she is aware of recent arguments against the essentialist view of language underlying some composition theories and practices. For example, she admits that error analysis is complex because there is "a crucial area of overlap" between *"encoding"* (defined by Epes as "controlling the visual symbols which represent meaning on the page") and *"composing* (controlling meaning in writing)" (6). She also observes that students are most likely to experience the "conflict between composing and decoding" when the "norms of the written code" are "in conflict" with "the language of one's nurture" (31). Given Epes's recognition of the conflict between encoding and composing, she should have little disagreement with compositionists who argue that learning to use the "codes" of academic discourse would constrain certain types of meanings, such as the formulation of feelings and thoughts toward cultures drastically dissonant from academic culture. Yet, when Epes moves from her theory to pedagogy, she argues that teachers of Basic Writers can and ought to treat "encoding" and "composition" as two separate areas of instruction (31). Her rationale is simple: separating the two could avoid "exacerbating" the students' experience of the "conflict" between these activities (31). The key terms here (for me, at any rate) are "exacerbating" and "conflict." They illustrate Epes's concern to eliminate conflict, disagreement, tension, and complexity from the Basic Writing classroom (cf. Horner, "Rethinking" 179–83).

Ann Murphy's essay "Transference and Resistance" likewise demonstrates the residual power of the earlier view of conflict and struggle as the enemies of Basic Writing instruction. Her essay draws on her knowledge of the Lacanian notion of the decentered and destabilized subject. Yet Murphy argues against the applicability of such a theory to the teaching of Basic Writing on the ground that Basic Writers are not like other students. Basic Writers, Murphy argues, "may need centering rather than decentering, and cognitive skills rather than (or as compellingly as) self-exploration" (180). She depicts Basic Writers as "shattered and destabilized by the social and political system" (180). She claims that "being taken seriously as *adults* with something of value to say can, for many Basic Writing students, be a *traumatic* and *disorienting* experience" (180; emphasis mine). Murphy's argument demonstrates her desire to eliminate any sense of uncertainty or instability in Basic Writing classrooms. Even though Murphy is willing to consider the implications of the Lacanian notion of individual subjectivity for the teaching of other types of students (180), her readiness to separate Basic Writing classrooms from other classrooms demonstrates the residual power of earlier views of conflict and struggle.

Such a residual view is all the more difficult to contest because it is supported by a new generation of minority educators. For example, in "Teacher Background and Student Needs" (1991), Peter Rondinone uses his personal experiences as an open admissions student taking Basic Writing 1 at CCNY during the early '70s and his Russian immigrant family background in the Bronx to argue for the need to help Basic Writers understand that "in deciding to become educated there will be times when [basic writers] will be forced to . . . reject or *betray* their family and friends in order to succeed" ("Teacher" 42). Rondinone's view of how students might best deal with the conflict between home and school does not seem to have changed much since his 1977 essay describing his experience as a senior at City College (see Rondinone, "Open Admissions"). In his 1991 essay, this time writing from the point of view of an experienced teacher, Rondinone follows Bruffee in maintaining that "learning involves shifting social allegiances" ("Teacher" 49). My quarrel with Rondinone is not so much over his having opted for complete deracination (for I honor his right to choose his allegiance even though I disagree with his choice). I am, however, alarmed by his unequivocal belief that his choice is the *a priori* condition of his academic success, which reveals his conviction that conflict can only impede one's learning.

Shelby Steele's recent and popular *The Content of Our Character* suggests similar assumptions about experiences of cultural conflict. Using personal experiences, Steele portrays the dilemma of an African American college student and professor in terms of being caught in the familiar "trap" bound by "two equally powerful elements" which are "at odds with each other" (95). Steele's solution to the problem of "opposing thrusts" is simple: find a way to "unburden" the student from one of the thrusts (160). Thus, Steele promotes a new, "peacetime" black identity

which could "release" black Americans from a racial identity which re-
gards their "middle-class" values, aspirations, and success as suspect
(109).

    To someone like Steele, the pedagogies of Bruffee, Farrell, and
Rondinone would make sense. In such a classroom, the black student
who told Steele that "he was not sure he should master standard English because then he 'wouldn't be black no more'" (70) would have the
comfort of knowing that he is not alone in wanting to pursue things "all
individuals" want or in wishing to be drawn "into the American mainstream" (71). Furthermore, he would find support systems to ease him
through the momentary pain, dislocation, and anxiety accompanying
his effort to "unburden" himself of one of the "opposing thrusts." The
popular success of Steele's book attests to the power of this type of thinking on the contemporary scene. Sections of his book originally appeared
in such journals as *Harper's, Commentary,* the *New York Times Magazine,*
and *The American Scholar.* Since publication of the book, Steele has been
touted as an expert on problems facing African American students in
higher education, and his views have been aired on PBS specials,
Nightline, the *MacNeil/Lehrer News Hour,* and in *Time* magazine. The popularity of his book should call our attention to the direct and indirect ways
in which the distrust of conflict and struggle continues to be recycled
and disseminated both within and outside the academy. At the same
time, the weight of the authority of the Wagners and Hellers should
caution us to take more seriously the constraints the Rondinones and
Steeles can exert on Basic Writing teachers, a majority of us still occupy-
ing peripheral positions in a culture repeatedly swept by waves of new
conservatism.

    But investigating the particular directions taken by Basic Writing pio-
neers when establishing authority for their expertise and the historical
contexts of those directions should also enable us to perceive alternative
ways of conversing with the Rondinones and Steeles in the 1990s. Because of the contributions of pioneers like Bruffee, Farrell, and
Shaughnessy, we can now mobilize the authority they have gained for
the field, for our knowledge as well as our expertise as Basic Writing
teachers. While we can continue to benefit from the insights into students' experiences of conflict and struggle offered in the writings of all
those I have discussed, we need not let their view of the cause and function of such experiences restrict how we view and use the stories and
pedagogies they provide. Rather, we need to read them against the grain,
filling in the silences left in these accounts by re-reading their experiences from the perspective of alternative accounts from the borderlands
and from the perspective of new language and pedagogical theories.

For many of these authors are themselves products of classrooms which promoted uncritical faith in either an essentialist view of language or various forms of discursive utopia that these writers aspired to preserve. Therefore, we should use our knowledge and expertise as compositionists to do what they did not or could not do: re-read their accounts in the context of current debates on the nature of language, individual consciousness, and the politics of basic skills. At the same time, we also need to gather more oppositional and alternative accounts from a new generation of students, those who can speak about the successes and challenges of classrooms which recognize the positive uses of conflict and struggle and which teach the process of repositioning.

The writings of the pioneers and their more established contemporaries indicate that the residual distrust of conflict and struggle in the field of Basic Writing is sustained by a fascination with cures for psychic woes, by two views of education—as acculturation and as accommodation—and by two views of language—essentialist and utopian. We need more research which critiques portrayals of Basic Writers as belonging to an abnormal—traumatized or underdeveloped—mental state and which simultaneously provides accounts of the "creative motion" and "compensation," "joy," or "exhilaration" resulting from Basic Writers' efforts to grapple with the conflict within and among diverse discourses. We need more research analyzing and contesting the assumptions about language underlying teaching methods which offer to "cure" all signs of conflict and struggle, research which explores ways to help students recover the latent conflict and struggle in their lives which the dominant conservative ideology of the 1990s seeks to contain. Most of all, we need to find ways of foregrounding conflict and struggle not only in the generation of meaning or authority, but also in the teaching of conventions of "correctness" in syntax, spelling, and punctuation, traditionally considered the primary focus of Basic Writing instruction.

3 Importing "Science": Neutralizing Basic Writing

Min-Zhan Lu

When discussing the "support" sociolinguistic research provided for composition, Lester Faigley observes that Shaughnessy's "landmark" study of error "almost on its own established basic writing as an important subfield within composition" (*Fragments* 61). This paper contextualizes Shaughnessy's contribution to composition by sketching the discursive terrain shaping Basic Writing's institutional birth.[1] I argue that the birth of Basic Writing cannot be separated from its success in constructing "science" as a means for neutralizing the politics of writing, teaching, and research at a time—the 1970s—and an educational site—the basic writing classroom—when the dominant found issues of difference and power most difficult to contain. One way of understanding Basic Writing's ability to establish itself as one of the ten topics "central to the teaching of composition" (Tate viii) during the seventies is to examine its active participation in a move across a range of academic disciplines and fields—including composition, literary studies, education, linguistics, sociology, and psychology—to maintain the "scientific" objectivity of the researcher/critic/teacher's language, methods, and knowledge. That is, we need to examine Basic Writing's venture outside English into "science" in terms of the teacher/researcher's often contradictory concerns to know the "aliens" in more realistic/neutral terms and to know the "aliens" with the language and from the perspective of a "settler."

Importing "Science": *Errors and Expectations* and "Basic Writing"

Critics have long observed the "seminal influence" of Shaughnessy's writing on Basic Writing (Courage 247). As Robert Lyons points out, in a field often marked by controversy and division, her work was invariably accorded attention and respect ("Mina Shaughnessy" 172). We might contextualize this phenomenon by analyzing the empiricist, idealist assumptions concerning language underlying the story of "science" told in two of Shaughnessy's most widely read writings, *Errors and Expectations* and her 1976 bibliographical essay on Basic Writing. "Science" in these texts works to align Basic Writing with dominant views on the neutrality of research, writing, and teaching, including the ideals of "scientism" in social sciences and composition (Phelps), the myth of "natural literacy" in higher education (Phelps 108; Scribner), a subject position of the "writer" centered on a New Critical "creative inwardness" (Miller) or "flight from politics" (Ohmann, *English*), and the expressive/empiricist metaphor of language underwriting the process approach to composition as well as realism, romanticism, and New Criticism (Faigley, *Fragments* 112). It operates to focus attention on the realism of the knowledge of the teacher/researcher/critic and to shift attention away from the politics of her perspective and language.

In *Composition as a Human Science*, Louise Wetherbee Phelps argues that the ideals of "scientism" often find their way into summaries of the "scientific method" offered in the social disciplines and composition (11, 12). She characterizes "scientism" as practices assuming an equation of "knowledge, truth, and proof," thus promoting a "logical empiricism" with its philosophical bases in "sense data" and "universal reason" (9). One of the consequences of such premises is, of course, the idealization of the "objective" attitude of the neutral scientist and of a neutral—"exact, formal, literal, and univocal"—observation language (10). "Science" in Shaughnessy's bibliographical essay "Basic Writing" is fixed within the parameters of "scientism." The relevance of "science" to Basic Writing, Shaughnessy maintains, resides in the validity not only of what the scientist said but also "the way he observed" and the way "thought is communicated in his work" (154). I read her to be urging basic writing teachers and researchers to look to "the *documents* of science" not only for truth but also methods of producing as well as presenting it (154, emphasis mine). In reviewing the "highly circumscribed literature" (142) on basic writing, Shaughnessy laments that "in English there is no tradition of *observation* and cumulative publication, as there is in the sciences" (142, 141, my emphasis). By calling this literature "information . . . tempting us to premature judgments" (142), she implies that "the tradition of observation and cumulative publication" yields "truth": produces "documents" (154) grounded *in* sense data—"files of student writing" or "case studies of student writers" (141).

A neutral observational perspective and language is also an ideal Shaughnessy aspires to for Basic Writing. For example, in her bibliographical essay, she justifies her preference for the designation "basic writer" by ranking various forms of identification—disadvantaged, handicapped, remedial, developmental, basic, severely unprepared—in terms of which is "more neutral" (137). She thus implies that a "neutral" approach to and presentation of the "new" students is not only possible but also preferable—the rightful goal of Basic Writing. As Lyons has cogently pointed out, *Errors and Expectations* strives to enact in its language, structure, and tone the academic ideal of "fairness, objectivity, and formal courtesy" (1980, 9–10).

This emphasis on observation and more fair, objective, longitudinal descriptions of actual students and their writing and learning is unquestionably subversive, representing the interest of basic writing teachers to acknowledge the intelligence of students deemed unfit by the gatekeepers, whose prejudices, ignorance, and arrogance toward basic writing teachers and students were repeatedly captured and critiqued in Shaughnessy's work, including "Diving In," "The English Teacher's Malady," and *Errors and Expectations.* On the one hand, given the authority of "science" on the discursive horizons of the gatekeepers, the move to deploy the story of "science" to produce—publish and make publishable—alternative, more in-depth and complex portraits of the "aliens" can be perceived as purely "rhetorical." That is, it could be perceived as an effort to shift the debate on the institutional place of basic writing students and teachers by casting alternative knowledge in a framework familiar to and deemed acceptable by the dominant. In writing without "a trace of revolutionary rhetoric," Shaughnessy is, and has succeeded historically in, making "a political statement" (Lyons, "Mina Shaughnessy" 185): the need to "uphold" and welcome the new students "within" the academic tradition (Lyons, "Mina Shaughnessy and the Teaching of Writing" 7). On the other hand, given the constitutive power of language, such a move can never remain purely "rhetorical" or escape other equally political statements and consequences. Rather, invoking the prevalent faith in logical empiricism and the neutrality of teaching, writing, and research signified by "science" also works to occlude attention (on the part of both the writer and reader) to the historical, political situatedness of the teacher/researcher: the complex and often contradictory interests motivating the observation and description. As a result, a set of "new" knowledge is perceived as replacing old prejudices as the objective Truth of basic writing rather than as provisional truths inscribed in specific social political motives and having specific social, historical consequences.

This might particularly be the case during Basic Writing's birth because of the residual power of the New Critical approach to writing on the discursive horizon of the gatekeepers in English studies, Basic Writing's home. For an essentialist view of language conjoins New Criticism with scientism. The assumed equation of knowledge, truth, and proof underlying scientism inevitably endows language with a "linguistic innocence," implying that it is a transparent medium for sensing reality and reasoning rather than being itself a site of social conflict and struggle (Lu, "Redefining"). Therefore, a venture into a "science" dominated by the ideals of scientism is but a "new" route back into the center of an English dominated by the master plots of expressive realism. As Catherine Belsey argues in *Critical Practice,* an expressive realism runs through dominant approaches to literature in English Studies from the nineteenth century to the 1970s: romanticism, Realism, and New Criticism. Both the mimetic and expressive views of art assume that the world of natural objects is unproblematically given and that the mind of the spectator is ready to perceive and re-present these natural objects (9). Thus, both the mimetic and expressive metaphors of language assume that language exists outside of history and is innocent of politics (Faigley, *Fragments* 112). The New Critics, in failing to recognize that meaning exists only within a specific language, "are forced back on" the naive empiricism-idealism conjoining romanticism and realism (Belsey 19). The same can be said about Basic Writing's venture outside of "English." The essentialist view of language conjoining scientism and New Criticism suggests that we need to read Basic Writing's participation in what Connors has termed composition's "yearning" toward scientific status not only in terms of what Elizabeth Flynn has described as a "defense in the struggle against its chief adversary, literary studies" (Flynn, "Feminism" 355); we need also to approach it in terms of its ability to establish Basic Writing's allegiance with New Critical projects within literary studies and mainstream composition. We need to examine the ways in which the figure of the "scientific" researcher conjoins the figure of the New Critic to ground the teacher's knowledge *in* the object of study—the text and/or the writer—and to render irrelevant attention to the teacher/critic/researcher's choice of language and perspective.

It is not coincidental but a logical consequence of the expressive realism conjoining scientism and New Criticism that Shaughnessy's "groundbreaking" approach to error would simultaneously deploy the knowledge of "sciences"—namely linguistics and cognitive psychology—and the "literary" method of close reading that critics have seen in her work (Miller 116–17; Bartholomae, "Writing" 70–71). For the same reason, the institutional currency of *Errors and Expectations* cannot be separate from its success in using the figure of the "scientific" researcher to authorize the neutrality of the New Critical scholar/teacher at a time when, as Miller observes, the hold of New Criticism in literary studies is "relaxing" (118). "Science" operates to justify not only the need for teacher/researchers to abandon some of the old beliefs and practices inherited from home (such as prejudice against non-standard English and the intelligence of its speakers) but also the need to renew other familiar beliefs and practices, including the myths of the political inno-cence of "writing" and "teaching" underlying the New Critical approach. Therefore, the efficacy of "the tradition of observation and cumulative publication . . . in sciences" for Basic Writing is not just, as Shaughnessy presents it, to legitimize—publish and make publishable—new knowl-edge *about* the new students ("Basic Writing" 141) but could also often work to legitimize—objectify and neutralize—familiar ways of know-ing the Other and evading the politics of intellectual efforts.

Furthermore, we need to keep in mind that the neutralizing power of "science" is invoked at a historical junction and educational site where issues of power and differences are at the center of all debates. In the context of illustrating the "academic" underpreparedness of the teach-ers, Shaughnessy points to the "urgent conditions, both political and economic," that led to the rash institution of "remedial wings" in col-lege campuses during the late sixties ("Basic Writing" 140). To argue for the need for teachers to read up on literature on "language in various social settings," Shaughnessy again admits that the basic writing class-room is simply one of the places where the fact of diversity has become not merely an "academic" topic but a complex and troubling issue af-fecting what English teachers teach and how they teach it (159). If issues of diversity and power are at the center of debate on the who, what, and how of teaching, then the status of "documents of science" can work to absolve the teacher/researchers from the need to reflect on the politics of their choice of perspective and language. For example, in *Errors and Expectations,* one "science"—linguistics—is used to provide support for a notion of writing and teaching which dissolves the political content of linguistic differences and which encourages students to approach dif-ferences through acculturation and accommodation rather than nego-tiation (Lu, "Redefining," "Conflict and Struggle"). Yet, the expressive realism authorizing the teacher/researcher's knowledge of the who, what, and how of teaching renders attention to the politics of such a resolution to differences and power irrelevant.

However, if we are to understand such pioneering work as Shaughnessy's writings on basic writing as not an example of an indi-vidual feat in instituting a professional field, we need to also reject see-ing it as an example of individual bad faith or conceptual failure. Rather, we need to approach the dominance of expressive realism in Shaughnessy's view of "science" and its political efficacy in terms of what Pierre Bourdieu has termed the dilemma of progressive intellectuals, i.e., the role of a "dominated among the dominant." The work of the basic writing teacher/researcher is inevitably riven by her identification with the dominated, generated by a commitment to the education of students deemed by the academy as aliens, and her inscription within the dominant in her function as a teacher and intellectual. In *Fragments of Rationality*, Faigley argues that the changing politics of composition studies during the 1970s cannot be separated from the political Right's exploitation of the anxiety of the professional middle class over the possibilities of "falling down the social incline" (54–63). His discussion of the various challenges and possibilities posed for the process approach by the right wing back-to-basics movement might be used to sketch the social, historical scene shaping Shaughnessy's interest in "scientific" knowledge, methods, and language. On the one hand, the so-called literacy crisis posed real threats to the institutional place of teachers and students associated with academic underpreparedness, presenting them as the villains personifying the invasion of "politics" (radical or guilt-ridden liberalism) on American education. The back-to-basics movement fueled an accountability movement during the early 1970s. States started to require schools to publish achievement test scores and passed laws requiring exit exams and frequent performance testing (Faigley, *Fragments* 63). These mandates generated extra pressure on English teachers, driving them to follow in step the drills-and-skills curriculum packages supplied by textbook publishers. For basic writing teachers like Shaughnessy, the conviction that the drills-and-skills curriculum does not work with their students and that standardized testing fails to do justice to the students' expertise and intelligence would motivate them to articulate an alternative approach. At the same time, the hegemony of the Right delimited how such an approach could be posed. Negatively, as Faigley reminds us, the marginalized status of many writing teachers led most to shy away from taking public political stands even when they disagreed with prevailing attitudes toward literacy (*Fragments* 66). This concern to pose one's alternative approach to literacy with a seemingly neutral knowledge base and language would be even more urgent for teachers like Shaughnessy since the institutional places of both the basic writing teachers and the students were even more precarious. Therefore, the interest in scientism surfacing in Shaughnessy's writing is intellectual—an indication of her inscription in New Critical expressive realism—as well as sociohistorical. Faigley also reminds us that, positively, the back-to-basics movement brought favorable conditions for writing teachers in their struggle to change their marginalized status in English (66). New positions for writing specialists were created and new resources of funding became available (67). But in their effort to take advantage of such possibilities, composition teachers would again need to place their research and teaching within the dominant views of "research" and "teaching" held by those with authority to grant such funding (see Horner, "Discoursing" 208–10). Therefore, Shaughnessy's deployment of "science" also needs to be read alongside the institutional reception of research and pedagogy which maintains and/or challenges the neutrality of writing, teaching, and research across disciplines.

In the following sections, I map the discursive terrain shaping the institutional birth of Basic Writing by delineating a pervasive move in composition to shift attention from the politics of writing, teaching, and research. I do so by tracing the story of "science" recurring across a range of canonical texts in composition, including Janet Emig's *The Composing Processes of Twelfth Graders* (1971), Peter Elbow's *Writing Without Teachers* (1973), Young, Becker, and Pike's *Rhetoric: Discovery and Change* (1970), Frank O'Hare's *Sentence Combining* (1973), James Moffett's *Teaching the Universe of Discourse* (1968), the Conference on College Composition and Communication's Statement on "Students' Right to Their Own Language" (1974), and I. A. Richards's *Practical Criticism* (1929). I argue that although quite a few of the texts enact stances toward "academic" discourse significantly different from Shaughnessy's *Errors and Expectations* both in their style (e.g., the "anti-academic" tone and language of *Writing Without Teachers*) and argument (e.g., the CCCC resolution on students' "right" to their "own" language), the concern to maintain the political "innocence" of teaching and research runs through them.[2] I further map the constraints such a concern poses for basic writing teachers and researchers by examining the ways in which U.S. educators impute "scientific" status to texts across English, education, and the social sciences which have been often cited by compositionists as useful resources, including the writings of Kenneth Burke, Paulo Freire, Basil Bernstein, Richard Ohmann, William Labov, and Lev Vygotsky. I argue that the pervasive move to separate these writers' thinking on the relations of language, subjectivity, differences, and power from their "scientific" knowledge of linguistic and cognitive structures and then to dismiss the former as "irrelevant" might likewise route Basic Writing's venture into "science" back into an English dominated by New Critical close reading.

Objectifying Process Research

One way of mapping the discursive terrain shaping Basic Writing's birth is to examine the story of "science" in what Shaughnessy calls a "pioneering study" capable of "saving us from *false* dichotomies," Janet

Emig's 1971 *The Composing Processes of Twelfth Graders* ("Basic Writing" 165–66, my emphasis). This monograph has generally been perceived as having played an "influential" or "precedent"-setting role in turning "process" into a key term and composition into a "legitimate" discipline (Faigley, *Fragments* 58, Miller 143). In "Competing Theories of Process," Faigley calls attention to the "mixture of social science and literary idioms" in Emig's writing (532). I'd like to argue that, as in Shaughnessy's work, this mixture needs to be examined in relation to the essentialist view of language underlying both Emig's definition of "phenomenological" research and the New Critical notion of writing. *Composing Processes* is "pioneering" not only because it gives composition a way into mainstream education and cognitive psychology but also because it gives composition a "fresh" way out: it proffers an "objective" rationale for composition to "entrench itself," as Miller puts it, in the dominant English subject/subject positioning at a time when "liberal" education is having difficulty maintaining the myth of its separation from politics (118; see also Ohmann, *English in America*).

"Process" in Emig's work is used interchangeably with words such as "phenomena," "entities," (*The Web of Meaning* 159), "actuality" (*Web* 160), or "behavior." Thus, "process" is essentialized into an independent entity inherent in the referent, an object which "we" (teachers and researchers) investigate, explain, perceive, select, gather, arrange (*Web* 159). Emig's characterization of "phenomenology," a tradition within which she places her case study (*Web* 163), illustrates the way in which "science" in Emig's work operates to free the construction and teaching of "process" from issues of power and difference. Quoting Elliot G. Mishler, Emig notes that "phenomenologists" assume that the "[phenomenon] contains multiple truths, each of which will be revealed by a shift in perspective, method, or purpose" (*Web* 162). The words "contain" and "reveal" ground the knowledge of the teacher/researcher in the "phenomenon" and make attention to the politics of the researcher's choice of how, when, and where to "shift" irrelevant even as she acknowledges the partiality of phenomenological knowledge.

Emig's goal in performing a "naturalistic examination" (*Web* 163) is to formulate universal constants: "delineating *the*, even *a*, writing process" and "ascertain[ing] whether the process has constant characteristics across writers" (*Composing* 15). However, the politics of her search for constants is made irrelevant by words such as "data" and "finding," which she uses consistently in association with verbs such as "elicit," "collect," or "reveal," which imply that the characteristics are essences inherent to—*within*—the "phenomenon" (4–5, 33). "Objectivity" is further invoked by presenting her method of research, "composing aloud," as a means to "ascertain" and "externalize" (5) and as *"reflect*[ing], if not parallel[ing], [the student's] *actual inner* process" (40, emphasis mine). In establishing the expressive realism of the "process," these verbs shift attention to what is *within* the object of study and away from the ways in which the researcher's "shift" of perspective, method, or purpose mediates the kind of truth she produces.

However, such discursive choices, such as the binary of "fact" and "feelings," significantly mediate both the data she gathers and her evaluation of such data. The following is an exchange between an Investigator and Lynn, one of the eight students studied by Emig, which is included in the appendix:

> Investigator: Ah, you were saying that, ah, you felt more comfortable when your writing concerned *facts*, or *the organization of facts*, rather than some expression of *feelings*, why do you think this is so?
>
> Lynn: I really have no idea. That is, this is just something about me. I would rather . . . *I'm a great organizer*, and I'm going to run into trouble maybe on the yearbook this year . . . I've always . . . I've always had trouble talking to people about my *feelings* on something. I can quote from other people I can . . . talk about, ahm . . . I can talk about *facts* more easily than I can talk about abstract things . . . . (*Composing* 123, my emphasis)

In a chapter entitled "Lynn: Profile of a Twelfth-Grade Writer," Emig summarizes the above exchange as follows:

> [T]he investigator asks Lynn why she thinks she feels more comfortable writing about *facts* rather than *feelings*. At first, she *claims* she has no idea and changes the subject; later she *admits* that she finds expressing her feelings painful:
>
>> I've always . . . I've always had trouble talking to people about, my feelings on something. . . .
>
>> (*Composing* 49, my emphasis)

Emig's summary highlights the binary of fact/feeling and glosses over the reference to "organization" in both the investigator's question and Lynn's reply. It also ranks the validity of the "data" Lynn yields through the contrast between "claim" and "admit." The truth value of what Lynn "claimed" is made suspect in comparison to what she "admits" (46). The word "admit," in invoking the equation of reality-truths-(self)-knowledge, shifts attention away from the ways in which the language of the researcher (the Investigator as well as Emig) mediates the way Emig, the Investigator, and Lynn construct the composing process. Notice the Investigator's qualification, "or the organization of facts," when posing the binary of "fact" and "feeling." This qualification momentarily signals to Lynn that "organization," another standard approach in writing pedagogy, is also an appropriate approach to "her" composing process. The fact that Lynn promptly took up that option to talk about her experience editing the yearbook illustrates the ways in which the language of the Investigator mediates the kind of "data" produced by the research. Likewise, Emig's depiction of that exchange as "claim" making and digression illustrates the extent to which the researcher's choice of perspective mediates her evaluation of the data. Furthermore, Lynn's eventual ability to get back to the issue of fact/feeling also suggests that the externalization of "her" composing process is mediated by both her familiarity with the language and perspective of the researcher and her willingness to view and talk about her composing process with that language. As Lynn points out, the "kids" at the "institute" she once attended had repeatedly told her that she "never seem[s] to be talking about [her]self, about [her] own feelings. . . " (123). In other words, Lynn might have "proved an exceptionally interesting subject" to the researcher because of "her ability to verbalize the process of her thinking and writing" (46) *with* the language and *from* the perspective of the researcher. However, the objective rhetoric underwriting Emig's monograph renders attention to the mediating power of the researcher's discursive choices irrelevant.

We might examine the politics of preempting attention to such mediating power by considering the white, middle-class alignment established by the criteria this study uses when selecting its cases. Emig states that the eight twelfth graders are chosen because they have above average and average "ability" (3) and "intelligence" (29). The criteria she uses for judging "intelligence"—school records, grades, scores on College Entrance Board Examinations and the comments of teachers (*Composing* 29)—are procedures which, as Ohmann has argued in *English in America,* represent the interests of white middle-class America. Yet, the "scientific" rhetoric overwriting the study renders moot reflection on the politics of using such criteria, which turn Lynn—the daughter of a lawyer and a high school history teacher, a student in the top five percent of her class, co-editor of the yearbook and a study hall monitor— into a representative case in a "truly cross-cultural district" consisting of "Jewish doctors, dentists, and professors" and workers at steel mills, including "blacks and newly arrived Mexicans, and Puerto Ricans" as well as "second generation Polish- and Serbian-Americans" (45). Likewise, it enables the researcher to state as self-explanatory why out of communities and schools with different "sociological characteristics" she has chosen eight cases from families with "marked likenesses in certain formal characteristics of their families," even though, as research by Bernstein and Heath has indicated, "formal" characteristics such as "verbal interaction with adults as an only child" and being "read to frequently" (76) are class specific. The announced purpose of the study is "to describe how student writers usually or typically behave as they write" (21) with the hope that "the" process presented by the study can be used to draw implications for how writing is to be taught "across" American high schools (97). In short, the goal of this "scientific" search for *the* typical writing behavior is to dissolve differences in writing behavior through teaching. The political efficacy of such a "scientific" endeavor therefore resides exactly in its ability to make the teacher/ researcher's depiction of the behavior of student writers like Lynn "typical," i.e., "scientific" or "objective," rather than socially and historically situated. Given the currency of neutrality in the United States of 1971, when "education" was daily being forced to confront its participation or complicity in racial and class inequality, the popularity of Emig's "process" research seems predictable. It offers composition, mainstream and basic, "fresh" ways for dissolving issues of differences and power in research, teaching, and writing.

Attention to the politics of teaching and research is further dissolved in Emig's writing through her construction of a "we"—members of the composition "community"—as people living in a world consisting solely of "intellectual ancestors," an "explanatory matrix," and "academic fields or disciplines" (*Web*). Choices of perspective are confined by "intellectual" and "academic" traditions that are seemingly unrelated to specific social and political conflicts. To detach the knowledge of these "intellectual ancestors" from the social contexts of their work, Emig reduces their work into one-liners. Vygotsky is mentioned as one of the "ancestors" yielding "observations" on "gesture" as the "origin of writing" (*Web* 166). Freire gets mentioned as one of the six "phenomenologists" working in philosophy, social sciences and literacy education (*Web* 161). Such sweeping generalizations enable Emig to group the work of Vygotsky and Freire with that of Piaget and Bruner (*Web* 160, 165) within the same "intellectual" tradition and to detach all of them from the particular and drastically different political contexts in which the four "ancestors" work (more of this later). Two types of teacher inhabit Emig's "educational system" in "disarray." The bad guys are the "dinosaurs, with their dismaying ratio of tail to brain" (*Web* 171), who "do not write" (*Composing* 98), "underconceptualize and oversimplify the process of composing" (*Composing* 98), are consumed by the "neurosis" over "peripherals" such as spelling, punctuation, or length, and hold on to a "teacher-centered presentation of composition." This type of portrait turns the conflict between the so-called process and product approaches or the teacher-centered and student-centered approaches into a struggle solely between haves and have-nots of particular "intellectual" traits: size of brain and brawn, real "writing" experience, or true knowledge of *the* process.

Attention to issues of difference and power is also displaced by Emig's deployment of the binary of the social vs. human/natural, a binary which critics have argued has hegemonic power in an English studies dominated by the New Critical approach (Ohmann, Miller, Lentricchia). *The* writing process is portrayed as "interrupted" in "major" ways by interveners and interventions (*Composing* 40). Emig defines the interveners as "persons who *enter into* the composing process of another" (40, emphasis mine). The phrase "enter into" sets "the process" up as a self-evident "phenomenon" with independent proceedings. In Emig's other and later work, a developmental frame is deployed to cast the "writing" process into something "natural" and "innate" in all people. "[A]s evidence from many disciplines now suggests, writing is developmentally a natural process" (*Web* 136). One essay, "The Tacit Tradition," concludes with a Credo which claims that "not writing or not wanting to write is unnatural; that, if either occurs, something major has been subverted in a mind, in a life" (*Web* 155). In turning "writing" into a natural phenomenon rather than a culturally constructed practice, Emig turns all teaching based on her definition of *the* writing process into practices sanctioned by natural laws. By the same token, differences in teaching can be evaluated in terms of their ability to enable a natural, human process rather than in terms of difference in socially, historically specific positions. Furthermore, such differences are decontextualized by the plot of human evolution: "the teacher-centered presentation of composition . . . is pedagogically, developmentally, and politically an anachronism" (*Composing* 100). Thus, politics of *the* process approach is presented as motivated by the natural course of ontogenic and phylogenic progression rather than also as shaped and shaping historically and socially specific relations of power within and outside the academy.

Yet, we arrive at a very different reading of the "natural" good of "process" research if we approach it in terms of its alignment with various hegemonic positions within and outside higher education during the 1970s. Emig presents "writing" defined through the process knowledge as a means to "freedom" on two levels: a freedom of mobility in society and a freedom to fully realize one's innate, "human" potential: a "way *up,* a way *out,* a way *in*" (*Web* 176, my emphasis). This faith in the myth of functional literacy and natural literacy is clearly political in its silence on the political interests shaping and shaped by its particular definition of literacy, its silence on other non-"literacy" conditions for individual social and political freedom or survival, and its deterministic portrayal of the individual as one acting passively according to social or natural laws. It also aligns Emig's process approach solidly with the dominant positions on the nature and function of literacy critiqued by such theorists as Scribner and Stuckey.

Emig's bi-modal approach to writing—extensive vs. reflexive—also sets up alignments with two power bases within English: the New Critical approach in literary studies and the "expressive" approach in composition. Emig's account of the "reflexive" mode suggests that writing in it allows students to be more "expressive" and natural: the choice of audience in that mode is the self or a trusted peer, it utilizes one's own experience and style, and it is affective, personal, and exploratory. In comparison, the extensive mode is repressive for setting "rigid parameters to students' writing behaviors"; assigning them "abstract," i.e., social topics such as the draft, drug addiction, the ABM missile system; and keeping the student from writing about "self" and "human relations" (*Composing* 92, 93). These opposing chains align Emig's "process" approach with "expressivists" such as Elbow and Macrorie in their shared emphasis on the personal and their anti-establishment sentiments, a move which, in its romantic valorization of the natural expression of authentic voice, is in keeping with the New Critical privileging of poetry as the medium for true experience. Emig suggests that we think of the "reflexive" in terms of the "contemplative role" of the writing self exploring the question "What does this experience mean?" The self writing in the extensive mode, by contrast, takes an "active role" motivated by the question of "How . . . do I interact with my environment?" (*Composing* 37). The distinction between introspection and interaction overlaps with a concern Richard Ohmann delineates in his analysis of the "cultural values inherent in close reading" (*English* 70–71). It teaches readers to view "aesthetic experience" in terms of "intransitive attention" and "emphatically not by acting to change the society that gives rise to experience" (Ohmann, *English* 74, 77). Thus, it sanctions a "flight from politics" for American "liberal humanists" during the post-war period (79). Ohmann points to the politics of such a subject positioning by contextualizing it in a range of social conditions exerting pressures to divorce "academic" work from politics, including the political repression of the McCarthy era (80), the enormous growth of American universities in the post-war period (86), and the accompanying improvement in income among English professors with its "almost-earned upper middle-class self-image" (81). He thus suggests that the New Critical approach to "writing" gains power in English because the material conditions of the time give it social and historical relevance. Likewise, the popularity of Emig's work for composition, mainstream and Basic

Writing, cannot be separated from its ability to renew the relevance of the New Critical subject positioning, especially since it joins other "popular" pedagogies, such as Elbow's 1973 *Writing Without Teachers,* in promoting a "creative inwardness" (Miller 91). As Faigley points out, the move to emphasize the value of autonomy, anti-authoritarianism and a personal voice in approaches such as Elbow's (and, we might add, Emig's) needs to be understood in view of what he calls the "anxiety of the middle class," the fear that "the dreaded loss of individualism under communism had occurred in the midst of capitalist prosperity," the anti-establishment sentiments of the 1960s, student activism during the Vietnam War years, and the crossfire of the right and the left on the political function of education (*Fragments* 56–57). In short, Emig's choice of purpose, method, and perspective must be perceived as an active response to very specific social, historical conflicts within and outside higher education. Therefore, the efficacy of Emig's "pioneering study" for Basic Writing resides not merely in the "fresh," "scientific" data and methods it brings to Basic Writing's understanding of its subject but also in its creative use of "science": its ability to provide methods and knowledge for making a neutralized New Critical subject positioning relevant to the teaching of the "aliens."

Humanizing Writing and Teaching

In this section, I map the discursive terrain shaping Basic Writing's birth by analyzing the ways in which the assumptions of expressive realism conjoining scientism and New Criticism work to neutralize—humanize—diverse canonical approaches to writing and teaching during the 1970s. I argue that the landmark status of texts like *Errors and Expectations* is in part ensured by the story of science it shares with a whole range of well-received texts on the teaching of writing, including *Teaching the Universe of Discourse* (1968), *Sentence Combining* (1970), *Rhetoric: Discovery and Change* (1970), *Writing Without Teachers* (1973), *A Conceptual Theory of Rhetoric* (1975), and the College Composition and Communication policy statement "Students' Right" (1974). Historians of composition theory have offered several frameworks for identifying the differences across these texts: forms of rhetoric (Berlin), perspectives of composing (Faigley, "Competing"), modes of making knowledge (North) and diverse combinations of components—axiological, procedural, pedagogical, and epistemological (Fulkerson). Richard Fulkerson argues when commenting on the formation of composition studies before 1980 that "genuine and extensive conflicts existed" across expressivism, formalism, mimeticism, and the rhetorical approach on the question of what constituted good writing (411–14). In the following section, I examine the ways in which a story of "science" conjoins a whole range of composition texts by establishing a common thread across the differences in the definition of good writing they pose. I argue that in different ways, "science" in these texts works to empty writing of the social and historical, operating to authorize a notion of "good" writing structured on the binary of "human" universality vs. social, historical differences. At a time in U.S. history when issues of differences and power are at the center of all public and academic debate, these texts reach canonical status in composition partially because they offer "new," "scientific" justifications for maintaining the neutrality of "good" writing and thus, the teaching of "writing."

Although Elbow has been traditionally housed in a different camp from Emig, identified as a "practitioner" rather than a "researcher" (North 22, 197) and as an "expressionist" rather than a "cognitivist" (Berlin 485–87 and Faigley, "Competing" 530), *Writing Without Teachers* intersects with *The Composing Processes of Twelfth Graders* in its concern to neutralize teaching and writing. Elbow markets his pedagogy as a means for the "people" to claim, through writing, more personal and political control (vii, 182). However, if we examine the expressive realism underlying *Writing Without Teachers,* we might argue that instead of empowering the little people, it can work to provide a seemingly "nice or sociable" or "easier and more natural" (176, 187) means for hegemonic power to control differences through writing and teaching.

At the core of *Writing Without Teachers* is the "believing game," which, according to Elbow, "yields *the* truth" (176). The pedagogy of believing is built on the assumption that there is "real"—"*hard,* commonsense, *empirical*" truth "*about*" the object of study, whether it is an utterance, text, dog, tree, or community (157, 159, 162, my emphasis). The association of truth with the empirical and hard invokes the plot of scientism through the equation of knowledge, truth, and facts. The link of the "hard" and "empirical" with "commonsense" ought to instruct us on the politics of the believing game. *Writing Without Teachers* defines common sense as that which "conforms to," "grows out of" or is "permitted by" the community rules (157, 170). Such a definition ensures that the search for truth would conform to rather than contest the interests of those within or across communities in positions of power to prescribe rules. However, the politics of such a subject positioning is effectively neutralized by the "scientific" rhetoric built on the equation between common sense and hard, empirical facts.

Expressive realism is also at the heart of another foundation to the believing game: an unequivocal faith in an "organism" *within* the writer to guarantee unmediated access to truth. "Your organism," *Writing Without Teachers* assures the students, "can do a lot of sifting that you cannot do consciously" (177). Therefore, the writer, "like the owl eating the mouse" (177), ought to "trust his organism to make use of what's good and get rid of what isn't" (103). By implication, the pedagogy of believing is neutral: it merely facilitates a natural process innate in all life forms. It helps us to access "a believing muscle *in* our head" (162) or "the organic, developmental process" (43). To further neutralize such a pedagogy, *Writing Without Teachers* grounds the teacherless class in a "paradigm" imported from "science": the "fetus going through all its stages," Freud's model of psychic unfolding, Erikson's seven-stage model, Piaget's cognitive growth (43).

However, the neutrality of writing-without-teachers crumbles as soon as we consider how it might work for students with different subject positionings cutting along lines of race, gender, class, or sex (see Jarratt 110–11). For example, the "writing" process requires writers to respond to competing ideas in "an atmosphere of acceptance and trust" (*Writing* 185). It seems that requirements such as "sleep[ing] with *any* idea that comes down the road" and becoming "someone who can be made to believe *anything*. A large opening that anything can be poured into. Force-fed. Raped" (185) would bring different challenges to a student aligned with racist and sexist positions (I'll call this student Student A) and a student (Student B) determined to fight racism and sexism. As the guru himself admits, the teacherless classroom is a "game" room with a "surreal, underwater vision of social reality" (121). To play successfully in the believing game, the students would have to willfully forget that different ideas are inscribed with unequal social, historical powers in the United States in which they live. Student B's awareness that "sleeping with" the ideas of a sexist or a racist is not only an unpleasant "game" but has resulted and still can result in real violence toward people of minority race and gender outside the game room would make course requirements to perceive the believing game as a "game" ("not real life") and to participate in it wholeheartedly suspect (175). On the other hand, Student A's awareness that within the context of today's United States, for a racist or sexist to *play* at "being taken over" by oppositional ideas could remain nothing more than an intellectual "game" would make such course requirements both viable and "pleasurable" for him (185, 175). However, within the organic/empiricist frame of *Writing Without Teachers,* Student B's hesitance to accept and trust opposing ideas could only be interpreted as a sign of her failure to get in touch with, or her alienation from, "organic" traits or processes supposedly inherent in all life forms, including herself.

Consider also the kind of resolution to differences likely to be fostered by the believing game. Given the unqualified celebration of the innate organism for discriminating truth, it is highly unlikely that the "game" process of "listening, silence, agreeing" and "yielding" would produce any real change in the writers' goals or subject positionings. Even the guru admits to having "really changed [his] mind" on "too few" occasions (184). Most likely, the "teacherless classroom" would be more successful in delivering its promise of helping the student reach that "blessed state of not worrying" when she would feel free to make her "own" decisions as to what is good and bad, using the responses of others to help her fulfill her "own goals" or "own private purposes" (126, 140). Yet, the empirical/organic rhetoric would have taught teachers and students to view these decisions as authorized by innate laws within the writer and the referent rather than constructed by specific class, race, gender, sex and/or intellectual alignments. Thus, it would also keep them from investigating the political motivations and consequences of such decisions.

How would such game rules work differently for Students A and B? The "teacherless classroom," in asking the student to play at being "non-aggressive," allows both students the privilege of viewing themselves as open-minded and cooperative (179). In telling the students to listen to the heart, it teaches both to turn inward when dealing with differences and seeking political control. However, such teaching would work differently for the two students once they take that "writing" outside the classroom. For Student A in today's United States, the political and personal "control" he gained through "good," "free writing" will remain "real" as well as "intellectual." Not arguing or not knowing how to argue within or outside the classroom alone would not decrease the hegemonic power of "his" racist and sexist ideas. Rather, it would increase his complacency over his open-mindedness. Student B, however, would gain the illusion of having gained personal and political control: the rules of the game would make her feel that she had been listened to and lead her to believe that she is calling the shots when "writing." This kind of "control" could not prepare her for negotiating power outside the game room where the rules of believing do not prevail. As James Berlin argues, the ideology of expressivist rhetoric is likely to be pleasing to the ruling elites and debilitating for effective resistance (487). Or, as David Bartholomae puts it, expressivist rhetoric "makes [students] suckers and . . . it makes them powerless, at least to the degree that it makes them blind to tradition, power and authority as they are present in language and culture" ("Reply" 128–29).

For an educational site where the "fact of diversity" is at the center of all pedagogical decisions (Shaughnessy, "Basic Writing" 159), writing-without-teachers can have political currency in several respects. The rules of the believing game can be used to turn the classroom into a conflict-free space where different ideas are tolerated—voiced and "listened" to without "arguing," nor effecting any change on the others (*Writing Without Teachers* 179). In teaching the writer to view her discursive decisions as dictated by laws innate in the writer and the referent, the pedagogy continues to shift attention from the ways in which subject positioning mediates thinking and writing and the ways in which the rules of the believing game endorse subject positionings which confirm rather than contest "community rules" and personalize the social and historical contents of goals and values. Such a seemingly neutral resolution to social conflict and power would seem to be especially valuable for educational sites such as the basic writing classroom, where the students' heterogeneous discursive practices and positionings make issues of diversity and power particularly difficult to contain. We might argue that Elbow's model is perceived as having "effect" upon basic writing teaching partially because in teaching the "art of getting started" it is also instructing in the art of dissociating power from differences, writing conflict and struggle out of Basic Writing (Shaughnessy, "Basic Writing" 151). The popularity of *Writing Without Teachers* cannot be separated from its empirical/organic rhetoric, a rhetoric proffering "human" justifications for believing in an introspective flight from differences and thus consolidating composition's alignment with both scientism and New Criticism.

The pedagogy of believing, contrary to what Elbow would have us believe, is socially and historically constructed rather than a purely personal and organic expression of the author's "own" beliefs and purposes, nor is it a product of an author trusting his "organism" for shifting the good from the bad. We can make this case by contextualizing *Writing Without Teachers* in the discursive scene of its production and reception, such as examining the empirical/organic rhetoric of another popular pedagogy, *Rhetoric: Discovery and Change* by Young, Becker, and Pike (1970). Several of the essays in Tate's *Teaching Composition* identify *Discovery and Change* as one of the most important texts in "new" rhetoric (Tate 57, 228, 234). This "new" rhetoric projects a "writer" living in a "new" world—an "extraordinarily diverse and disturbed world"—and conducting arguments in situations that involve "confrontations between old and young, East and West, white and black" (Young et al. 8, 9, 274). According to the authors, "human differences" are the cause of "misunderstanding" and must be "overcome," "resolved," or "reduced" until communication can take place (26, 30). The pedagogy of "discovery and change" promises to do just that by teaching students to reach "an accurate image of the world" as well as the "elimination of conflict between writer and reader" (275). Sustaining this promise are a set of rules— "heuristic procedures" and "Rogerian strategies." Although, as Berlin has argued, the approach of *Rhetoric: Discovery and Change* is more "social-epistemic" than expressionistic (173), I'd argue that the rules of "new" rhetoric, like the rules of Elbow's "teacherless classroom," would work to dissolve differences in the name of "human" empathy and truth.

Rhetoric: Discovery and Change posits a set of heuristic procedures supposedly authorized by the "observations" of linguists and anthropologists (26). Efforts to deploy the authority of "science" to neutralize these procedures is most explicit in the authors' defense of the validity of tagmemics, the "basis" of the book (xi). One of the authors, Kenneth Pike, maintains that his is "a theory of the structure of human behavior which is grounded in a set of axioms about human nature" (quoted in Young, "Invention" 31). Another author, Richard Young, likewise asserts that tagmemics "embodies psychological universals." Their "universality" rests on their "demonstrated usefulness in analysis of highly diverse linguistic data" and "on the mind's inability to function without them" (Young, "Invention" 31). Such assertions imply that teaching the "heuristic procedures" is neutral because these procedures are developed in accordance with the universal laws of *human* behavior and *human* nature.

However, the particular meanings these procedures generate suggest that they are social constructs rather than inherent structures. The procedures teach students to objectify ideas, values, experiences, people, communities, or cultures into repeatable "units" with identifiable features which can be "isolated and studied" (225). The power relationship between the writer and the reader is dissolved by the images of "separate human particles" (225) and of society as "a bag of marbles" (176). In short, these procedures work to ensure that the student would approach different ideas, people, or cultures as fixed and discrete entities rather than also in terms of power conflict and struggle across competing social forces. A similar move is made in Young's reading of Burke's dramatistic method in his bibliographical essay (Young, "Invention" 13). Treating Burke's dramatistic method as "a clear instance" of the "heuristic procedure," he presents it as a means of "discovering *essential* features of the behavior of groups or individuals" (15). This interpretation presents "motive" as an essence *within* the "individual" and "group" and downplays Burke's concern with the sociopolitical structure of the "scene" of writing (I discuss this below).

To ensure that the meaning "discovered" by the heuristic procedures would be accepted by—"change" the minds of—people with different viewpoints, the pedagogy poses a set of Rogerian strategies supposedly based on an "image of man" authorized by theory and practice in "psychotherapy" (6–7). From Carl Rogers, *Rhetoric: Discovery and Change* borrows the assumption that "man has *free* will, but his ability to consider alternative positions is limited if he feels threatened" (8). Based on such an assumption, the pedagogy poses a set of strategies to "reduce" the reader's sense of threat. One rule, like the rule of never arguing in the believing game, is to "convey" to the reader that he is understood (275). Another is to "induce him to believe that he and the writer share similar moral qualities (honesty, integrity, and good will) and aspirations (the desire to discover a mutually acceptable solution)" (275). Yet another is the requirement that "opponents confront each other as equals in an atmosphere of mutual trust" (280). The Rogerian model turns the writing classroom into the kind of "surreal" vision of social reality the "teacherless" classroom aspires to reinforce. It places decisions to resist or accept alternative positions solidly within the realm of a "personal" ("psychological") divested of social and historical content: a "free will" inherent in "man" and his "senses" of trust. And the Rogerian strategies place such decisions in the realm of the "textual" by implying that the reader's senses of threat can be reduced by nothing more than a set of "writing" gestures. In placing decisions to "change" in the realm of the "personal" and the "textual," *Rhetoric: Discovery and Change* joins the New Critical project in defining writing as an inward flight from the social and historical. It implies that "confrontations between young and old, East and West, White and Black" can be dissolved by nothing more than a set of thinking and writing strategies. The political efficacy of the pedagogy of "discovery and change" is of course its implication that "senses of threat" resulting from competing ideas are purely formal (perceptual or conceptual) and psychological (private and instinctual) and thus can be treated—"reduced"—through formal strategies. That is, social and historical differences can be treated—"reduced" and resolved—textually by a "content" of writing discovered through heuristic procedures and a "style" of writing modeled after group therapy, without any effort to tackle the existing socioeconomic structures leading to and sustained by such differences. Therefore, the "new" rhetoric of Young, Pike, and Becker is not likely to offer teachers of basic writing a different route outside English than Emig's composing process or Elbow's writing without teachers. Likewise, the popularity of Emig and Elbow as well as Young et al. must be understood in the context of their deployment of "science" to offer English "new/neutral" rationales for continuing established positions.

Interest in importing "science" to "humanize" teaching and writing can also be seen operating in another popular text on the discursive scene, Moffett's *Teaching the Universe of Discourse* (1968). *Teaching the Universe of Discourse* is not only cited by Shaughnessy for "its insights into the forms of discourse and the readiness of students at different ages to produce and enjoy them" (305) but also reviewed in two other essays in *Teaching Composition* for its "*new* way of classifying discourse" and its "value" in setting up a curriculum at "almost any level of education" (Tate 126–29, 230). North distinguishes Moffett as a "philosopher" (94, 104–05) from "practitioners" like Elbow (22) or "researchers" like Emig (97). Nonetheless, North observes, Moffett "seems to want to grant [the philosophical premises of his argument] special status because of their empirical origins [in psychological research on child development]" and so to make his argument "into knowledge of a different order. . . unassailable" (104). I'd like to take this observation a step further to argue that Moffett's move to authorize the philosophical premises of his argument with their empirical origins indicates a concern to use "science" to neutralize the particular resolution to differences promoted by his premises.

The foundation of *Teaching the Universe of Discourse* is the claim that a correspondence exists across "modes of discourse," "levels of abstraction" and "stages of growth" (v, 13). A pedagogy which hierarchizes diverse forms of abstraction necessarily resolves differences through privileging certain forms over others. For example, the "concentric circles" representing various "rhetorical contexts" posed in the book privilege thinking and writing from the "biological" perspective by depicting it as not only the "largest" and most "universal" but also as the "determining" context for all the other contexts, including the "cultural," "national or ethnic," "social sub-group" and "family" (68). Teaching students to move up the hierarchy of abstraction thus involves teaching them to shift their perspective from the specific social and historical conditions of their life towards the "universal"—biological. Thus, "teaching the universe" participates in the construction of creative inwardness dominating English studies during the late '60s and '70s. However, Moffett claims to have "recast" or "assimilated" elements of "English" (rhetoric, grammar, literary technique) into the "psychological" terms of human growth (vi–vii, 14, 15). The "scientific" frame thus neutralizes the political of teaching "writing" which turns students away from the social/historical toward the "universal"/biological, casting it instead into a pedagogy of "liberation" rather than "acquisition" (28), "naturalistic" teaching (159), or "organic learning" (178).

A similar move to "recast"—psychologize/neutralize— writing and teaching is made in Moffett's reading of Bernstein and Piaget (58). Although Moffett acknowledges that Bernstein's restricted and elaborated codes are intended to describe social class differences in the use of language and not developmental differences, he maintains that differences between the two codes are "remarkably parallel to general growth irrespective of class" (58) and suggestive of "how much the language of disadvantaged students seems to be *arrested* at a stage that middle-class children go easily beyond" (59, emphasis mine). Reading Bernstein in terms of Piaget's developmental frame enables Moffett to present different family and class backgrounds as having different effects on the child's "normal" growth, with some (working-class) disadvantaging the child by "arresting" that growth.

This reading points to the social content of Moffett's interest in "psychology." This tendency to use a developmental frame to hierarchize class differences is, ironically, also articulated in Moffett's effort to combat racial and class segregation among school children (157). According to Moffett, the "disadvantaged" urban children can benefit from the "mixing" by learning "new" uses of language while the "advantaged children" of the suburbs can benefit by "*re*learn[ing]" the emotive and communal uses of language that middle-class upbringing tends to destroy (94, my emphasis). By implication, the socially "advantaged" have already had, although lately having lost, the skills possessed by the "disadvantaged," while the latter have yet to acquire the skills the former possess. Even though both the "familial" and "cultural" are here seen as "contexts" which restrict rather than expand the fullest development of the children, they seem to restrict in different ways, some keeping the child from "higher" and some from "lower" levels of development (94). At a time when, as Shaughnessy put it, the War on Poverty put headings such as "cultural deprivation" and "cultural differences" in the Education Index ("Basic Writing" 138) and given the dominance of empirical/organic rhetoric on the discursive scene, the popularity of *Teaching the Universe of Discourse* cannot be separated from its ability to recast into "scientific"—"biological," "natural," and "universal"—terms a pedagogy which hierarchizes class differences.

Frank J. D'Angelo's *A Conceptual Theory of Rhetoric* (1975) is another work repeatedly cited in *Teaching Composition* for its "original" discussion of customary methods of development in writing (57, 100, 230). The concern to locate a totalizing structure inherent in the "human" mind in both D'Angelo's rhetorical study and Moffett's study on forms of discourse again points to the political currency of expressive realism on the discursive scene. D'Angelo presents his "new" rhetoric as "invigorated" by the insights of the "new sciences": linguistics, psycholinguistics, semantics, neuropsychology, psychotherapy, anthropology, biology (162). Deploying the authority of the "new sciences," D'Angelo projects a "universe" in which *the* process in every area (of composing, psychological or physiological) has its "counterparts" in every other area (16), and each "mirrors" or "repeats" in microcosm the larger "evolutionary process" of the universe (vi–vii). The equation of knowledge, truth, and data is evoked through characterizing modern linguistics, the foundation of *Rhetoric*, as "descriptive" (18). Furthermore, D'Angelo maintains that his "theory" is grounded in "empirical testing," has "empirical evidence for hypotheses" and some sort of correlation between "observable facts and the constructs of the logical system" (24). Not surprisingly, the empirical rhetoric works hand in hand with an organic rhetoric. He depicts the patterns of discourse he "describes" as "symbolic manifestations of underlying mental processes" (57, 10?) which are "genetically inherited" and innate in every "human organism" (26). By implication, the concern to "describe" essentialized—universal and innate—structures (26, 27, 57), which D'Angelo presents as crossing disciplines such as linguistics, anthropology, and literary criticism, is driven by the "realities" of human nature and therefore neutral rather than social and historical.

The empirical/natural rhetoric exempts D'Angelo from the need to reflect on the politics of confining research and the teaching of writing to "recurring," "formal" patterns (19). More specifically, it occludes attention from the power relations and struggle inscribed in the "recurring" formal patterns or the social and historical forces sustaining their power to recur. Rather, it allows D'Angelo to claim that in "describing" only the "recurring" patterns, he is merely making more self-conscious and more economical operations and properties innate in all "human organisms" and universally practiced (47). And it absolves D'Angelo from the need to justify the politics of a pedagogy which dissolves differences in forms of discourse by urging teachers to "direct" students to "observe" and "imitate" recurring formal patterns (158). Given this rhetoric, it should not be surprising that he presents his pedagogy as complementary to pedagogies which are "related to" the exploration of "psychologists" and "psychotherapists" including Freud and Carl Rogers (158–59). It is indeed the recurring attempt to use "science" to detach "writing" and "teaching" from issues of power and differences that makes texts as seemingly diverse as *A Conceptual Theory of Rhetoric, Writing Without Teachers,* and *Rhetoric: Discovery and Change* compatible to one another and useful for a composition eager to establish its institutional place.

The hegemony of expressive realism on the discursive scene of Basic Writing's birth can also be construed from the story of "science" in O'Hare's *Sentence Combining,* another popular text cited in five of the ten essays in *Teaching Composition* and praised by Shaughnessy as one of the "most useful sources of information on sentence combining as a method of instruction" for Basic Writing (Tate 157, 105, 206, 267). Although North classifies O'Hare as a "researcher" rather than a "practitioner" (Elbow) or "philosopher" (Moffett) and as an "experimental" rather than a "clinical" (Emig) researcher (143, 97), an objective/natural rhetoric aligns O'Hare's monograph with all the texts I discuss in this section. This rhetoric might also explain how this monograph can share canonical status with other texts that explicitly critique sentence-combining, most notably Moffett's *Teaching* (see Moffett, Chapter Five).

The central question organizing O'Hare's study is "whether sentence-combining practice will enhance the normal growth of syntactic maturity" (20). "Science" again functions as direct and indirect "support" for this move to recast hegemonic definitions of "mature" sentence structure into a "natural" and "universal" developmental frame. O'Hare markets his study as providing an "objective" measure which can be used to "describe" in "quantifiable terms" or to "readily identify" and "objectively verify" what English teachers have always been vaguely aware of (19, 20). Thus, the researcher/teacher's definitions of "normal growth" and "syntactic maturity" are presented as facts innate in the objects of study—the students and their writing—and independent from the perspective and language of the researcher/teacher.

The works of "leading linguists" and "behavioral scientists" are also cited to authorize the pedagogy (v). The link between T-unit length and embedded sentences and syntactic/cognitive "maturity" is presented as legitimized by "language development studies" (24) or cognitive theories (31). The "scientific" base works to shift attention away from the study's tendency to dismiss differences across the students chosen by the study and to ignore the social consequences of subjecting all students to the rules of "mature" syntax. O'Hare seems to admit to at least two factors leading to a correlation between "normal growth" and "syntactic maturity": the "child's" cognitive development and "his" enculturation through reading and schooling (24). Yet, he quickly shifts attention from the latter factor by zeroing in on the "developmental trend: the increase with age." O'Hare consistently refers to his subjects in terms of "biological growth," as older or younger or as an adult or child, rather than in terms of their place in the educational system (23–24). Such references occlude attention to their enculturation, even though the students under study are selected because of the grades they are in—i.e., they appear to be in the same "age" group because specific social conventions result in all "children" in the United States beginning schooling at the same age.

A similar move to neutralize one's position on how and what to teach is also articulated in another text with a seemingly opposite stance on the importance of written syntactic forms to O'Hare's *Sentence Combin-*

ing: the 1972 resolution by the Executive Committee of the Conference on College Composition and Communication, "Students' Right to Their Own Language." This position statement also seems to differ from texts such as *Errors and Expectations* on the question of whether academic discourse should be the means and goal of writing classrooms. However, an explanation of the "linguistic and social knowledge" grounding the 1972 resolution drafted by the Committee in 1974 suggests that "science" serves a similar neutralizing function in all three texts ("Students' Right" 3). The "scientific" status of "linguistics" is invoked by references to the "actual available linguistic evidence" (1) and "insight from linguistic study" (6). The committee's interest in *"actual* available linguistic *evidence"* (1, my emphasis) seems to reside strictly in the binary of deep structure vs. surface details and the "new" rationale this binary offers for maintaining the neutrality of teaching and writing, a move conjoining the CCCC policy statement with pedagogies as seemingly disparate as Shaughnessy's error study, O'Hare's sentence-combining exercises, and Elbow's believing game.

For example, one of the "insights from linguistic study" grounding the policy statement is the assertion that "differences among dialects are always confined to a limited range of surface features that have no effect on what linguists call deep structure" (1, 6). The committee "roughly" translates, for composition, "deep structure" as "meaning" (6). Such a translation separates "meaning" from "linguistic forms" or "dialectal features" and turns it into an essence existing beyond the realm of "controversy" over differences and diversity.[3] In reducing discursive differences to a "limited range of surface features," the teaching of "meaning" is divested of its social, historical content. Composition finds a "new"—"scientific"—rationale for maintaining education's transcendence over social and historical power struggle.

This "linguistic" knowledge allows the committee to maintain a "new understanding of the English teacher's function" (7): the official function of English teachers is to teach skills which help students "acquire" meaning and help students "gain confidence in communicating in a variety of situations" in a variety of forms (11) and not to "reproduce meaning" in any given surface forms, such as the forms of a "dialect" called Edited American English (EAE) (7). On the one hand, this "new" understanding can help relieve the back-to-basics right wing pressure on writing teachers convinced that drills on "correct" form cannot improve students' ability as readers and writers. On the other hand, this understanding allows for a continual separation of the transmission of "meaning" from issues of differences and power through the imagery of "coding" and "decoding" (7). That is, it enables the committee to argue that issues of diversity are present only in the teaching of "dialectal features." Defining diversity as a mere surface feature further allows the committee to pose a binary pedagogical solution: either "obliterating" (2) or "eliminating" differences by forcing students to read and write only in EAE (10) or upholding diversity by allowing students to read and write in any dialect.

The imagery of a "deep structure" or stable "meaning" thus effectively frees all processes of meaning-making—whether structured on the rules of believing, heuristic procedures, or the universe of discourse—from issues of power and difference. Of course, the neutrality of meaning-making processes cannot stand on its own without the support of an equation between the "deep," the "innate," and the "universal," which is established by claims such as "it follows" that if all languages are the product of the same "instrument"—the "human brain"—then "all dialects are essentially the same in their deep structure" (9). By implication, "meaning" remains stable because it has its origin in the "biological" rather than social and historical. Among the criteria the committee explicitly points to as the basis for teaching reading and writing is the discovery of meaning through both "logic and metaphor" (8). Taken outside the frame of biological law, we can argue that notions of "logic and metaphor" are social and historical constructs. Particular definitions of "logic" and "metaphor"—as in the case of Young, Becker, and Pike's heuristic procedures and of New Critical definitions of poetic language—can significantly control the kind of "meaning" these help to discover. However, attention to the politics of promoting particular processes of meaning-making is rendered moot by the "scientific" authority of "linguistic" knowledge. In short, the efficacy of "linguistics" for composition resides not only in its support for the "students' right to their own language" but also in its support for the teachers' right to teach processes of meaning-making supposedly backed by "natural," "human" laws. That is, the separation of meaning and form ensures that English teachers preserve the power to control the process of meaning-making without having to address the politics of their choice of approach to writing and teaching.

Another dictum imported from "science," "no dialect is inherently good or bad" (5), is also used to neutralize the teaching of "linguistic" forms. While it serves to deconstruct social prejudices toward nonacademic discourses, it also works to turn EAE into just another "dialect" which can be used to transmit "meaning" without mediating its production (see Lu, "Redefining"). Teachers can claim that in teaching students to "experiment" with new dialectal forms such as EAE, they are upholding diversity, offering students "additional options" or "greater flexibility and versatility in the choices they make" (11) rather than mediating the student's subject positioning across competing discursive powers. Such a rhetoric is seductive because it invokes both liberal pluralism and the myth of functional literacy. It presents the teaching of academic discourse as in keeping with a "nation proud of its diverse heritage and its cultural and racial variety" (3). Since our "pluralistic society requires many varieties of language to meet our multiplicity of needs" (5), teaching of EAE is motivated by the students' "need" and "want": their being and desiring to be functioning citizens of a "pluralistic" nation (15). At the same time, an implicit hierarchy is established in the document's depiction of language variety: only "the written dialect" is viewed as serving the "larger, public community" and meant to carry information about our "representative problems and interests" (3, 5). The binary of public/private, larger/narrow, as I have argued, ensures that efforts to respect diversity will and can only result in everyone's "needing" and "wanting" to learn and use EAE (15). Again, the efficacy of "linguistics" for composition is its ability to neutralize the dissemination of hegemonic linguistic forms as well as to find new reasons for perpetuating myths of pluralism and functional literacy.

The move to import "science" to neutralize writing and teaching in the name of innate "human" linguistic or cognitive laws across texts I examine in this section has institutional currency for composition because it can work to confirm the place of composition within English Studies. It renews the story of "science" in New Critical projects such as I. A. Richards's *Practical Criticism,* one of the texts cited by Shaughnessy as useful for Basic Writing (Shaughnessy, "Basic Writing" 164; *Errors* 208). *Practical Criticism* presupposes a story of a "natural" tendency in "man" toward, on the one hand, greater complexity and finer differentiation of responses and, on the other, increased order (268–69). Since "poetry" is supposedly that unique instrument by which "our minds have ordered their thoughts, emotions, and desires," in making such a technique "accessible," the "new" criticism becomes by implication one of those "deliberately contrived artificial means of correction" needed for the well-being of "human mentality" (301). This organic plot enables *Practical Criticism* to market a "new," clearly socially and historically situated technique of reading and writing as a neutral means for containing—ordering and controlling—differences. On one hand, *Practical Criticism* explicitly calls attention to several aspects of the "contemporary social and economic conditions" the "new" technique is interested to contain: an increasing heterogeneity of ideas, feelings, and perspectives; "more troubling still, *our* handling of these materials varies" and "vehicles of tradition, the family and the community, for example, are dissolved" (301, 318). The move to uphold the figure of a poet/critic, one who handles difference through "exposing" ambiguities to "observe" and "analyze" them "systematically" rather than ignoring them through stereotyping and standardizing interpretations (319, 320) is therefore also a move to contain different ways of handling differences across class—"*descending* from the scholar's level to the kitchen-maids" (318)—and institutional sites, such as literature, science, politics, and commerce (253–54). Yet, reflection on the politics of this "poetic" resolution to differences is rendered moot within the frame of the story of "a too sudden diffusion of indigestible ideas" disturbing the "order of *human* mentality" (301, my emphasis).

This story of the law of "human mentality" is likewise grounded in the authority of "scientific" knowledge and methods. For example, emphasis on order, organization, and coherence is grounded in "scientific" knowledge of living "organisms": "a good idea of some of the possibilities of order and disorder in the mind may be gained from Pavlov's Conditioned Reflexes" (268, footnote 8). Statements such as "[our] minds have developed with other human beings" are supported by reference to Piaget's *The Language and Thought of the Child* along with a verse from Wordsworth's Prelude (191, note 4). An empirical/organic rhetoric also runs through statements such as "central, most stable, mass of our ideas has already an order and arrangement fixed for it by the *facts* of Nature" (260). The hegemony of scientism also surfaces in Richards's faith in the "empirical" foundation of meaning. He asserts that "every interesting abstract word (apart from those that have been nailed down to phenomena by the experimental sciences) is inevitably ambiguous" (319). By implication, the meaning of words "nailed down to phenomena" by "experimental sciences" is transparent and stable. Thus, the meaning of key words such as "human mentality" is unequivocal since it has been nailed down by "sciences." The equation of truth, knowledge, and data is also evoked in Richards's effort to ground his "practical" criticism in the authority of "scientific methods." It can hardly be coincidental that he presents close reading as a break from the "history of criticism"—arriving from "research" rather than "argument" (7). The technique of close reading is a "corrective" based upon an "investigation" of how actual readers read—"protocols" gathered from "several hundreds of opinions upon particular aspects of poetry." He indicates being "anxious" to meet as far as may be the objections of the best psychologists over whether the protocols "supply enough evidence" (9).

The story of science emerging from *Practical Criticism* indicates that the popularity of the pedagogies I discuss in this section have to do not merely with the institutional power of science over the humanities but also with the residual power of an empirical/expressive view of language within English. As both Phelps and Faigley have pointed out, the hegemony of scientism in fields such as linguistics during the 1970s, like that of New Criticism in English, is being actively challenged by emerging perspectives and practices. The dominance of scientism in these canonical texts indicates that composition's venture into "science" is in part driven by a concern to maintain the neutrality of the scholar/teacher/researcher at a time when the presumed separation of the academic from the social and political was under fire both within and outside U.S. higher education. Therefore, the contribution of the compositionists I have been discussing to the institutional status of Composition in general and Basic Writing in particular must also be reviewed from the stance they take on issues of differences and power. Likewise, the difficulties of breaking the hegemony of empirical/expressive views of language on the discursive scene of Basic Writing's birth is not only intellectual in the narrow sense but deeply social and historical.

Dissolving Attention to the Social and Historical: Translating Knowledge across Disciplines and Continents

To further explore the pervasive move to naturalize writing and teaching on the discursive terrain shaping Basic Writing's birth, we need to also examine composition's appropriations of the work of researchers and critics across disciplines which to various degrees explicitly addresses the relations of language, power, and subjectivity. In the following section, I will read the works of authorities frequently cited in composition—Kenneth Burke, William Labov, Basil Bernstein, Richard Ohmann, Lev Vygotsky, and Paulo Freire—to highlight the ambivalence of each toward, and/or oftentimes pronounced critiques of, essentialist views of language and the myth of the neutrality of teaching writing. I discuss the ways in which composition during Basic Writing's birth effectively glossed over such elements in these works through various forms of excerpting and translating. I argue that the social, historical nature of the hegemony of expressive realism across science and English can be illustrated by U.S. educators' effort to maintain the "objectivity" of the knowledge posited by these authority figures when translating, editing, introducing, and citing their works. This effort takes two directions: on one hand, zeroing on aspects of the text which can appear to support the essentialist framework, and, on the other, dismissing aspects of the studies where writing is presented as mediated by rather than transcending its social, historical contexts.

Treatment of Kenneth Burke's work is exemplary in this regard. Several of the composition texts I discuss above perceive Burke's pentad to be one of the most influential "literary" resources for the "new" rhetoric. The Burke appearing in these texts is often someone interested in upholding the objectivity of his structural knowledge. This reading of Burke, however, dissolves a tension marking Burke's writing. As Frank Lentricchia puts it cogently in *Criticism and Social Change,* in Burke's work, a desire to move to a perch above historical process in an effort to find a single master structure is consistently contradicted by a concern to be critical of such a "structuralist" project (56). The essentialist impulse is most evident in *A Grammar of Motives,* where Burke posits "dramatism"—five key terms supposedly exhausting the structural possibilities of textual expression (Lentricchia 66–67). Using other sections from Burke's *Grammar,* Lentricchia argues that even in the process of formulating this ur-form, Burke introduces theoretical qualifications that open up his method to a level of historical analysis (Lentricchia 69). Lentricchia concludes that as a reader of history, Burke is a "critical structuralist," one who investigates ruthlessly his own terminological resources (71). On one level, "man" in Burke is the autonomous subject of liberal humanism, with its corollary values of freedom, creativity, self-possession, and self-presence. On another level, this autonomy is deconstructed because the "agent" and his "action" are located within a system, as having a constraining context (Lentricchia 71). In Burke's own words, the actor is "motivated," acting as well as being "acted upon by his state of being acted upon" (cited in Lentricchia 73). Meaning is made and unmade, enforced and subverted, assented to and resisted in collective acts of will, where nothing (or very little) is natural, fixed, and eternal (Lentricchia 69). This line of Burke's thinking presents writing as constitutive of rather than transcending the hegemonic process in the Gramscian sense (Lentricchia 76). By implication, Burke the critical structuralist would perceive all intellectual acts, including the act of positing the pentad, as involved in power in every way.

However, as Lentricchia points out, Burke the critical structuralist "has consistently slipped through" the attention of critics and modernist writers because of the hegemony of the New Critical flight from politics between the two world wars (86). This selective reading of Burke seems to have continued in composition's appropriation of Burke during Basic Writing's birth. For example, D'Angelo's reading of Burke centers on passages which allow D'Angelo to dissolve Burke's ambivalence toward universalizing structures and to conclude, "for Burke, it matters *not* whether these patterns are psychological universals or merely conventional or acquired forms, the idea being that once we have obtained them, they can become the means of organizing discourse" (D'Angelo 19, emphasis mine). A similar move is made by Young in his bibliographical essay on "Invention" (13). Young refers us to passages where Burke presents the "pentad" as "never to be abandoned" since "all statements that assign motives can be shown to arise out of them and to terminate in them." Foregrounding the essentialist impulse marking Burke's work enables Young to present the dramatistic method as a means of "discovering essential features of the behavior of groups or individuals" (15), a procedure which "shares features" with essentialist programs such as Pike's tagmemics (30–31).

Young does acknowledge that compositionists such as W. Ross Winterowd and William Irmscher have turned the pentad into "a heuristic independent of the context of Burke's theory" ("Invention" 16) and, in doing so, have made it lose some of its power, intelligibility, and reason. But he quickly maintains that this "excerpting" of Burke's work has "adequate justifications": it does "us" service in making even part of the theory available to "composition" (16). Given the domination of expressive realism in composition, we might say that the service performed by the strategy of excerpting is to make it possible for "composition" to overlook Burke's position on the politics of intellectual activity such as the posing and disseminating of structural laws, and thus to avoid reckoning with the challenge Burke's work poses for the concern of "us" to neutralize writing and teaching.

Of course, the move to excerpt Burke's pentad is largely made possible because of Burke's own concern to stage a scientist/critic/writer capable of transcending the social and historical entrapping "man" that conjoins the author and his disciples. This concern is latent in both articles Burke wrote explicitly for the composition teaching community: "Questions and Answers about the Pentad" (*College Composition and Communication* 1978) and "Rhetoric—Old and New" (1950, *Journal of General Education*). Before turning to Burke's attempt to write his own work outside history, let me begin by mapping out the move to contextualize writing and teaching embedded in Burke's discussion of the implications of his "literary" theory for the teaching of "composition" and "communication." Burke distinguishes his "dramatism" from the more "positive" use of the pentad in Irmscher by rehearsing themes such as "attitude" ("Questions" 330), "identification" ("Rhetoric" 203), "gods quarreling" and "contracts" with gods ("Questions" 333). As Lentricchia's reading of Burke suggests, these themes are central to Burke's critical structuralist views. They highlight the relationship between form, rhetoric, and power, thus pointing to the social and historical context of the production, dissemination, and deployment of structural knowledge, including "dramatism." That is, these themes invoke passages in Burke that Lentricchia has recalled to our attention where Burke examines the production of structural laws in relation to "bureaucratization of the imaginative" (Lentricchia 61), where the "imaginative" is depicted as "embodied in the realities of a social texture, in all the complexities of language and habits, in the property relationships, the methods of government, production and distribution, and in the development of rituals that re-enforce the same emphasis" (Burke, *Attitudes Towards History* 225–26). And they recall passages depicting the "gods contract[ing]" the "dispossessed person" by making him feel that "he 'has a stake in' the authoritative structure that dispossesses him" (*Attitudes* 329–30). Attention to these themes in Burke would lead us to view all discursive structures, the "'dramatistic' nomenclature" ("Questions" 334) as well as the "various specialized nomenclatures (of physics, chemistry, biology or the like)" ("Questions" 335)—as social, historical forces and the teaching of such structures, the act of "contracting" for "gods."

Burke's critical structuralist position is also operative in his claim that his "'new' rhetoric" is reinvigorated by fresh insights of the "new sciences" ("Rhetoric—Old and New" 203). Part of the use of "new sciences" for Burke, contrary to their use for Elbow's "believing game" or Young, Becker, and Pike's "new" rhetoric, is the insights these disciplines shed on the social, historical content of the psychological and biological. Burke depicts "psychosomatic medicine" as concerned with the ways in which our "physiques are led to take on attitudes in keeping with the rhetorical or persuasive aspects of ideas" ("Rhetoric" 203). This suggests that the "new sciences" interest Burke because they shed insight on the ways in which ideas are "worked into the very set of nerves, muscles, and organs" (203), i.e., the extent to which the hegemonic process "bureaucratizes" our unconscious and physical body as well as the conscious. Thus, to Burke, a "'new' rhetoric" reinvigorated by the "new sciences" would acknowledge rather than deny the social and historical in the "psychological" and "biological" origin of meaning.

At the same time, the challenge to composition's concern to find support for neutralizing writing and teaching posed by these passages can be easily glossed over because they coexist with passages clearly driven by Burke's concern to write himself—the "literary," "structuralist" critic—outside the historical process in which he depicts the acting of other agents of writing—the "writer" of the texts he analyzes. He presents his "job" as helping a "critic perceive what was going on *in* a text" by "asking of the work the explicit questions to which its structure had already implicitly supplied the answers" ("Questions" 332, 335). In depicting the pentad as a means of making explicit what is implicit *in* the structure of the object of study, Burke endows his structural knowledge with an empirical base. The "objective" rhetoric exempts the Author of the pentad from the kind of historical analysis of the rhetorical motive and grammar of writing he applies to other writers. In moving the critic and his knowledge outside the historical process to a transcendental plane, it renders moot all attention to the politics of teaching that finds support from the "pentad."

However, the grammar and motive of maintaining the objectivity of "dramatism" is socially and historically situated. As Lentricchia argues, this desire to write the critic outside history cannot be separated from the sociocultural matrix of the 1930s, indicating alignment with formalism's concern to "escape" the worst socioeconomic crisis this country has known and to contest the hegemony of the aesthetic of social realism (56, 64). Likewise, the political efficacy of Burke's pentad for composition resides in the dominant role formalism has played in English from the 1930s to the 1970s and in composition's search for a new/ neutral rationale for its existence at a time when issues of power and difference are most difficult to contain in academic as well as public debate. It is composition's alignment with a certain kind of reception theory dominating modernism and humanist literary theory that makes composition's excerpting of Burke viable and a "service" to composition. That is, the move to excerpt Burke puts composition at the center of an intellectual enterprise dominated by "a concern for the abiding patterns of human subjectivity whose universal structures bind us all across the ages, cultures, and societies" (Lentricchia 93).

Composition's importation of William Labov's study of "nonstandard English" also illustrates its tendency to dissolve the tension between a concern to essentialize structural knowledge and a concern to situate discursive practices in the social and historical. Using the Chomskian distinction between competence and performance, Labov studies the "abstract and complex" organization of "language rules" in varieties of English (9). His defense of the systematic nature of "nonstandard" English has served as support for composition teachers interested in arguing for recognition of the intelligence and competence of students whose home English is "nonstandard." For example, his study is featured in Shaughnessy's bibliographical essay as one of the texts which basic writing teachers ought to read illustrating "basic differences" in languages (159). Labov's research suggests that knowledge of the "vernacular" can help teachers to perceive the student's seeming "mistakes" and "misbehaviors" as signs of the "difference" between the rules in nonstandard and standard English (of pronunciation [44], grammar [48], modes of mitigation and politeness [51], vocabulary [46]) rather than as signs of the student's lack of intelligence or her resistance to learning.

Ironically, in his concern to pin down the structures of nonstandard English, Labov and his team come up with a rich collection of data on the dialogical nature of discursive practices—the ways in which power mediates our perception and performance of linguistic rules. He notices that the informants' perception and enactment of the rules of the non-standard English are always "shifting" toward the standard: the researcher has difficulty catching them in situations when these two systems are not in "interaction." Labov cautions us to consider the ways in which "social forces," including the social prestige of the language and the power relationship between the researcher and informants, "affect linguistic behavior" (11). He laments that languages are not so carefully partitioned from each other in the speakers' heads that the right hand does not know what the left hand is doing: their rules "are bound to interact" (36). However, these references to the ways in which power relations mediate our knowledge and application of "linguistic rules" is overwritten by a concern to naturalize the author's structural knowledge.

Expressive realism in Labov's work is most explicitly demonstrated by the assumption that the "sociolinguistic investigator" can and ought to "obtain a record of the subjects' *natural* speech" (50, emphasis mine): "The grammars we are concerned with must be grammars of a language which is actually used for communication *within* the speech community" (39, emphasis mine). Imagery of the "real" neutralizes the investigator's structural knowledge by grounding it within the referent, the "speech" of the "speech community." However, when evaluating the quality of information and informants, Labov demonstrates a clear interest in erasing differences across discursive practices to stabilize the "grammars" of that speech community. For example, he depicts information as having a "major defect" (42) if it does not allow us to distinguish regular rule-governed behavior from rare or variable behavior (42). Informants are "poor" or "unreliable" (36, 11) when diverse systems interact on the scene of the interview or in their minds (11, 36). The concern for regularity and purity articulates Labov's alignment with modern linguistics' desire to posit a "speech community"—a unified and "maximally homogeneous" social world—as the object of its study (see Pratt, "Linguistic Utopias" 50). In positing such a "speech community," the rules surfacing in the exchange between people of least linguistic, social, political difference in most monodialectal situations are construed as the "norm." In homogenizing the discursive practices of a "community," such a construct also reinforces the hegemonic power of those at

the center of individual discursive sites. As feminist critic Deborah
Cameron argues, it marginalizes the less powerful of the group, including its female members. That is, such an approach to "community" and
linguistic norms is not neutral, as implied by the rhetoric of the "natural" and "actual," but situated in the power struggle across lines of class
and gender as well as race and ethnicity.

We may argue that it is the expressive realism underlying Labov's
study which makes it possible for "authorities" like Labov and Moffett
with seemingly directly opposite takes on Bernstein's work to both serve
as useful sources for composition. As I have argued earlier, Moffett reads
Bernstein's research on the different codes of middle-class and working-class students as evidence of differences in the students' cognitive
skills. Labov refutes that position in his critique of Carl Bereiter and his
program for preschool children (Labov 47). In spite of the differences,
the service both offer composition is the support for isolating the formulation and dissemination of "forms" of discourse—"abstraction" in
the case of Moffett, "linguistic rules" in the case of Labov—from their
social and political contexts.

A similar move to dissolve an ambivalence toward the neutrality of
writing and teaching in the conceptual horizon of the writer also takes
place in composition's excerpting of the work of Richard Ohmann. Being the editor of *College English*, Ohmann could not be easily dismissed.
He is cited in five of the ten bibliographical essays in *Teaching Composition* (Tate 75, 88, 97, 325, 227, 249). On the one hand, there seems to be a
concerted effort in these essays to present Ohmann as a trailblazer in
English's venture into linguistics—one of the representatives of "linguis-
tic-analysts" in America (75), a "transformationalist" (88), and a "speech
act" theorist—and, on the other, to ignore his cultural analysis of the
professional ethos of English departments, especially those articles (published before 1973) which serve as the basis of much of his argument in
English in America. That is, these leading voices in composition seem to
suggest that the only Ohmann relevant to composition is the Ohmann
who is, in Ohmann's own words, "intending" to write "professional
books" "advancing 'our' knowledge and my career" (*English in America*
4). At the same time, the Ohmann who admits to feeling "uncomfortable about where careers were taking me and the people I worked with"
and beginning to "give strident talks, criticizing the profession and pro-
posing reforms" is unanimously dismissed (5).

Let me examine the essentialist strain in Ohmann's writing from the
earlier part of the 1960s to understand how such an amputation of
Ohmann's work is possible. Among Ohmann's articles cited as useful
resources in *Teaching Composition* is "In Lieu of a New Rhetoric" (1964),

in which Ohmann sketches out the assumptions of a New Rhetoric to which he admits to "adhere" ("In Lieu" 20). Ohmann depicts the writer as holding "the mirror up, not only to nature or to the audience, but to himself," which indicates an alignment with expressive realism (19). Like other promoters of the "new" rhetoric, Ohmann naturalizes the "new" writing as helping readers to "share . . . a way of being human" (22). Likewise, he maintains that postulating a hierarchy of world views is "easy" if we start from those "conceptual modes . . . *dictated* by our biological makeup" and move through the "smaller" ones of nation and culture down to the "smaller subgroups" of profession and class (19). In "Literature as Sentence" (1966), another article cited in *Teaching Composition,* Ohmann uses the Chomskian binary of deep and surface structure to encourage efforts to "anchor" our "elusive intuition" of form and content in the framework of generative grammar and study the "cognitive and emotional processes" literary work sets in motion (261, 265, 267). In "Speech, Action, and Style" (1971), a third article endorsed by the contributors to *Teaching Composition,* Ohmann uses speech act theory to argue that we study the rules for illocutionary acts (246–47) and actions "basic to the continuity of human society" or "norm of human interactions" (248) which are performed by illocutionary acts. And he is concerned to find correlations between styles of illocutionary action and "fundamental literary types" (252). In none of these articles does Ohmann reflect on the politics of his "professional" interest in "deep" rules and structures in the context of the academic, cultural, and social conditions of the 1960s, as he does a decade later in *English in America.*

It is worth spending some time analyzing Ohmann's critique of the politics of English in two essays ignored by the bibliographical essays. In "The Size and Structure of an Academic Field: Some Perplexities" (1967), Ohmann evinces an uneasy tension between an unequivocal faith in the neutrality of "science" and a concern to acknowledge the politics of English. The history and forum of its presentation (first as a talk at the 1966 NCTE convention and then as an essay published in *College English*) and its topic (the relationship between English and science) make it unlikely that any of the compositionists I discuss here would have missed encountering it. In the essay, Ohmann makes the argument that "science" is a "bad," "inappropriate" model for English because the former is neutral while the latter has its cultural functions (362, 366). His definition of "science" illustrates the hegemony of scientism on the internal as well as external scene of his writing. Ohmann makes no qualification when stating that "science seeks to achieve a neutrality towards particular events" and the "activity of theorizing *is* essentially neutral" (364). He maintains that "scientific inquiry has a certain ethic—that of disinterestedness," and "its results are morally neutral"—"it maintains a moral neutrality towards the objects of its attention" (365). In short, to Ohmann in this article, "science" is a bad model for "English" because the latter cannot be "science" but not also because Ohmann questions the master plots of scientism. On the other hand, "English" cannot be neutral because it is interested in "the fostering of literary culture and literary consciousness"—the building of a "corporate identity" (363). Given the pervasive concern to turn composition into a "science" and the tendency to think of English/science or literature/composition in binary oppositions on the discursive horizon, it is conceivable that leading compositionists might view Ohmann's comment on the social function of "English" as relevant only to the other component of English—those committed to "literary" culture and consciousness—and therefore as having little to do with those of "us" committed to "science" and the fostering of universal, natural "literacy."

In another essay ignored by the bibliographies, "Teaching and Studying Literature at the End of Ideology" in *The Politics of Literature* (1970), which serves as the foundation of his chapter on the "Professional Ethos" in *English in America,* Ohmann launches an even more cogent and extended analysis of the politics of English through unpacking the "cultural values inherent in close reading" (135). He not only calls attention to the "flight from politics" (143) it promotes but also puts New Critical "reading" in the context of a general evasion of social conflict in American culture in its two-hundred-year history (143), the particular social historical conditions of the 1950s (144), and the myth of "academic freedom" dominating education (152). The word "literature" in the title of both the essay and the book might again be used to justify "composition's" silence on Ohmann's view of the politics of reading and teaching. However, composition's reception of *English in America,* in which Ohmann explicitly points to composition's participation in the New Critical flight from politics, suggests that this silence needs to be examined in relation to the history of composition's concern to maintain its neutrality. As John Trimbur argues in his 1993 review of *English in America,* "the field [composition] had collectively misplaced its copy of *English in America*" by 1980, only three years after its publication (389). Composition's reception of *English in America* during the birth of Basic Writing suggests that the excerption of Ohmann the structuralist linguist from Ohmann the social critic would have taken place even if he had explicitly demystified the neutrality of composition in his earlier essays.

This case is likely given the comparable U.S. reception given Bernstein's elaborated and restricted codes. Bernstein's own review of his research from 1956 through 1987 puts in cogent terms an ambivalence toward the neutrality of structuralist knowledge marking his work. Bernstein maintains that there has been a "movement" in his thinking and research "from the *giving of definitions* in terms of general linguistic indices" to emphasizing the *"relation* between meanings, realizations, and context" ("Elaborated" 101, emphasis mine). He feels it "important to point out (because it is normally ignored)" that this movement has been "continuous," beginning from a series of papers in 1964 (98). After 1971, it has led him to put more emphasis on the linkage between the "macro power relations and micro practices" (119). It is this emphasis, he argues, which distinguishes his code theory from the deficit and language variety/difference position (118). In emphasizing the "movement" in his research, Bernstein repeats his reservations, voiced as early as 1969 in a paper delivered at Columbia (*Class* 1: 191), concerning how U.S. educators have "used (and more often abused)" his work, by drawing "only upon very early work" (18) or amputating his concern to define linguistic indices from his developing interest in the link between codes, meaning, and power. Moffett's reading of Bernstein via Piaget, which I have analyzed in the previous section, exemplifies the kind of "abuse" Bernstein has in mind.

As Bernstein argues in the Introduction to the 1971 edition of a collection of his writings, this form of amputation has to be "ideological" since "research in the social sciences arises out of the social context, is organized within a social context and, of critical significance, is given its various meanings by receiving social contexts" (1: 18). The social context constraining the U.S. reception of Bernstein's work, Bernstein goes on to argue, is the domination of the deficit model in both the left and right wing position on what Shaughnessy has depicted as issues giving birth to Basic Writing: the War on Poverty and the debate on "cultural deprivation" and "difference" during the 1960s (Shaughnessy, "Basic Writing" 138). In calling the U.S. amputation of his work "inadvertent" (*Class* 1: 194), Bernstein suggests that it is a comment on the "receiving social contexts" rather than the social contexts producing his research. However, we can argue that the U.S. "abuse" of his earlier writings is also made possible by a contradictory impulse toward the figure of the researcher operating in his work, which speaks to the hegemony of scientism in the "social science" shaping his research context. As Ohmann has argued, the concepts of class and code in Bernstein's work, as in mainstream social science, are "structural and static" ("Reflections" 11). They are heuristic concepts obtained by "calibrating" factors and looking for correlations across variables (8–9).[4] Furthermore, Bernstein's choice of adjectives for distinguishing the two codes participates in the empirical, natural rhetoric dominating "science" across the continents. Words such as "universalistic" (vs. "particularistic") orders of meaning, "meta-" (vs. "descriptive") languages of control and innovation, and "public" (vs. "private") knowledge (*Class* 1: 196-97) implicitly privilege the codes of the middle class while explicitly arguing for the educability of those socialized to the "restricted" codes. Furthermore, this cluster works to displace attention from the politics of teaching in arguments such as the following:

> The introduction of the child to the universalistic meanings of pub-
> lic forms of thought is not compensatory education—it *is* educa-
> tion. It is in itself *not* making children middle class. (*Class* 1: 199, my
> emphasis)

In implying that there is a form of education which transcends the so-cial and historical, this cluster of words sustains the myth of natural literacy in much the same way expressive realism neutralizes Emig's composing process, Richards's "close reading," Elbow's writing with-out teachers, or the "new" rhetoric of Young et al. This aspect of Bernstein's thinking makes his work susceptible to his U.S. (ab)users.

However, Bernstein's insistence that the U.S. refusal to acknowledge the "movement" in his work illustrates the ideological framework of his U.S. readers is nevertheless to the point, especially if put alongside the U.S. importation of the work of Vygotsky and Freire during Basic Writing's birth. Vygotsky's "linguistic knowledge" is cited by Shaughnessy as a valuable source for basic writing in both *Errors and Expectations* and "Basic Writing." U.S. exposure to Vygotsky's work was mostly confined to the 1962 publication of his *Thought and Language* (Hanfmann and Vakar), which remained until the late 1970s his only work available in English to U.S. readers. In the "Translators' Preface," Hanfmann and Vakar state that "in favor of straightforward *exposition*," they have eliminated "certain *polemical* discussions that would be of little interest to the contemporary reader" (Hanfmann and Vakar xii, my em-phasis). The dichotomy between "exposition" and "polemical discus-sion" posits an ideal reader who perceives "research" as separate from and above "politics." This "reader" is materialized by Jerome S. Bruner in his "Introduction" to the translation, in which he uses the dichotomy between a "Marxist theorist" and a reader like himself to undercut Vygotsky's view on the relation between language, thought, and power (Bruner, Introduction x). Bruner praises Vygotsky for his "mediational" point of view and for introducing an "historical perspective" to the de-velopment of thought: depicting "man as shaped by the tools and in-struments that he comes to use" and having the "capacity to create higher order structures" (ix). The "striking fact" about Vygotsky's developmental theory, Bruner claims, is its description of the "many roads to individuality and freedom" (x): turning "the effort to learn and master" various "mediating structures" into "a mechanism whereby one becomes free of one's *history*" (ix). Bruner's reading suggests that he is interested in an "historical"—i.e., transhistorical—perspective, one which neutralizes the teaching of specific linguistic and cognitive "mediating structures" in the name of "human" development and transcendence of "history." To justify his move to translate Vygotsky's book into a support for such a transhistorical perspective, Bruner has to make irrelevant Vygotsky's recognition of the role of "one's history"—society and social specificities giving shape to mediating structures. Bruner does so by invoking the equation of "Marxist" and the "political" with the "nonscientific." Portraying Vygotsky as a "theorist of the nature of man" who "transcends" rather than participates in "ideological rifts" dividing "our world so deeply today" (x), Bruner marks that portion of Vygotsky's thinking which does not fit into Bruner's transhistorical perspective as "what pleases Marxist theorists" (x). By implication, the portion of Vygotsky's work which can be read as coming from the "theorist of the nature of man" can and ought to be excerpted from that portion of his work which pleases the "Marxist theorists" in Stalin's totalitarian U.S.S.R. and the United States. Such a rationale can work only if "contemporary readers" share with Bruner and the translators a belief in the transcendental power of "scientific" research and the myth of the West as "a pluralistic world where each comes to terms with the environment in his own style" (x). Since, as I have argued in the previous sections, such readers populated composition during Basic Writing's birth, it is not surprising that only the "scientific" Vygotsky was effectively translated and introduced into U.S. education during the late sixties.

In hindsight, we might argue that Vygotsky became a "useful" source for Basic Writing precisely and only because his *Thought and Language* had been so effectively amputated by Bruner and the translators of the 1962 edition. That is, Vygotsky's use for composition and Basic Writing partially rests on the fact that U.S. readers had to wait for more than a decade for different introductions, as set forth by the publications of *Mind in Society* (1978) and the 1986 edition of *Thought and Language*. The Introductions in both of these later publications urge us to approach Vygotsky's developmental theory in the context of his interest in applying a dialectical and historical materialist frame to psychology. These readings call attention to Vygotsky's concern with "the consequences of human activity as it transforms both nature and society" (*Mind* 129). Situating Vygotsky in the tradition of Marx and Engels, Cole and Scribner argue that for Vygotsky, "the mechanism of individual developmental change is rooted in society and culture" (Introduction 7), and the focus of Vygotsky's theory and research is "the historically shaped and culturally transmitted psychology of human beings." However, given the power of expressive realism on the discursive terrain shaping Basic Writing, it is doubtful that U.S. readers would have received *Thought and Language* with the same enthusiasm if the book was first imported in such terms.

Predictably, U.S. (ab)use of *Thought and Language* often glosses over Vygotsky's critique of "old schools of psychology" (*Thought and Language* [1986] 212) and of Piaget. Vygotsky explicitly distinguishes his view of language from the "associationists' view," which Vygotsky argues assumes a bond between meaning, a certain sound, and a certain object or referent and a bond between meaning and the transcendental laws of the spirit or soul (*Thoughts and Language* [1986] 212–14). Furthermore, in a chapter called "Piaget's Theory of the Child's Speech and Thought," Vygotsky explicitly criticizes the intersection between Piaget's theory and "psychoanalysis" in perceiving the relationship between "the biological and social factors of development" as a "breakdown"—in terms of a dichotomy of "inherent" and "external, 'alien,'" forces (44–45). A field concerned to neutralize notions of linguistic and cognitive processes cannot afford to hear this portion of *Thought and Language*, even though Piaget himself explicitly acknowledges a difference between his theory of "cognitive egocentrism" and Vygotsky's notion of "inner speech" in a short pamphlet titled "Comments." As Trimbur argues in his reading of Piaget's response to Vygotsky in "Comments," the core of the difference between the two is their different attitudes toward the social and historical. Piaget cannot accept Vygotsky's view "that the egocentric and communicative functions of language are equally socialized and that intellectual life is therefore social throughout its development" (Trimbur, "Beyond Cognition" 214). The differences between Piaget's cognitive egocentrism and Vygotsky's inner speech reside in Piaget's reliance on the "inner/outer" polarity and Vygotsky's concern to dismantle it (Trimbur 212). Vygotsky views "inner speech" in the Bakhtinian sense, as inscribed in and contributing to socially and historically specific power struggles (Trimbur 218; see also Wertsch). To Piaget, speech and cognition develop "from the inside out, from cognitive egocentrism to social cooperation," while for Vygotsky, the binary of inner and outer is deconstructed because the "outer world of public discourse has already entered as a constitutive element into the inner world of verbal thought" (Trimbur 215). However, given the hegemony of expressive realism and the myth of "scientific" neutrality on the discursive terrain during Basic Writing's birth, readings like Trimbur's would have little political currency even if they had been produced. Rather, Emig's move to group Vygotsky and Piaget within the same matrix would appear more reasonable.

U.S. amputation of Vygotsky's work also takes the form of removing his research from its social, historical contexts, even though Vygotsky explicitly calls attention to both the political content and contexts of research in his critique of Piaget. As Cole and Scribner argue in their introduction to *Mind in Society*, "historical materialism," the assumption that historical changes in society and material life produce changes in "human nature" (consciousness and behavior), plays a fundamental role in Vygotsky's thinking (Introduction 7). Viewing Vygotsky as a "Marxist theorist" as well as a "theorist of the nature of man" would help us hear Vygotsky's critique of Piaget's tendency to stay within the "safe ground" of "pure empiricism" (*Thought and Language* [1986] 14) differently than if we were to follow the direction set by Bruner. Vygotsky argues that "facts are always examined in the light of some theory and therefore cannot be disentangled from philosophy" (15). Piaget's effort to keep his work within "the bounds of pure factual science" and to deliberately avoid philosophy "is itself philosophical" (Vygotsky 41). Attention to Vygotsky's historical materialist perspective would lead us to read him as saying that the perspective and language of research is never neutral because the choice of "philosophy" is always social and political. That is, the differences between the research of Vygotsky and Piaget reside not only in the insights each constructs concerning the nature of linguistic and cognitive practices but also on the perspective of each on the neutrality of "science." Given the hegemony of the Politburo in Stalin's U.S.S.R., situating experimental cognitive psychology within a Marxist framework was imperative for all intellectual practices during Vygotsky's time (Cole and Scribner 6). We need to view Vygotsky's choice of a historical materialist frame as an active response—an attempt to cope with the constraints of "official" interpretations of Marxism dictating "scientific" research by revising and challenging its dogmatism. However, this reading is unlikely in the West given the cold-war mentality, the tendency to essentialize knowledge, and the myth of a "free" West fighting "Marxism" in the minds of contemporary readers in the 1960s and early 1970s. Rather, the equation between Marxism, communism, and Stalin's U.S.S.R. upheld by the 1962 translation of *Thought and Language* would have more currency and therefore was more likely to shift attention from the ways in which Vygotsky's deployment of the historical materialist framework illustrates a creative response to the social, historical contexts constraining his research.

Ironically, in dismissing the social and historical contexts of Vygotsky's research, the 1962 translation might also have led us to overlook a shared constraint pressuring the work of Vygotsky, Bruner, Piaget and readers such as Shaughnessy or Emig: namely, the shared need to negotiate with the pressure of fitting "research" within a totalizing narrative of "human" history: the "Marxist" narrative dominating Stalin's Soviet Union of historical progression through the feudal-capitalist-socialist-communist economic structures and the story in "our" so-called pluralistic society of the road to bourgeois individual autonomy. To put it another way, we can see in both the need to find creative ways of responding to the domination of expressive realism across the Marxist discourse dictating Stalin's U.S.S.R. and the liberal humanistic discourse of the West. In choosing a "historical materialist" interpretation of Marxism, Vygotsky can be perceived as implicitly challenging the universalizing story of "human" progress toward "proletarian" dictatorship by situating the production of all knowledge—historical, linguistic, or psychological—in the social and historical—as socially and historically constructed thought or language. At the same time, *Thought and Language* also bears the mark of the official "Marxist" plot dictating all areas of life in Stalin's U.S.S.R. For example, the move to displace attention from differences along lines of race, gender, class, and ethnicity conjoins *Thought and Language* with the work of Bruner and Piaget. Vygotsky, too, labels the "three hundred" subjects of his experimental study in terms of "biological" and "pathological" differences: as "children, adolescents, and adults, including some with pathological disturbances of intellectual and linguistic activities" (*Thought and Language* [1986] 105). This indicates that no research of "the nature of man," whether by Vygotsky or Piaget, could absolutely rise above but is always inscribed in the "ideological rift" of a particular time and place. At the same time, given the power of scientism, this aspect of Vygotsky's work would not be viewed in terms of the social, historical conditions of research but more likely as an expression of the ability of the "scientist" to transcend the political constraints of his time.

We might further contextualize composition's (ab)use of Vygotsky's *Thought and Language* by situating it alongside U.S. educators' metonymic reading of Freire's *Pedagogy of the Oppressed* (1970) (Aronowitz 9). As both Henry Giroux and Stanley Aronowitz have argued, U.S. readers during the seventies tended to "denude" Freire's work of its most important political insights (Giroux, "Paulo Freire" 177; Aronowitz 8; see also Bizzell, "Marxist"). The prevailing interest is to extrapolate a series of teaching "tools" from *Pedagogy of the Oppressed* which can be effectively used by democratic and humanist teachers to motivate students to imbibe the curriculum with enthusiasm instead of turning their backs on schooling (Aronowitz 11). Such an importation of *Pedagogy of the Oppressed* is bound to dismiss the echo of the humanist Marxism (McLaren and Leonard 3) in Freire's thoughts on history and human nature even though readers—including Aronowitz, Ira Shor, bell hooks, and Giroux—have argued in *Paulo Freire: A Critical Encounter* that his "understanding of subjectivity, experience, and power bears some resemblance to certain strains of poststructuralist thought," readings for which Freire himself has expressed appreciation (Freire, Foreword, x).

Given the hegemonic concern to neutralize composition during Basic Writing's birth, it seems hardly surprising that U.S. educators "humanize" Freire's social theory, i.e., turn it into a pedagogy concerned with individual salvation from dehumanizing social forces involving no fundamental social transformation. Indeed, it is possible to excerpt the following statements from *Pedagogy of the Oppressed* and appropriate them within the frame of composition's "new" knowledge of universal "human" cognitive and linguistic laws to assume a convergence between Freire's pedagogy of the oppressed and much of the "new" pedagogy I examine above:

> [Problem-posing education] affirms men as beings who transcend themselves (72);

> The humanist, revolutionary education must be imbued with a profound trust in men and their creative power (62).

Taken out of context, neither passage would look out of place in the work of Emig, Elbow, or Young et al. However, if we re-read these passages in the context of Freire's discussion of the nature of consciousness and the goal of problem-posing education, we would have to acknowledge a drastic difference between the meaning of the word "human" in Freire's pedagogy and in the "new" pedagogy of composition. The "man" empowered by problem-posing education and the "human" potential it facilitates is not the bourgeois subject of liberal humanism. "Humanist" education is "revolutionary" in the context of Freire's work not because it liberates "man" from the alien forces of "society" through "intellectual" flight but because it helps man to fight injustice and transform all relations of domination operating on the social, historical scene and in one's mind. This difference is most obvious if we consider Freire's explicit attention to the political content of individual consciousness and of problem-posing education. The consciousness of the oppressed, Freire argues, is "divided." Having "internalized" the consciousness of the oppressor, their ideal is to be "man"—the oppressor (*Pedagogy* 32). At this stage, their vision of the new man is individualistic, and they tend to be more interested in "private revolution": reverse their place and role while leaving oppression unchanged (30–31). Freire calls this the "tragic dilemma of the oppressed" (33). Such descriptions of consciousness indicate that human subjects in Freire's *Pedagogy of the Oppressed* are, "as in Marx, rooted in historical struggle" (*Pedagogy* 3). Human cognitive and linguistic practices are implicated in the relations of domination played out in the social, historical scene. Human consciousness is not a shelter against alien social forces but a site where socially and historically specific power struggle takes place.

Because of the power struggle within the consciousness of the teacher and students, neither can the classroom in Freire's work be seen as transcending the social and historical. As Freire reminds us, the "practice of problem-posing education" only "entails at the *outset* that the teacher-student contradiction be resolved" (*Pedagogy* 67). It only resolves the oppressor-oppressed contradiction at the "outset" because in creating a space for "cognitive actors to cooperate" (67) through the format of teaching, it has not resolved "the oppressor-oppressed contradictions" on the external scene of cognition—the "concrete situation" in which "the oppressor-oppressed contradiction is established" (35)—nor on the internal scene of cognition—the consciousness of the cognitive actor. Therefore, the "vocation" of problem-posing is helping students and teachers struggle against the oppressors by struggling to "eject" the oppressor from within, which cannot be achieved without fundamental change in the distribution of power on the social and historical scene (33). These descriptions of the social content of human consciousness and problem-posing education remind us that pedagogies which help students to exercise believing muscles and heuristic procedures in the name of inherent human laws cannot liberate students from relations of domination because it is not involving them in "incessant struggle against the structure of oppression within" their consciousness (33). They are not "liberatory" in the Freirean sense. The implicit but sharp criticism this aspect of Freire's pedagogy performs on composition's effort to neutralize "human" consciousness and the teaching of "human" cognitive and linguistic processes suggests that it would not be to the interest of authors whose work I examine in the previous sections to read Freire's social theory carefully. Rather, *Pedagogy of the Oppressed* can only be useful to composition in general and Basic Writing during its "birth" when it is denuded of its insights on the politics of humanistic education.

At the same time, the effort to "humanize" Freire's pedagogy is made possible by the tradition of separating the production and reception of knowledge from its social, historical contexts and the myth of a "free" West. Together, that tradition and myth operate to endorse a dismissal of Freire's social theory as the product of, as Aronowitz points out, a "local [Brazilian] phenomenon" therefore not relevant to the "core of Freire's teaching" (Aronowitz 10). By the same token, given the "thoroughly democratic context" marking the political systems of North America and Western Europe, the "core" of Freirean teaching can be practiced in its essence free from the encumbrance of local politics.

The Politics of Re-telling Basic Writing's "Birth" via "Science" in the 1990s

In constructing a recurring story of "science" dominating the discursive terrain of Basic Writing's birth, I have tried to portray the teacher/researcher of basic writing in her function as a dominated within the dominant: riven by her commitment to the interests of students labeled as academic "aliens" and her professional inscription within the dominant. My purpose for re-telling this story is to argue that historically, our commitment to posing fairer and more objective portraits of these students has been mediated by social, historical pressures to treat such alternative knowledge as neutral, universal Truth grounded solely in the "reality" inherent in the objects we study and teach—the students and their writing. The "scientific" rhetoric, in occluding our attention to the contradictory political motives and consequences of our research and teaching, has exempted us from the need to rigorously struggle against our alignments with the dominant when addressing issues of differences and power. While commitment to a fairer and more objective representation of the dominated is central to the work of basic writing, we need always to keep in mind, as we demand of our opponents, that "objectivity" and "fairness" are socially, historically constructed concepts and cannot be isolated from the question of who is speaking to whom, for whom, why, when, and where. That is, if we are to rigorously address issues of differences and power in our research and teaching, we must refuse the tendency to essentialize knowledge, new and alternative or established and hegemonic.

This attempt to re-search the history of Basic Writing's participation in neutralizing research, teaching, and writing is itself not politically innocent but motivated by a specific reading of the current discursive terrain. It is my concern that the pressure to depoliticize the perspective of the teacher/researcher in the 1990s has not lessened. On one hand, the emerging authority of theories of language which acknowledge issues of power and differences in discursive practices in composition, literary studies, linguistics, and the sciences increasingly makes pub-

lishable and published "new" representations of students and teachers
labeled "basic," legitimizing alternative knowledge which contests the
Truth of expressive realism. On the other hand, the neoconservative move
to renew its hegemony in the United States of today is increasingly making any attempt to call attention to the politics of teaching, writing, and
research vulnerable to the terrorism of labels such as "political correctness."

The emergence of alternative representations of students and teachers labeled as "basic" since the late 1970s can be illustrated by the differences in the style and content of Shaughnessy's bibliographical essay
and some of the bibliographical essays in the 1990 *Research in Basic Writing.* Andrea Lunsford and Patricia Sullivan's essay "Who Are Basic Writers?" begins by acknowledging the circularity of definitions of basic
writers as students in basic writing courses and the "more complete and
richer definitions" provided by scholars of basic writing (18). Their review of the literature aimed at defining basic writers, however, leads
them to conclude not only that "in a real sense, [they] do not know"
who basic writers *are* but also that, in a different sense, the questions
themselves are wrong: "trying to answer these questions . . . only led us
to new ways of asking the questions and even to questions about questions. . . . to explore the rich complexities of the questions rather than to
search for certain or simple answers" (27). This tentative questioning at
the end of the bibliographical survey destabilizes the hegemony in Basic Writing research and teaching of questions such as who *are* the basic
writers and what *are* their writings, questions which often work to focus
attention on the realism of "new" knowledge *about* the object of study
and teaching while exempting attention to the politics of the researcher/
teacher's choice of language, perspective, and methods. Thus the conclusion implicitly legitimizes questions about these questions, potentially including questions about the expressive realism embedded in the
posing of these questions in existing research and pedagogy.

Donna Haisty Winchell's essay "Developmental Psychology and Basic Writers," included in the same volume, reviews researchers' attempts
to place basic writers at particular "stages" of cognitive development. It
similarly ends by calling such attempts into question, noting the "problem of dictating values" that results from such efforts. Citing critiques
of the "cognitive" approach to understanding writing by Patricia Bizzell,
Mike Rose, and others, Winchell warns that "when teachers attempt to
accelerate their students' cognitive development, . . . [t]hey are asking
their students to accept a value system" (43). Although she maintains
that "a background in developmental psychology is an essential part of
the training of teachers of basic writers," she nonetheless accompanies

this statement with an extensive reference to Rose's cautionary note warning that such research encodes "social and political hierarchies . . . in sweeping cognitive dichotomies" (43).

In their essay on "Literacy Theory and Basic Writing," Mariolina Salvatori and Glynda Hull adopt a more radical position. Insisting at the outset that "[literacy] is permanently and deeply ideological, and teaching it necessarily means inculcating and reproducing a specific set of values and evaluations," they reject the possibility even of writing a politically neutral bibliographical essay on literacy and basic writing. As they put it in explaining their categorizations of the literature they review, they intend their categorizations to

> set up a context where theory and practice interrogate, test, and monitor each other, where different theories and practices read their own and each other's differences critically, where researchers, theorists, and teachers create for themselves and measure up to the responsibility that literacy thrusts upon them. (52)

They thus renounce at the outset the assumptions of scientism by calling attention to the politics of their own choice of language, perspective, and methods.

In thus explicitly challenging the "academic" tone characterizing Shaughnessy's bibliographical essay, researcher/teachers like Salvatori and Hull risk becoming the target of current Right charges of academic "political correctness." To a great extent, the hegemony of the binary of academic vs. political dominating the birth of Basic Writing is still with us, as attested to by conservative moves to kill the so-called "politicized" composition curriculum at the University of Texas at Austin. Economic retrenchment in states like New York likewise takes the form of targeting teachers, students, and programs viewed as most "expendable"— the most marginal and least resistant to "academic" cooptation—comparable to recent attacks on U.S. welfare programs. In such a climate, the pressure to ground one's alternative knowledge (including representations of the students' need to negotiate differences and power when writing and learning) solely in the authority of "reality" inherent in the object—the students and their writing—and to shift attention away from the politics of one's choice of language, perspective, and methods (including one's preferences for theories which acknowledge the relation of power, subjectivity, and language) is real: social, historical, as well as intellectual. For no academic project in today's United States, including this one, can transcend concerns over student admission and support services as well as teachers' own job security, tenure, and promotion. We might even regard calls within composition to eliminate first-year composition courses or to mainstream basic writing, rather than being motivated purely by new perspectives on students' needs, to be responses as well to newly imposed financial constraints on English departments and writing teachers' fatigue from long institutional exploitation.

Re-searching the history of Basic Writing's alignment with "intellectual" traditions such as scientism and New Criticism in the context of similar "professional" pressures during the late 1970s can help us grasp the differences in the social, historical contexts of basic writing teaching and research then and now, so that we might explore different strategies for wrestling with these pressures. I hope to illustrate in this version of that history that the desire to authorize the perspective and knowledge of the dominated cannot benefit from the assumptions of expressive realism, for only the dominant has the power to objectify—neutralize and universalize—truth. In order to not lose sight of our concern to identify with the dominated, we must be willing to grapple with our inscription in the dominant and rigorously contextualize our knowledge with the question of who is speaking for whom, when, where, and why. That is, we have no option but to meet head-on the Right terrorist accusations of "political correctness." On the one hand, we need to more actively take advantage of the differences in the conditions of work during the late 1970s and the 1990s: the emerging power of "academic" discourses which recognize the relation of power, subjectivity, and language offers us an alternative "intellectual" tradition and the legitimacy of Basic Writing as an academic field. On the other hand, we must nevertheless be vigilant toward the pressure to objectify the knowledge produced from such alternative discursive and institutional positions. Most of all, we should keep in mind that this history of Basic Writing's birth is deeply social and historical. It is provisional and strategic, serving as a point of departure for re-searching ways of contextualizing new knowledge in basic writing in the social, historical specificity of not only the students we study and teach but more important, of the teacher/researcher producing and receiving that knowledge.

4 Redefining the Legacy of Mina Shaughnessy: A Critique of the Politics of Linguistic Innocence

Min-Zhan Lu

The aim of this paper is to critique an essentialist assumption about language dominant in the teaching of basic writing. This assumption holds that the essence of meaning precedes and is independent of language, which serves merely as a vehicle to communicate that essence. According to this assumption, differences in discourse conventions have no effect on the essential meaning communicated. Using Mina Shaughnessy's *Errors and Expectations* as an example, I examine the ways in which such an assumption leads to pedagogies which promote what I call a politics of linguistic innocence: that is, a politics which preempts teachers' attention from the political dimensions of the linguistic choices students make in their writing.

My critique is motivated by my alignment with various Marxist and poststructuralist theories of language.[1] In one way or another, these theories have argued that language is best understood not as a neutral vehicle of communication but as a site of struggle among competing discourses. Each discourse puts specific constraints on the construction of one's stance—how one makes sense of oneself and gives meaning to the world. Through one's gender; family; work; religious, educational, or recreational life, each individual gains access to a range of competing discourses which offer competing views of oneself, the world, and one's relation with the world. Each time one writes, even and especially when one is attempting to use one of these discourses, one experiences the need to respond to the dissonance among the various discourses of one's daily life. Because different discourses do not enjoy equal political power in current-day America, decisions on how to respond to such dissonance are never politically innocent.

From the perspective of such a view of language, Shaughnessy's stated goal for her basic writers—the mastery of written English and the "ultimate freedom of deciding how and when and where" to use which language (11)—should involve at least three challenges for student writers. First, the students need to become familiar with the conventions or "the stock of words, routines, and rituals that make up" academic discourse (198). Second, they need to gain confidence as learners and writers. Third, they need to decide how to respond to the potential dissonance between academic discourse and their home discourses. These decisions involve changes in how they think as well as how they use language. Yet, most pedagogies informed by the kind of essentialist assumption I defined earlier, including the one Shaughnessy presents in *Errors and Expectations,* tend to focus attention on only the first two of these challenges.

I choose *Errors and Expectations* as an example of such pedagogies because, following Robert Lyons, I interpret the operative word in that book to be "tasks" rather than "achievements." As Robert Lyons cogently points out, Shaughnessy's work "resists closure; instead, it looks to the future, emphasizing what needs to be learned and done" (Lyons, "Mina Shaughnessy" 186). The legacy of Shaughnessy, I believe, is the set of tasks she maps out for composition teachers. To honor this legacy, we need to examine the pedagogical advice she gives in *Errors and Expectations* as tasks which point to the future—to what needs to be learned and done—rather than as providing closure to our pedagogical inquiry. One of the first tasks Shaughnessy sets up for composition teachers is that of "remediating" ourselves ("Diving In" 238). She urges us to become "students" of our students as well as of new disciplines. Reading *Errors and Expectations* in light of current theories of language is one way of continuing that "remediation." Shaughnessy also argues that a good composition teacher should inculcate interest in and respect for linguistic variety and help students attain discursive option, freedom, and choice. She thus maps out one more task for us: to carry out democratic aspirations in the teaching of basic writing.[2] Another task she maps out for composition teachers is the need to "sound the depths" of the students' difficulties as well as their intelligence ("Diving In" 236). If, as I will argue, some of her own pedagogical advice indicates that an essentialist view of language could impede rather than enhance one's effort to fulfill these tasks, then the only way we can fully benefit from the legacy of Shaughnessy is to take the essentialist view of language itself to task.

In *Errors and Expectations,* Shaughnessy argues that language "is variously shaped by situations and bound by conventions, none of which is inferior to the others but none of which, also, can substitute for the others" (121). Using such a view of language, she makes several arguments key to her pedagogy. For example, she uses it to argue for the "systematic nature" of her students' home discourses, the students' "quasi-foreign relationship" with academic discourse, and thus, the logic of some of their errors. She also uses this view of language to call attention to basic writers' existing mastery of at least one variety of English and thus, their "intelligence and linguistic aptitudes" (292). She is then able to increase the confidence of both teachers and students in the students' ability to master a new variety of English—academic English.

Shaughnessy's view of language indicates her willingness to "remediate" herself by studying and exploring the implications which contemporary linguistic theories have for the teaching of basic writing.[3] However, in looking to these fields for "fresh insights and new data," Shaughnessy seems to have also adopted an essentialist assumption which dominates these theories of language: the assumption that linguistic codes can be taught in isolation from attention to the production of meaning and from attention to the dynamic power struggle within and among diverse discourses.[4]

We see this assumption operating in Shaughnessy's description of a writer's "consciousness (or conviction) of what [he] means":

> It seems to exist at some subterranean level of language—but yet to need words to coax it to the surface, where it is communicable, not only to others but, in a different sense, to the writer himself. (80)

The image of someone using words to coax meaning "to the surface" suggests that meaning exists separately from and "at some subterranean level of language." Meaning is thus seen as a kind of essence which the writer carries *in* his or her mind prior to writing, although the writer might not always be fully conscious of it. Writing merely serves to make this essence communicable to oneself and others. As David Bartholomae puts it, Shaughnessy implies that "writing is in service of 'personal thoughts and styles'" ("Released" 83). Shaughnessy does recognize that writing is "a deliberate process whereby meaning is crafted, stage by stage" (Shaughnessy, *Errors* 81), even that "the act of articulation refines and changes [thought]" (*Errors* 82). But the pedagogy she advocates seldom attends to the changes which occur in that act. Instead, it presents writing primarily as getting "as close a fit as possible between what [the writer] means and what he says on paper," or as "testing the words that come to mind against the thought one has in mind" (*Errors* 79, 204). That is, "meaning is crafted" only to match what is already in the writer's mind (*Errors* 81–82).

Such a view of the relationship between words and meaning does not allow for attention to the possibility that different ways of using words—different discourses—might exercise different constraints on how one "crafts" the meaning "one has in mind." This is probably why the pedagogical advice Shaughnessy offers in *Errors and Expectations* seldom considers the possibility that the meaning one "has in mind" might undergo substantial change as one tries to "coax" it and "communicate" it in different discourses. In the following section, I use Shaughnessy's responses to three student writings to examine this tendency in her pedagogy. I argue that such a tendency might keep her pedagogy from achieving all the goals it envisions. That is, it might teach students to "write something in formal English" and "have something to say" but can help students obtain only a very limited "freedom of deciding *how* and when and where" to "use which language" (11, emphasis mine).

The following is a sentence written by one of Shaughnessy's students:

> In my opinion I believe that you there is no field that cannot be effected some sort of advancement that one maybe need a college degree to make it. (*Errors* 62)

Shaughnessy approaches the sentence "grammatically," as an example of her students' tendency to use "fillers" such as "I think that . . . " and "It is my opinion that . . . " (62). She argues that these "fillers" keep the writers from "making a strong start with a *real subject*" and make them lose their *"bearings"* (62, my emphasis). The distinction between a "real subject" and "fillers" suggests that in getting rid of the "fillers," the teacher is merely helping the writer to retrieve the real subject or bearings he has in mind. I believe Shaughnessy assumes this to be the case because she sees meaning as existing "at some subterranean level of language." Yet, in assuming that, her attention seems to have been occluded from the possibility that as the writer gets rid of the "fillers," he might also be qualifying the subject or bearing he originally has in mind.

For instance, Shaughnessy follows the student's original sentence with a consolidated sentence: "A person with a college degree has a better chance for advancement in any field" (63). Shaughnessy does not indicate whether this is the student's revised sentence or the model the teacher might pose for the student. In either case, the revised sentence articulates a much stronger confidence than the original in the belief that education entails advancement. For we might read some of the phrases in the original sentence, such as "in my opinion," "I believe that you," "some sort of," and "one maybe need," as indications not only of the writer's inability to produce a grammatically correct sentence but also of the writer's attempt to articulate his uncertainty or skepticism toward the belief that education entails advancement. In learning "consolidation," this student is also consolidating his attitude toward that belief. Furthermore, this consolidation could involve important changes in the writer's political alignment. For one can well imagine that people of different economic, racial, ethnic, or gender groups would have different feelings about the degree to which education entails one's advancement.

In a footnote to this passage, Shaughnessy acknowledges that "some would argue" that what she calls "fillers" are "indices of involvement" which convey a stance or point of view (62 n. 4). But her analysis in the main text suggests that the sentence is to be tackled "grammatically," without consideration to stance or point of view. I think the teacher should do both. The teacher should deliberately call the student's attention to the relationship between "grammar" and "stance" when teaching "consolidation." For example, the teacher might ask the student to consider if a change in meaning has occurred between the original sentence and the grammatically correct one. The advantage of such an approach is that the student would realize that decisions on what are "fillers" and what is one's "real subject" are not merely "grammatical" but also political: they could involve a change in one's social alignment. The writer would also perceive deliberation over one's stance or point of view as a normal aspect of learning to master grammatical conventions. Moreover, the writer would be given the opportunity to reach a self-conscious decision. Without practice in this type of decision making, the kind of discursive options, freedom, or choice the students could obtain through education is likely to be very limited.

Attention to this type of deliberation seems just as necessary if the teacher is to help the student who wrote the following paper achieve the style of "weav[ing] personal experience into analytical discourse" which Shaughnessy admires in "mature and gifted writers" (198):

> It can be said that my parents have led useful live but that usefulness seems to deteriorate when they fond themselves constantly being manipulated for the benefit of one and not for the benefit of the community. If they were able to realize that were being manipulate successful advancements could of been gained but being that they had no strong political awareness their energies were consumed by the politicans who saw personal advancements at the expenses of dedicated community workers. And now that my parents have taken a leave of abscence from community involvement, comes my term to participate on worthwhile community activities which well bring about positive results and to maintain a level of consciousness in the community so that they will know what policies affect them, and if they don't quite like the results of the policies I'll make sure, if its possible, to abolish the ones which hinder progress to ones which well present the correct shift in establishing correct legislation or enactments. In order to establish myself and my life to revolve around the community I must maintain a level of awareness to make sure that I can bring about positive actions and to keep an open mind to the problems of the community and to the possible

manipulation machinery which is always on the watch when progressive leaders or members of the community try to build effective
activities for the people to participate. (197)

Shaughnessy suggests that the reason this writer has not yet "mastered
the style" is because he has just "begun to advance into the complexity
of the new language" and "is almost certain to sound and feel alien with
the stock of words, routines, and rituals that make up that language"
(198). The "delicate task" of the teacher in such a situation, Shaughnessy
points out, is to "encourag[e] the enterprise and confidence of the student" while "improving his judgment about both the forms and meanings of the words he chooses" (198).

I believe that there is another dimension to the teacher's task. As
Shaughnessy points out, this writer might be "struggling to develop a
language that will enable him to talk analytically, with strangers, about
the oppression of his parents and his own resolve to work against that
oppression" (197). If what Shaughnessy says of most of her basic writers is true of this writer—that he too has "grown up in one of New York's
ethnic or racial enclaves" (3)—then the "strangers" for whom he writes
and whose analytical discourse he is struggling to use are "strangers"
both in the political and linguistic sense. To this writer, these "strangers" are people who already belong to what Shaughnessy calls the world
of "public transactions—educational, civic, and professional" (125), a
world which has traditionally excluded people like the writer and his
parents. These "strangers" enjoy power relationships with the very
"politicans" and "manipulation machinery" against whom this writer
is resolved to fight. In trying to "talk analytically," this writer is also
learning the "strangers'" way of perceiving people like his parents, such
as viewing the oppression of his parents and his resolution to work
against that oppression with the "curiosity and sentimentality of strangers" (197–98). Thus, their "style" might put different constraints than
the student's home discourse on how this writer re-views "the experiences he has in mind" (197). If all of this is so, the teacher ought to acknowledge that possibility to the students.

Let me use the writings of another of Shaughnessy's students to illustrate why attention to a potential change in point of view might benefit
students. The following are two passages written by one of
Shaughnessy's students at the beginning and the end of a semester:

Essay written at beginning of semester

Harlem taught me that light skin Black people was better look,
the best to suceed, the best off fanicially etc this whole that I trying
to say, that I was brainwashed and people aliked.

I couldn't understand why people (Black and white) couldn't get alone. So as time went along I began learned more about myself and the establishment.

Essay written at end of semester

In the midst of this decay there are children between the ages of five and ten playing with plenty of vitality. As they toss the football around, their bodies full of energy, their clothes look like rainbows. The colors mix together and one is given the impression of being in a psychadelic dream, beautiful, active, and alive with unity. They yell to eachother increasing their morale. They have the sound of an organized alto section. At the sidelines are the girls who are shy, with the shyness that belongs to the very young. They are embarrased when their dresses are raised by the wind. As their feet rise above pavement, they cheer for their boy friends. In the midst of the decay, children will continue to play. (278)

In the first passage, the writer approaches the "people" through their racial and economic differences and the subject of childhood through racial rift and contention. In the second paper, he approaches the "children" through the differences in their age, sex, and the color of their clothes. And he approaches the subject of childhood through the "unity" among children. The second passage indicates a change in how this writer makes sense of the world around him: the writer has appeased his anger and rebellion against a world which "brainwashed" children with discriminatory perceptions of blacks and whites. Compared to the earlier and more labored struggle to puzzle out "why people (Black and white) couldn't get alone [sic]," the almost lyrical celebration of the children's ability to "continue to play" "in the midst of the decay" seems a much more "literary" and evasive form of confronting the world of "decay."

Shaughnessy characterizes this writer as a student who "discovered early in the semester that writing gave him *access* to thoughts and feelings he had not *reached* any other way" (278, my emphasis). She uses these essays to illustrate "the measure of his improvement in one semester." By that, I take Shaughnessy to have in mind the changes in length and style. By the end of the semester, the student is clearly not only finding more to say on the subject but also demonstrating better control over the formal English taught in the classroom. This change in length and style certainly illustrates the effectiveness of the kind of pedagogical advice Shaughnessy gives.

Yet, these two passages also indicate that the change in the length and style of the student's writing can be accompanied by a change in thinking—in the way one perceives the world around one and relates to it. This latter change is often political as well as stylistic. I think that

Shaughnessy's responses to these student writings overlook this potential change in thinking because she believes that language will only help
the writers "reach" but not change how they think and feel about a certain subject or experience. Thus, attention to a potential change in one's
point of view or political stance seems superfluous.

If mastery of academic discourse is often accompanied by a change
in one's point of view, as my reading of these three student writings
suggests, then it ought to be the teacher's task to acknowledge to the
students this aspect of their learning. However, teachers may hesitate to
do so because they are worried that doing so might confirm the students' fear that education will distance them from their home discourses
or communities and, as a result, slow down their learning. As
Shaughnessy cogently points out, her students are already feeling over-
whelmed by their sense of the competition between home and college:

> Neglected by the dominant society, [basic writers] have nonethe-
> less had their own worlds to grow up in and they arrive on our
> campuses as young adults, with opinions and languages and plans
> already in their minds. College both beckons and threatens them,
> offering to teach them useful ways of thinking and talking about
> the world, promising even to improve the quality of their lives, but
> threatening at the same time to take from them their distinctive ways
> of interpreting the world, to assimilate them into the culture of
> academia without acknowledging their experience as outsiders. (292)

Again and again, Shaughnessy reminds us of her students' fear that college may distance them from "their own worlds" and take away from
them the point of view they have developed through "their experience
as outsiders." She argues that this fear causes her students to mistrust
and psychologically resist learning to write (125). Accordingly, she suggests several methods which she believes will help students assuage
that fear.

For example, when discussing her students' difficulty in developing
an "academic vocabulary," Shaughnessy points out that they might resist a new meaning for a familiar word because accepting it would be
like consenting to a "linguistic betrayal that threatens to wipe out not
just a word but the reality that the word refers to" (212). She then goes
on to suggest that "if we consider the formal (rather than the contextual) ways in which words can be made to shift meaning we are closer
to the kind of practical information about words BW students need"
(212). This seems to be her rationale: if a "formal" approach (in this case,
teaching students to pay attention to prefixes and suffixes) can help students learn that words can be made to shift meaning, then why not avoid
the "contextual" approach, especially since the "contextual" approach

will only activate their sense of being pressured to "wipe out not just a word but the reality that the word refers to"?

But taking this "formal" approach only circumvents the students' attention to the potential change in their thinking and their relationship with home and school. It delays but cannot eliminate their need to deal with that possibility. As a result, students are likely to realize the change only after it has already become a fact. At the same time, because the classroom has suggested that learning academic discourse will not affect how they think, feel, or relate to home, students are also likely to perceive their "betrayal" of home in purely personal terms, the result of purely personal choices. The sense of guilt and confusion resulting from such a perception is best illustrated in Richard Rodriguez's narrative of his own educational experience, *Hunger of Memory*. Rodriguez's narrative also suggests that the best way for students to cope constructively with their sense of having consented to a "betrayal" is to perceive it in relation to the politics of education and language. The long, lonely, and painful deliberation it takes for Rodriguez to contextualize that "betrayal" suggests that teachers might better help students anticipate and cope with their sense of "betrayal" if they take the "contextual" as well as the "formal" approach when teaching the conventions of academic discourse. In fact, doing both might even help students to minimize that "betrayal." When students are encouraged to pay attention to the ways in which diverse discourses constrain one's alignments with different points of view and social groups, they have a better chance to deliberate over how they might resist various pressures academic discourse exercises on their existing points of view. As Shaughnessy points out, "English has been robustly inventing itself for centuries—stretching and reshaping and enriching itself with every language and dialect it has encountered" (13). If the teacher acknowledges that all practitioners of academic discourse, including those who are learning to master it as well as those who have already mastered it, can participate in this process of reshaping, then students might be less passive in coping with the constraints academic discourse puts on their alignments with their home discourses.

In preempting Shaughnessy's attention from the political decisions involved in her students' formal or linguistic decisions, the essentialist view of language also seems to have kept her from noticing her own privileging of academic discourse. Shaughnessy calls formal written English "the language of public transactions—educational, civic, and professional"—and the students' home discourse the language one uses with one's family and friends (125). Shaughnessy insists that no variety of English can "substitute for the others" (121). She reassures her students that their home discourses cannot be substituted by academic discourse, but neither can their home discourses substitute for academic discourse. Thus, she suggests that academic discourse is a "necessary" and "advantageous" language for *all* language users because it *is* the language of public transaction (125, 293). This insistence on the nonsubstitutive nature of language implies that academic discourse has been, is, and will inevitably be the language of public transaction. And it may very well lead students to see the function of formal English as a timeless linguistic law which they must respect, adapt to, and perpetuate rather than as a specific historical circumstance resulting from the historically unequal distribution of social power and as a condition which they must recognize but can also call into question and change.

Further, she differentiates the function of academic discourse from that of the students' home discourses through the way she characterizes the degree to which each discourse mobilizes one's language learning faculty. She presents the students' efforts to seek patterns and to discriminate or apply rules as "*self-sustaining* activities" (127, emphasis mine). She argues that the search for causes, like the ability to compare, is "a constant and deep *urge* among people of *all* cultures and ages" and "part of an *unfolding intellective power* that begins with infancy and continues, at least in the lives of some, until death" (263, emphasis mine). Academic discourse and the students' home discourses, Shaughnessy suggests, unfold their "intellective power" differently. The home discourses of basic writers are seen as allowing such power to remain "largely intuitive," "simplistic" and "unreasoned" (263), while the conventions of written English are seen as demanding that such power be "more thoroughly developed," "more consciously organized" (261). Thus, academic discourse is endowed with the power to bring the "native intelligence" or the "constant and deep urge" in *all* language learners to a higher and more self-conscious level.

This type of depiction suggests that learning academic discourse is not a violation but a cultivation of what Basic Writers or "people of all cultures and ages" have in and of themselves. Shaughnessy thus suggests basic writers are being asked to learn academic discourse because of its distinctive ability to utilize a "human" resource. Hence, her pedagogy provides the need to learn academic discourse with a "human," and hence with yet another seemingly politically innocent, justification. It teaches students to see discursive decisions made from the point of view of academic culture as "human" and therefore "innocent" decisions made absolutely free from the pressures of specific social and historical circumstances. If it is the student's concern to align himself with minority economic and ethnic groups in the very act of learning academic discourse, the politics of "linguistic" innocence can only pacify rather than activate such a concern.

Shaughnessy's desire to propose a pedagogy which will inculcate respect for discursive diversity and freedom of discursive choice articulates her dissatisfaction with and reaction to the unequal social power and prestige of diverse discourses in current-day America. It also demonstrates her belief that education can and should attempt to change these prevailing unequal conditions. However, the essentialist view of language which underlies her pedagogy seems also to have led her to believe that a vision of language which insists on the equality and nonsubstitutive nature of linguistic variety, and an ideal writing classroom which promotes such a view, can stand in pure opposition to society, adjusting existing social inequality and the human costs of such inequality from somewhere "outside" the sociohistorical space which it is trying to transform. As a result, her pedagogy enacts a systematic denial of the political context of students' linguistic decisions.

The need to critique the essentialist view of language and the politics of linguistic innocence it promotes is urgent when viewed in the context of the popular success of E. D. Hirsch Jr.'s proposals for educational "reforms." Hirsch argues for the "validity" of his "vocabulary" by claiming its political neutrality. Hirsch argues that "it is used to support *all* conflicting values that arise in public discourse" and "to communicate *any* point of view effectively" or "in *whatever* direction one wishes to be effective" (*Cultural Literacy* 23, 102, 103; my emphasis). Hirsch thus implies that the "vocabulary" one uses is separate from one's "values," "point of view," or "direction." Like Shaughnessy, he assumes an essence in the individual—a body of values, points of view, a sense of direction—which exists prior to the act of "communication" and outside of the "means of communication" (*Cultural Literacy* 23).

Like Shaughnessy, Hirsch also argues for the need for *everyone* to learn the "literate" language by presenting it as existing "beyond the narrow spheres of family, neighborhood, and region" (*Cultural Literacy* 21). Furthermore, he assumes that there can be only one cause of one's failure to gain "literacy": one's unfamiliarity with "the background information and the linguistic conventions that are needed to read, write, speak effectively" in America (*Cultural Literacy* 22, "Primal Scene" 31). Thus, Hirsch also denies the students' need to deal with cultural differences and to negotiate the competing claims of multiple ways of using language when writing. He thereby both simplifies and depoliticizes the challenges facing the student writer.

Hirsch self-consciously invokes a continuity between Shaughnessy's pedagogy and his "educational reforms" ("Culture and Literacy" 27;

Cultural Literacy 10). He legitimizes his New Right rhetoric by reminding us that Shaughnessy had approved of his work. For those of us concerned with examining writing in relation to the politics of gender, race,
nationality, and class, the best way to forestall Hirsch's use of
Shaughnessy is to point out that the continuity resides only in the essentialist view of language underlying both pedagogies and the politics of
linguistic innocence it promotes. Critiquing the essentialist view of language and the politics of linguistic innocence in Shaughnessy's work
contributes to existing criticism of Hirsch's New Right rhetoric (see
Armstrong; Bizzell, "Arguing"; Moglen; Scholes; Sledd and Sledd). It
makes clear that if, as Hirsch self-consciously maintains, there is a continuity between Shaughnessy's work and Hirsch's ("Culture and Literacy"
27; *Cultural Literacy* 10), the continuity resides only in the most limiting
aspect of Shaughnessy's pedagogy. Recognition of some of the limitations of Shaughnessy's pedagogy can also be politically constructive for
the field of composition by helping us appreciate Shaughnessy's legacy.
Most of the lessons she taught us in *Errors and Expectations*, such as students' "quasi-foreign relationship" with academic discourse, their lack
of confidence as learners and writers, their desire to participate in academic work, and their intelligence and language-learning aptitudes,
continue to be central to the teaching of basic writing. The tasks she
delineates for us remain urgent for those of us concerned with the politics of the teaching of writing. Recognizing the negative effects that an
essentialist view of language has on Shaughnessy's own efforts to ex-
ecute these tasks can only help us identify issues that need to be addressed if we are to carry on her legacy: a fuller recognition of the social
dimensions of students' linguistic decisions.

5 Mapping Errors and Expectations for Basic Writing: From the "Frontier Field" to "Border Country"

Bruce Horner

Through *Errors and Expectations* and the founding, in 1975, of the *Journal of Basic Writing,* Mina Shaughnessy is largely credited with establishing both the field and the term "basic writing" (Gray, Troyka). Yet Shaughnessy ends *Errors and Expectations* by warning that the errors and expectations to which she refers are *teacher* errors and expectations, closing her study with the hope that "our enterprising new students will somehow weather *our* deficiencies and transcend our yet cautious expectations of what they can accomplish in college" (294). Describing the field of basic writing as a "frontier, unmapped, except for a scattering of impressionistic articles and a few blazed trails," she likens *Errors and Expectations* to a "frontier map" "certain to have the shortcomings of other frontier maps, with doubtless a few rivers in the wrong place and some trails that end nowhere" (4).

Much of the subsequent discourse in the field of basic writing can be located on the "maps" provided by Shaughnessy and some of her colleagues at CUNY. These maps identify basic writers in terms drawn from theories of cognitive development and from theories of discourse and second language acquisition. But such maps tend to place BW students at particular stages of cognitive development or language acquisition in ways that, unfortunately, continue what Susan Miller has observed as composition's tendency to treat students as "emerging, or as failed, but never as actually responsible 'authors,' . . . as only tentative participants in consequential learning about writing" (196). In such models, as David Bartholomae has recently complained, basic writing risks becoming "a reiteration of the liberal project of the late 60s early 70s, where in the name of sympathy and empowerment, we have once again produced the 'other' who is the incomplete version of ourselves, confirming existing patterns of power and authority, reproducing the hierarchies we had meant to question and overthrow" ("Tidy House" 18).

The growing field of basic writing in this way recapitulates the history of writing instruction given students of all ages, who have been

similarly identified as always "emerging" and/or "other" by their placement at a particular stage of cognitive development and literacy acquisition. However, recent work by teachers and researchers of the writing
of "established" writers, college students, high school students, and even
children offers an alternative model for locating students and their writing. For example, Harste et al., working with young children, call into
question the validity of notions of "developmental stages," "readiness"
and "emergent reading" for understanding how children learn to read
and write, finding that "one must approach all children as if they know
quite a bit about reading and writing" in order to "build upon the knowledge they have already acquired about literacy" (44). Boomer et al., arguing for educational programs that involve both teachers and students
in negotiating curricula, ask that we recognize children (K–12) "as decision makers, intenders, owners of their own ideas, willing partners with
their teachers in the active pursuit of their own learning" (15).

Such work, loosely categorized as the study of "border" writing and
"border" pedagogy for its attention to the negotiation of power and identities in writing and teaching, offers a way to resolve the conceptual and
ethical dilemmas on the horns of which basic writing teachers have found
themselves caught. For such work suggests a redefinition of the situation faced by basic writers as the situation of any writer. "Literacy," Harste
et al. argue, "is [for us as for the young] neither a monolithic skill nor a
now-you-have-it/now-you-don't' affair" (69). By adopting this view, we
can see the phenomenon of "basic writing" as a representative instance
of the history, theory, and practice of literacy instruction generally.

In this essay, I first trace the surfacing of the dilemmas posed by earlier conceptions of basic writing and then examine how "border"
conceptualizations of basic writing respond to those dilemmas. To illustrate the differences between earlier and more recent conceptualizations,
I discuss theoretical and pedagogical approaches to written "error" cor-
responding to each. I argue that redefining the "territory of basic writing" as "border" territory and writing as negotiation, while introducing
new difficulties for teachers and students, effectively resolves the dilemmas posed by earlier conceptions of basic writing by identifying both
students and teachers as active participants in negotiations of power
and thus improving the expectations of both for the work they face in
confronting one another.

Shaughnessy has urged two sets of terms to account for the writing
difficulties of her students. In an oft-quoted passage from the Introduction to *Errors and Expectations*, Shaughnessy states that "BW students
write the way they do, not because they are slow or non-verbal, indifferent to or incapable of academic excellence, but because they are *begin-*

ners and must, like all beginners, learn by making mistakes" (5, my emphasis). Consistent with her use of geographic metaphors to describe basic writing as a "frontier," however, she also describes BW students as foreigners, "true outsiders," "students whose difficulties with the written language seemed of a different order from those of the other groups [of students admitted to CUNY], as if they had come, you might say, from a different country," "strangers in academia" (2, 3). In such a view, the task confronting basic writers is to "move across the territory of language" (10) presumably through the uncharted territory of basic writing and in the direction of the land and language of the academy.

In the last half dozen years, compositionists have identified significant problems with conceiving of BW students, and those deemed illiterate generally, as either "beginners" or "true outsiders." Nonetheless, it is important to recognize the real advantages accruing from such conceptions. Most important, they allow us to see both the intelligence and educability of BW students (Lyons, "Mina Shaugnessy"). Viewing the writing of BW students as akin to either beginners or foreigners encourages, first, an acknowledgment of the students' educability or "linguistic aptitude"; second, a far more tolerant attitude toward students' errors (though not a dismissal of the importance of errors); and third, a model for discovering patterns in those errors, or the "logic" of the students' errors, and for addressing them (Lyons, "Mina Shaughnessy and the Teaching of Writing"). Just as foreign speakers and beginners make characteristic mistakes and go through characteristic stages in the process of learning an unfamiliar language, so BW students can be understood to make characteristic errors and to go through characteristic stages in the process of improving their writing. In short, both conceptions of BW students present the students and their writing as not fixed but *in process*. As Shaughnessy, describing "the view a teacher is more likely to have toward a foreign student learning English," explains,

> [The student's] errors reflect upon his linguistic situation, not upon his educability; he is granted by his teacher the capability of mastering English but is expected in the course of doing so to make errors in English; and certain errors, characteristic errors for natives of his language who are acquiring English as a second language, are tolerated far into and even beyond the period of formal instruction simply because they must be rubbed off by time. (*Errors* 121)

Much of the research on basic writers since 1975 represents attempts to understand them in at least one of these ways. Those viewing basic writers chiefly as beginners have looked especially to theories of cognitive development to explain such students' difficulties (Berg and Coleman; Elifson and Stone; Goldberg; Hays, "Development"; Kroll;

Lunsford, "Cognitive"; Tremblay). Basic writers, such research suggests, are somehow stuck at a lower level of cognitive development, unable to engage at a "formal-operational" level of thought (Berg and Coleman; Lunsford, "Cognitive"), or occupy a lower position on William Perry's scheme of intellectual and ethical development (Hays, "Socio-cognitive Development"; see Bizzell, "William Perry"; Slattery). Those viewing basic writers primarily as "foreign" or "outsiders" have looked especially to ethnographic studies, second-language acquisition, and discourse theory (Bartholomae, "Inventing"; Bizzell, "What Happens"; Kogen; Martinez and Martinez, "Who Is Alien"; Trimbur, "Beyond Cognition"). The problems of basic writers, these scholars have argued (often in response to studies drawing on theories of cognitive development), are signs not of cognitive immaturity; rather, they signal a difference in "world view" (Bizzell, "What Happens"), "values" (Martinez and Martinez, "Who Is Alien") or a lack of familiarity with certain discourse conventions. As Bartholomae has put it,

> Basic writers are beginning writers, to be sure, but they are not writers who need to learn to use language. They are writers who need to learn to command a particular variety of language—the language of a written, academic discourse—and a particular variety of language use—writing itself. . . . [Basic writing] is not evidence of arrested cognitive development. ("Study of Error" 254)

Joseph Harris has observed that in keeping with these two ways of viewing basic writers there have developed two different sets of metaphors for thinking about changes in the students' writing and the role of basic writing teachers: metaphors of "growth" and of "initiation." If we think of BW students as cognitively immature beginners, then "improvements" in their writing are signs of cognitive *growth,* with BW teachers *fostering* such growth. If we think of BW students as *foreigners,* then changes in their writing represent changes in their social or cultural identities *initiated* at least in part by writing courses ("Three Metaphors").

But both of these metaphors have been found to be problematic. Imagining students as cognitively immature denies the obvious facts of their status as adults (cf. Shaughnessy, *Errors*). Further, as Mike Rose has argued, identifying BW students in this way has functioned largely to exclude them and BW programs from the university ("Language"). Fostering cognitive maturity sounds like an unimpeachable, even commendable vocation, but not one appropriate for college. Finally, such a view, as Rose and others have argued, ignores the rich complexity and particularity of both cognition and writing (Rose, "Narrowing"; Berthoff; Bizzell, "Cognition," "William Perry"; Haswell; Kogen; Martinez and Martinez, "Reconsidering").

On the other hand, if learning to write is not a matter of becoming cognitively mature but of changing one's social and cultural identity, initiating such change seems liable to charges of cultural imperialism, converting the "natives" to *our* native ways by teaching them the rituals and gestures of academic discourse. Such conversions are difficult to justify ethically. Justifications that have been offered, such as Thomas Farrell's argument that "literacy," including the acquisition of the forms of Standard English, enables critical consciousness or a mode of thought necessary to Western culture, tend to fall back on "foundationalist" conceptions of literacy which the "social" view rejects (Bizzell, "Foundationalism"). In such foundationalist conceptions, literacy either as a medium or a practice is reified and idealized into the equivalent of what, in the nineteenth century, the West came to know as "art." Cultural critic Raymond Williams has described this nineteenth-century development as one in which "two processes—the idealization of art and the reification of the medium—were connected. . . . Art was idealized to distinguish it from 'mechanical' work" (*Marxism* 160). In this process, Williams explains,

> The properties of 'the medium' were abstracted as if they defined the practice, rather than being its means. This interpretation then suppressed the full sense of practice, which has always to be defined as work on a material for a specific purpose within certain necessary social conditions. (*Marxism* 159–60)

Claims that literacy yields significant cognitive rewards apply to "literacy" a similar abstraction of the written medium and thus suppress the full sense of literacy as a practice.

But those rejecting justifications based on such reifications of writing still face an ethical dilemma. Bizzell, perhaps foremost among compositionists confronting this dilemma, explains,

> an anti-foundationalist understanding of discourse would see the student's way of thinking and interacting with the world, the student's very self, as fundamentally altered by participation in any new discourse. These will not be changes the student can erase at will. Also, the ability to participate in a new discourse will change the student's relationship with other discourses—particularly in the case of academic discourse. Because academic discourse is identified with social power, to show familiarity with it can mean being completely alienated from some other, socially disenfranchised discourses. Thus the student's new ability to participate in academic discourse will condition his or her opportunities to participate in other discourses, and make some life paths more attractive than others. ("Foundationalism" 43–44)

However, teachers rejecting a reified, "foundationalist" view of literacy simultaneously deny themselves any foundation, or authority, for advocating or initiating such changes. As Bizzell puts it in a later essay, "We [teachers] exercise authority over [students] in asking them to give up their foundational beliefs, but we give them nothing to put in the place of these foundational beliefs because we deny the validity of all authority, including, presumably, our own" ("Beyond" 670).

As noted above, there are serious problems associated with viewing basic writers as "beginners"; such a view belies the evident maturity of BW students and the very complexity of their writing. But if it doesn't make sense to think of these students as beginners, it is becoming increasingly clear that it makes equally little sense to think of many of them as "foreign." And just as "cognitivist" approaches to understanding basic writing risk being exclusionary, so there are exclusionary implications in identifying native basic writers as "foreign." Writers adopting such identifications have sidestepped those implications by treating the contradiction of describing native students as "foreign" not as oxymoronic (i.e., "pointedly foolish" [*OED*]), but as a paradox ("a statement or tenet contrary to received opinion or belief, often with the implication that it is marvelous or incredible" [*OED*]), a marvel to be wondered at but not challenged or questioned. We can see this treatment obtaining when Shaughnessy states that basic writers seem to have "come from a different country" or states of them, "Natives, for the most part, of New York, graduates of the same public school system as the other students, they were nonetheless strangers in academia" (*Errors* 2–3).

Such a treatment of the situation of basic writers as *paradoxical* recurs in the more general debate on America's "literacy crisis"—at least, paradoxically, in the language of conservatives. Former Secretary of Education William Bennett warns that if students are not given access to the Western high cultural tradition, "they will become aliens in their own culture, strangers in their own land" (29–30). E. D. Hirsch Jr. laments that currently, though

> [young people] share a tremendous amount of knowledge among themselves, much of it learned in school, . . . from the standpoint of their literacy and their ability to communicate with others in our culture, what they know is ephemeral and narrowly confined to their own generation. Many young people strikingly lack the information that writers of American books and newspapers have traditionally taken for granted among their readers from all generations. (*Cultural Literacy* 7)

These authors, in eerie echoes of Shaughnessy and Bizzell, thus warn of the prospect of a curious phenomenon: natives who nonetheless belong to another country, members of a culture and a community who are yet nonmembers, knowledgeable youth incapable of communication, "aliens in their own culture, strangers in their own land." Such descriptions give a peculiar cast to Shaughnessy's likening of the "territory of basic writing" to a "frontier." Robert Lyons argues that Shaughnessy "uses this image . . . with great precision," explaining:

> The frontier is the place where everyone is a stranger, and where nobody is fully at home or settled in. In this new territory, everyone has to get his bearings, students and teachers alike, and everyone has to make adjustments in his habitual modes of thinking and acting. The frontier calls on everybody's resourcefulness and ingenuity in adapting his particular kind of knowledge to new situations. It also calls for a special openness and trust—in a difficult and sparsely populated land, people must cooperate for survival. And the frontier is finally a place where the future is necessarily more important than the past. ("Mina Shaughnessy and the Teaching of Writing" 11)

But this vision of basic writing as frontier ignores the prior, ongoing inhabitance of the "frontier" territory by a variety of "others," inhabitants from whose perspective the territory is not "frontier" but "home." Of course, the descriptions of basic writers cited above positing clear distinctions between those who belong and those who don't, the skilled and the unskilled, do recognize the presence of "others." Both visions, however, displace those "others" in a rehearsal of the American "frontier" experience and common representations of that experience. As Pierre Bourdieu observes of frontiers generally, "The frontier . . . produces cultural difference as much as it is produced by it" (*Language* 222). In the history of the American "frontier," not everyone was a stranger, but the strangers, with considerable firepower, on encountering native inhabitants of the territory, decided the natives were the strangers, "true outsiders," "outlandish," or "foreign." These they tried to convert when they weren't trying to eliminate them from the territory altogether. Subsequent mapping of the territory involved not only the delineation of rivers and paths but also the identification of what territory belonged to whom, with only tiny pockets of land allotted or "reserved for" the original inhabitants, if indeed their presence and need for any territory was acknowledged at all.

I recall the American frontier experience not in order to equate the teaching of basic writing with cultural genocide but to demonstrate that viewing students as "foreign" has led us to think about teaching in terms of conversion or deracination. The dilemma is both ethical and conceptual, arising from problematic identifications of both students and teachers which must be abandoned if the dilemma is to be resolved. It is foolish, finally, to identify native students as strangers and for those of us

teaching basic writing to identify ourselves as "natives"—whether of
the academic discourse community, the land of Standard English, or even
the Land of Literacy, and it is dangerous to deny the operation of power
(while enacting it) through denying the specificities of history and circumstance. As descriptors of language practice, such identifications are
counterproductive, for they encourage a reified sense of students and
teachers and their languages and "discourse communities" while mask-
ing power relations among those groups (Harris, "The Idea"; Horner,
"Rethinking" 185–88; Pratt, "Linguistic"). Just as conservatives like
Bennett and Hirsch can be attacked for positing and attempting to impose a particular, narrow, reified view of American culture as representative of all American culture, so theoretical discussions sometimes
present particularized, narrow, but most important, reified views of the
discourse of academic writing as representative of the literacy to be given
to students viewed as "other" by teachers imagined as "having" "literacy." The actual frontier of basic writing, and in particular the actual
writing of BW students, calls this view into question. As Bartholomae
has more recently observed,

> [Basic writers] are not the only ones who make mistakes and who
> present their work in ways that are inappropriate for a university.
> Mainstream freshmen, senior English majors, graduate students, our
> colleagues may all produce work that is naive, wrong, or off the
> track. The issue, then, is not who misses the mark but whose misses
> matter and why. To say this is to return attention to institutional
> processes of selection and exclusion. . . . The work of basic writers
> calls into question our assumptions about orderly presentation, stan-
> dards of copy editing, and the stability of conventional habits of
> thinking. This is not to say that order, correctness, and convention
> should not be goals of a literate education. It is to say, however, that
> the borderlines between our work and theirs are not as clear as we
> like to assume. ("Writing" 68–69)

Basic writing threatens our sense of our identity (as represented in our
written work), our possession of particular linguistic territory (and I am
uncomfortable invoking the first person plural here). This sense of threat
is all too similar to that sense of threat implicit in conservative appeals
to preserve a reified cultural legacy posited as *the* American culture, *the*
tradition. Conservative rhetoric implicitly responds to the threatening
sense that the culture they have posited is a pure construct in conflict
with other possible constructions of that culture. The pronouns, as usual,
are telling. For example, Hirsch argues that it is only through "shared
information" that "*we* learn to communicate effectively with one another
in *our* national community" (*Cultural Literacy* xvii; my emphases). But
he complains early in his book that *he* can no longer communicate via

allusions to Shakespeare, as his father once did, because he can no longer assume that others would recognize or understand such allusions (9–10). He admits that youth share other knowledge among themselves which he, evidently, does not know but presumably could learn. The problem for Hirsch, it seems, is thus not simply that he cannot communicate with them, but that their knowledge threatens to displace the legitimacy, even the communicative power, of his own. "They" have a shared community, and it is not "ours."

Correspondingly, the written language of basic writers threatens, or seems to threaten, to displace the language that teachers would have them use. "Their" conventions for writing are not "ours." Thus those of us teaching basic writing are caught between the horns of an ethical dilemma: if we "convert" students to "our" conventions, we are liable to charges of cultural genocide; on the other hand, ignoring differences between their conventions and those of Edited American English amounts to abandonment (cf. Philip 18–19; Delpit 291–97).

One resolution to this dilemma is represented in recent revaluations of "borderlands," "margins," and "negotiation" as terms to describe the writing, and responding to the writing, of young children (Harste et al. 27–79), high school students (Robinson and Stock), the full range of K–12 students (Boomer et al., Delpit), and professional writers (Hicks; hooks, "marginality"), as well as beginning college students (Bartholomae, "Writing," "The Tidy House"; Harris, "The Idea," "Three Metaphors"; Hill; Horner, "Rethinking"; McQuade; Rose, *Lives*; Sommers; cf. Giroux, *Border Crossings* 28–36). This resolution might be thought of as recuperating Lyons's utopian account of the "frontier" of basic writing cited above. What renders the "frontier" image utopian is the absence of any sense of power relations among the participants, the absence of any sense of their individual or collective histories, and its assumption of shared ideals for the future. All are equal and equally strangers (the territory belongs to no one as of yet), all must make adjustments, everyone must contribute, trust is essential, everyone looks to the future rather than brooding on the past. These render the account vulnerable to ridicule, whether as a representation of basic writing or indeed the teaching of any writing at any level, or as an account of the American frontier experience. Redefining that "frontier" as "borderland" and the cooperative efforts of "frontier settlers" as negotiations between border residents injects a healthy sense of power relations into the picture and refutes both the idea of the writer as autonomous individual and the notion of writers operating from a location indisputably at the center of organically unified discursive communities with shared goals, suggesting instead a conception of writing as the ongoing re-negotiation of positions in response to inevitable histories of conflict and contradiction, and a conception of the field of teaching writing as essentially a site of contestation.

Injecting such a sense of power relations into Lyons's depiction and questioning the particular future to be worked toward need not entirely eliminate it as an ideal. What is attractive in Lyons's depiction is its sense of give-and-take and of unpredictable change—"everyone has to get his bearings, students and teachers alike, and everyone has to make adjustments." In this phrase Lyons imagines a process of negotiation among the parties as to what will be offered and what will be accepted, the changes that each is willing to make and those which are rejected, a welcome lack of determination about the direction to which those changes will lead, and a sense that no one—neither students nor teachers—is comfortably "at home" or "native." By imagining the process in terms akin to negotiation, Lyons comes close to resolving the dilemma of requiring conversion or abandonment. For negotiation acknowledges conflict and power as integral components of the dynamics of change while positioning all parties as agents—allowing in education for what Boomer et al. describe as "ownership" of learning (15–16). In negotiation, the parties involved are interdependent on one another and on the outcome of the negotiation. In negotiating, both parties engage in a dynamic exchange of power in which both are changed in ways neither can predict beforehand (Gulliver xvii, 81). Through a process of exploration, revision, and learning, both parties reposition themselves in relation to each other and to their prior understandings of themselves and the issues negotiated (cf. Boomer 8).

Nor need the operation of power among parties of unequal status somehow falsify negotiations or predetermine their outcomes, as is sometimes imagined. As social theorist Anthony Giddens reminds us, "Power relations . . . are always two-way, even if the power of one actor or party in a social relation is minimal compared to another. Power relations are relations of autonomy and dependence, but even the most autonomous agent is in some degree dependent, and the most dependent actor or party in a relationship retains some autonomy" (93). That teachers in some ways wield more power than students thus does not mean that students lack power or autonomy (rendering them automatons). As the inability of teachers to predict the outcomes of their encounters with students illustrates, those encounters are engagements in negotiation, negotiations in which power operates in both directions in ways that can change both students and teachers.

Viewing basic writing as border country and the teaching of basic writing as negotiation is thus attractive for several reasons. First, unlike the cognitivist view, it acknowledges the position of students as agents in relations of power. Rather than being seen as so many hungry, naturally deplorable vacuums—beginners bringing with them little but the potential to learn—students are recognized as capable of and interested in exploring options and exercising choices in their work and requiring respect for their maturity and responsibility as adults. Second, this view makes explicit the historically and politically marginal, "border" status of basic writing courses, students, and teachers in relation to activities deemed more "central" while adopting a perspective that inverts that status, in effect redefining "border" as "leading edge." By adopting such a perspective on "marginality," as Jay Robinson and Patricia Stock explain, "the spatial location margin may be recognized for what it is—a generative site for making meaning, a generative site for building knowledge with the potential to benefit all of us wherever we reside" (273). Third, establishing the territory of basic writing as border country acknowledges more fully the fluidity of identities which basic writing students, teachers, and courses may occupy at any given moment. Henry Giroux describes "border pedagogy" as enabling students "to rewrite their own histories, identities, and learning possibilities" and as positioning teachers "as intellectuals whose own narratives must be situated and examined as discourses that are open, partial and subject to ongoing debate and revision" (*Border Crossings* 30, 35). Redefining basic writing as border country establishes both teachers and students as strangers to one another who nonetheless agree to meet to engage in what Ira Shor has described as "mutual re-creations" (*Critical Teaching* xxvii) in which students and teachers continually contest one another's positions and authority in ever-shifting relations of power. This view thus eliminates the ethical dilemma teachers have posed for themselves of whether or not to "convert" students by acknowledging students' own responsibility and choice in seeking change and the indeterminate nature of the changes to which any basic writing course might lead either students or teachers.

Finally, such a conception of basic writing corresponds closely to recent accounts of writing which stress the operation of conflict and power in the production of writing. Indeed, some writers have attested that it is only under such "border" conditions, fraught with conflict, that writing is possible. Gloria Anzaldúa, writing of both geopolitical and psychic borders, describes borders as

> set up to define the places that are safe and unsafe, to distinguish us from them. A border is a dividing line, a narrow strip along a steep edge. A borderland is a vague and undetermined place created by the emotional residue of an unnatural boundary. It is in a constant state of transition. The prohibited and forbidden are its inhabitants. (3)

Yet she argues that it is these very conditions that make her writing possible. As she explains,

> Writing produces anxiety. Looking inside myself and my experience, looking at my conflicts, engenders anxiety in me. Being a writer feels very much like being a Chicana, or being queer. . . .
>   Living in a state of psychic unrest, in a Borderland, is what makes poets write and artists create. (72, 73)

bell hooks, acknowledging that marginality is commonly identified as a "site of deprivation," argues from her own experience as a writer that it also be recognized as a "site one stays in, clings to even, because it nourishes one's capacity to resist. It offers the possibility of radical perspectives from which to see and create, to imagine alternatives, new worlds" ("marginality" 342, 341). Min-Zhan Lu, drawing on her own experience of conflict between the discourses of Mao Tse-tung's Marxism and Western humanism in her education in the People's Republic of China, recommends treating the writing classroom as a borderland in which students learn to negotiate and draw on such conflicts in their writing. Neither her parents nor her school teachers recognized the value of such experiences of conflict. Instead, home and school each insisted on maintaining its borders: "each contrived a purified space where only one discourse was spoken and heard. . . . [and] jealously silenced any voice that threatened to break the unison of the scene" ("From Silence" 445). As a result, she explains, "I was unable to acknowledge, grasp, or grapple with what I was experiencing, for both my parents and my teachers had suggested that, if I were a good student, such interference [between discourses] would and should not take place" (443). Nonetheless, she claims that "in spite of the frustration and confusion I experienced growing up caught between two conflicting worlds, the conflict ultimately helped me to grow as a reader and writer. Constantly having to switch back and forth between the discourse of home and that of school made me sensitive and self-conscious about the struggle I experienced every time I tried to read, write, or think in either discourse" (437–38). Consequently, Lu argues that rather than maintaining borders between discourses, we need to encourage students to explore ways of negotiating the conflicting discourses of home and school in their writing (447). Marlene Nourbese Philip similarly argues for Caribbean writers that they write in the contested space between the language varieties of demotic and Standard English. For Philip, "The excitement . . . as a writer comes in the confrontation between the formal and the demotic within the text itself" (18). "To say that the experience [of the Caribbean] can only be expressed in standard English (if there is any such thing) or only in the Caribbean demotic . . . is, in fact, to limit the experience. . . . It is in the continuum of expression from standard to Caribbean English that the veracity of the experience lies" (18). "It is not sufficient," she argues, "to write only in dialect, for too often that remains a parallel and closed experience, although a part of the same language. Neither is it sufficient to write only in what we have come to call standard English. The language as we know it has to be dislocated and acted upon—even destroyed—so that it begins to serve our purposes" (18–19).

The images these writers present of the scene and dynamics of writing correspond closely to the actual situation and experience of class meetings for basic writing courses, meetings in which strangers—both teachers and students—however warily, approach one another, learn and change from their encounters with one another, and learn and change the language in working with it. To demonstrate both the value of such images for teachers of basic writing and some of the problems which they present, I want to look at the implications which viewing the "territory" of basic writing as a borderland and the teaching of writing as negotiation has for the most high-profile issue in the teaching of basic writing, error (cf. Horner, "Rethinking"; Hull, "Research"). Those writing on error have taken approaches aligned with the different views of basic writers described above. Those influenced by theories of cognitive development have used basic writers' apparent inability to "see" their errors or correct them as further evidence of students' cognitive immaturity. In response, such teachers have devised exercises to develop cognitive and perceptual skills in students (Goldberg, Gorrell). Patricia Laurence, arguing from Piaget that "perception interferes with cognition and cognition interferes in perception," has argued that BW students' inability to recognize and correct their errors indicates that their "perception remains in the preliminary *centered* stage" ("Error's" 30, 32). In this stage, "A student sees a word or object in one way, his way, and visual and cognitive exploration is unfocused and unsystematic. This student may perceive letters and parts of words, but recognition will not itself result in meaningful interpretation. . . . perceptions are not analytic" (31). To encourage "*de-centration,* the ability to see words in new ways," she has recommended exercises in which students circle different examples of different grammatical constructions (35–37).

Other researchers, rejecting the notion that students suffer from cognitive immaturity, argue instead that basic writers' errors are comparable to the errors of anyone learning a second language. Researchers have used the technique of error analysis, borrowed from the field of second-language acquisition, to argue that BW students' errors are indications of their attempt to approximate written discourse (Bartholomae, "Study"; Kroll and Schafer; Schwalm; Shaughnessy, *Errors*; Tricomi). The advantage of this approach, Barry Kroll and John Schafer explain, is that "instead of viewing errors as pathologies to be eradicated or diseases to be healed, the error-analyst views errors as necessary stages in all language-learning, as the product of intelligent cognitive strategies and therefore as potentially useful indicators of what processes the student is using" (209). And other scholars have convincingly argued that we see the problems of basic writers in terms of different interpretive communities. Elaine Lees, for example, has argued that "errors" are socially constructed by the interpretive community of proofreaders ("Proofreading"). In this view, the problem for BW students is one of not yet belonging to that interpretive community, with its ways of seeing which allow members to construct and eliminate errors. In both these views, basic writers are granted a degree of respect as cognitively mature adults. Their problems are re-imagined as comparable to the problems of social outsiders—foreigners learning a new language, or pledges seeking initiation into a different interpretive community.

These latter views, however, confront the ethical dilemma of requiring native speakers of English to use the conventions of Edited American English to represent their own language. Lees has observed that one of the reasons basic writers have so much trouble with error is that "[i]n learning to identify a familiar form as an error . . . a learner not only moves into an interpretive community but moves out of one as well. . . . To make such a move at all, it appears the learner must give up a system, a set of assumptions, a way of proceeding: one that already works, or seems to" ("Proofreading" 226–27). Persuading such writers to make such sacrifices is hard work. Those attempting to justify the teaching of EAE to such students have alternatively argued the status of EAE as a separate, politically neutral language—the English "grapholect"—or argued for the acceptance of the dominance of EAE as an historical fait accompli (Epes, Eskey). Shaughnessy, for example, argues that "mastery of formal written English [is] the language of public transactions—educational, civic, and professional," "a claim upon a wider culture" (*Errors* 125, 126). But like those who reify the medium of "literacy," or American culture, this reifies the "language of public transaction" as a static entity to which students must needs submit: "*the* language of public transactions" (Lu, "Redefining").

Sarah D'Eloia, alternatively, defends teaching EAE not in terms of maintaining the status quo but in terms of the lives of individual students within it:

> If one is persuaded that the business of the English teacher is more properly teaching a radical critique of our present social order rather than equipping students with the language skills necessary to cope

successfully in it, there is, indeed, little point to teaching standard English. However, to pursue the former course of action as the more moral, one must assume that our social order is changing so rapidly that our students can safely ignore social dialect and class as well as racial discrimination and, more importantly, that they can safely ignore the demand for skills of a technological society. We do not believe either can safely be ignored. In the absence of this safety, two facts remain: It will be important that middle class Americans learn to tolerate a broader spectrum of linguistic diversity, at the same time that upwardly aspiring minorities make linguistic accomodations [sic] toward the standard, especially in writing. While it is true that broad scale linguistic change is the product of social change, it is equally true that linguistic change toward control of the standard facilitates social mobility and social change for individuals. ("Teaching" 9)

D'Eloia might well be accused of sidestepping the political controversy associated with issues of teaching EAE here, but such sidestepping is understandable given the kinds of choices that *seem* to be available. Either we abandon BW students to "their own" language conventions and the consequences which currently follow upon use of those conventions, or we accept the unjust dominance of EAE in order to enable "social mobility and social change for individuals."

But again, this dilemma results from a series of reifications: the student is imagined as belonging entirely to a particular language community itself imagined as completely separate from the language community and practices of academics or "literates," a community whose own ways are imagined as fixed and with members assumed to be in unconditional possession of those ways. But if, as Bartholomae claims, "the borderlines between our work and [the work of basic writers] are not as clear as we like to assume," then the problem of basic writing becomes not one of who belongs where, and the terms for granting possession of a fixed territory or membership in a given community, but rather how we and our students can negotiate in the border country to produce different sorts of work at different times and thus, construct different sorts of communities: what conventions or practices might be accepted, by whom, and under what conditions, for a given writing. One BW student, writing about the situation of a writer like himself, describes the problem thus: "He tries different methods to find out which makes society understand his work. He tries to reach this goal, so he can be on the border line of what society wants and what he wants" (quoted in Lees, "The Exceptable Way" 144). In response to such students, I don't think we should attempt to identify "what society wants," handing him a map of what we think goes where. Nor would I recommend offering such students maps of multiple sets of fixed conventions, each with its appropriate place, as is sometimes suggested (Shaughnessy, *Errors* 121; D'Eloia, "Teaching"; cf. Lu, "Redefining"; Pratt, "Linguistic"; Lees, "The Exceptable Way"). As Lees has recently argued, both such responses require that we pretend to a certainty about conventions that the history of writing and the research on reader responses to writing deny, and both thus treat the writer as powerless in the face of such conventions ("The Exceptable Way" 151–52). Testimony to the effect of such treatment is offered by the BW student quoted above, who, having outlined a "trial and error" method for a writer to use to survive on the "border lines," warns,

> but if the trial and error does not work, and [the student] is in my position of not knowing how to express himself my [sic] using the exceptive method of the society, he would have pity for himself, he would be up late at nights asking God for his help. . . . it would hurt him so bad that he would just don't know what to do. While the writer that is not stuck would have some freedom in the way he wrote his works. (quoted in Lees, "The Exceptable Way" 144)

Though such testimony could be used to support pedagogies aiming simply to teach "the exceptive method of the society," I would argue that the real problem for this student is that he imagines that such a method exists and that to progress on the road to writing freedom, he must somehow acquire it. Lacking that method, he imagines himself as powerless, pitiable, reduced to praying as a last resort. On the other hand, note that he characterizes the "writer that is not stuck"—the sort of writer he would presumably want to become—not as one in possession of such a method but as one with "some freedom in the way he wrote his works." To convince this writer that he is not powerless, we will have to also grant that he too has "some freedom" and respond to his writing accordingly. Giddens warns that "[a]n agent who does not participate in the dialectic of control, in a minimal fashion, ceases to be an agent" (149). As I have argued elsewhere, to prevent such an eventuality in students requires that we encourage their participation in such a dialectic, recognizing and getting them to recognize their potential as agents in their writing ("Rethinking"). This does not mean we ignore points of difference, problems we or other readers have with their writing. It means rather that both teachers and students need to focus on such points of contact, the borders where different and shifting sets of conventions conflict, and to practice negotiating those differences. This means drawing attention, in class, to conflicting ways particular readers have of responding to particular textual conventions, asking not just what difference a particular writing practice—say, fragmented free modifiers, or ways of citing another text—can make, but to whom, and when, and why it might make such differences (cf. Yelin; Harste et al. 27–29, 202–3; Delpit 293–96). We can make explicit the perspective we adopt in "proofreading" papers and ask students to compare that perspective with those which make less likely the "discovery" of errors. Rather than responding to their texts in isolation, we can interview students about why they have followed the particular notational practices they have, and we can explain what of those practices bothers us and which delight us and the reasons for those responses.

Let me illustrate with an excerpt from a student's paper. In response to an assignment, given about midterm, which asked students to discuss what Richard Rodriguez's *Hunger of Memory* suggested about education, one student in an "intensive writing" class for beginning college students wrote:

> In "Complexion" Rodriguez writes, "I consider the great victoms of racism to be those who are poor and forced to do menial labor" (117). Through his life, Rodriguez comes to view those minorities who are less fortunate as vicitms of racism. He goes on to say "He was surprised to meet manual laborers with college diplomas" (133). Rodriguez views education as a means of avoiding this labor associated with racism. When I worked in construction this summer I was also surprised to work with a laborer that had a college degree from the University of Texas. He said that office jobs weren't what he wanted to do, so he was a laborer. I didn't consider him poor or underpriveleged, because he had made the choice to stay in a profession that he enjoyed instead of using his education to pursue a job in which he could make more money. On the other hand, I also worked with several guys that were high school dropouts that I would consider poor, because they were working as laboroers not by choice, but because their lack of education had limited their career options.

The misspellings, awkward syntax, and unconventional use of quotation marks might well lead us to view this writer as suffering from faulty perception and cognition, or as an alien to the discourse of the academy. His three spellings "victoms," "vicitms," and "laboroers" might persuade us that he is unable to "de-center" his perception of his writing enough to see the letters he has written (as might his silent alterations of Rodriguez's original text in his first quotation). And so we might assign him exercises to improve his skill at perceiving words and letters. His confusion of direct and indirect quotations might persuade us that he is a writer to whom, ironically, the conventions of writing are "foreign" and to whom they must be taught. Or, to lump together these two perspectives, we might label the writer an outsider to the "interpretive community of proofreaders," to whose assumptions, values, goals and procedures he must be converted.

I would deny neither that the writer in some ways faces just these difficulties nor that the pedagogies suggested as remedies possess a certain utility for students facing such difficulties. However, I would object to the way in which both approaches position teachers as powerless conduits of hegemony and the student as an essentially powerless object on which that hegemony operates, a potential consumer of the products of the culture of high literacy but, like an impoverished nation, with little to contribute in return. We might better respond to this writer by acknowledging to him at the outset the reading of the relationship between the concepts of labor, poverty, and education he has produced and wants to offer. As Lees has recently argued, "The intriguing prospect for a developing writer may be, in the end, the possibility that someone will listen, that someone will hear what he or she has to say. . . . to seem someone worth listening to" ("The Exceptable Way" 161). And as Robinson and Stock have argued concerning marginalized high school students, "If we would be literate, and help others to become so, it is a time for thoughtful listening to those voices that come from the margins; it is time for reflective reading of texts that inscribe those voices as *centrally* human ones" (313, my emphasis). Such "thoughtful listening" requires that we position this student as a writer engaged in an attempt to make meaning. To do this would mean that we still attend to "errors" but in terms not of "de-centration" or "conversion" but of the specific forms of reading by particular readers. "Reflective reading" of his text would have to include explaining what might confuse or bother particular readers—most clearly for me in this case, the use of quotation marks to mark the citation to Rodriguez's statement about manual laborers with college educations. Without identifying his use of quotation marks as violations of some absolute law, I could explain what those marks signal to me and other readers like me and the confusion that results for readers to whom such marks signal such meanings: who, after all, was surprised? Who is Rodriguez talking about if not himself? Of course, in this instance, given the social and institutional status of "my" reading, and given the student's desire to persuade readers like me to appreciate his response to Rodriguez, he is likely to want to change to "my" ways of notation and spelling in spite of the fact that his own spellings and his marking of the second quotation clearly did not bother or confuse him. What we should be wary of unwittingly encouraging him to do, however, is to alter the reading he offers in obliging such "academic" readers. More than once in asking individual students about error-ridden passages, I have discovered how completely I have misinterpreted the student's meaning, and how my unconscious assumption of the correctness of my own interpretation has stalled the interview.

I have found it better, though less immediately efficient, to question the student as to why he or she uses a particular notation or syntax and the meaning he or she perceives from such notations and syntax (cf. Tricomi 64). This can often lead to explicit negotiations comparable to those between writers and editors: "Can I get you to see X if I do A or B?" And it can lead to disagreements. My suggestions, however clever and well-intentioned I believe them to be, are not always taken. Instead, they serve as points of departure for exploring options and making decisions. In any case, however, the student remains positioned as having some say and some role to play other than that of apprentice or mimic—some freedom. That this freedom is not absolute, is conditioned in part by the shifting and powerful demands of others, does not render it empty but dynamic. In reinforcing the students' sense of being in a position to negotiate, we enable them to see writing as a negotiating process of bargaining as to what might count as what, to whom, for what purposes, under what circumstances.

There are numerous difficulties in attempting thus to position students and teachers. Perhaps most obviously, it directly contradicts common teacher-student relations in which teachers are granted, and are expected to operate from, a position of absolute authority on their subject. As a consequence, students might well be tempted to dismiss such non-absolute "positioning" as mere posturing (Boomer 7–10; cf. Delpit 286–91). Maintaining the distinction is both vital and an ongoing task. Second, such positioning assumes the shifting identity of both teachers and students, an assumption with which few teachers or students are comfortable. Harris has remarked on the extraordinary persuasiveness of appeals to membership in a particular community ("The Idea"). Pedagogies denying the validity of such appeals must compete with pedagogies which make them; further, they must posit in place of such appeals a fluid, shifting sense of identity which flies in the face of what Harris calls the "myth of the autonomous essential self" (20). Though Harris claims social theories of reading and writing have helped deconstruct this myth for composition teachers, it remains dominant in much of American culture. Finally, acknowledging to students the indeterminacy of the outcomes of negotiations between readers and writers is to deny what many students presumably want—indeed, what any writer dreams of at least some of the time as an ideal: a sure thing, a proven method, the absence of conflict, contradiction, and tension, the achievement of perfect communication (cf. Lu, "Conflict"). Indeterminacy doesn't sell, a significant liability in a consumerist society.

In spite of these limitations, models of writing as negotiation and basic writing as a borderland offer significant advantages over previous conceptions of basic writers, basic writing, and the writing classroom. They acknowledge the play of power in language, the shifting nature of language practices, and the agency of both teachers and students. And more importantly, they position every student writer *as* a writer with "some freedom," akin to rather than different from other writers in residing "on the border line of what society wants and what he wants." I have been arguing that basic writers, like all writers, have "some freedom," and that to act on that freedom is not a matter of sloughing off immaturity; nor does it require students to sell their souls. Students, like all writers, can negotiate *as* writers for particular positions for particular occasions, vis-à-vis particular readers, if only we can persuade them, and ourselves, that they can.

II Professing Basic Writing

6 Re-thinking the "Sociality" of Error: Teaching Editing as Negotiation

Bruce Horner

That errors in writing are somehow "social" is no news to the field of composition. Yet there is a recurring discrepancy in the approach compositionists take toward this dimension of written error. On the one hand, what counts as an "error" (or as "correct") in writing *is* generally recognized as "social": most compositionists freely acknowledge the history of the controversial imposition of standards of "correct" notation as a set of arbitrary conventions. On the other hand, the production of particular errors is regularly identified and treated not as social but as individual, evidence of an individual writer's cognitive or perceptual difficulties, trouble knowing and/or seeing error. We might account cynically for the discrepancy between recognition of what might be called the "sociality" of errors and the focus of research and teaching on error as a sign of ethical irresponsibility. I would argue, however, that this discrepancy results from an impasse in how the "sociality" of error has been theorized. To acknowledge that errors are "social" seems to mean primarily that one acknowledges the history of the regularization of conventions for writing English, a regularization which, not coincidentally, has favored the syntactic forms of dialects spoken by more powerful social groups. But all this seems to be viewed as a fait accompli, "history" in the sense of something in the past about which there is little now to be done, a digression that takes attention away from the immediate problems of our students and their writing. The proper focus of attention for researchers and teachers of writing, it seems largely to be assumed, is on matters of student cognition and perception.

In her 1985 review of "Research on Error and Correction" Glynda Hull testifies to this state of affairs. Hull acknowledges that "[m]ost of the controversy surrounding correctness in writing has finally to do with power, status, and class," but observes that much recent research on error "can be viewed as walking a middle ground in the controversy, neither despairing that students must learn a privileged language nor grieving overlong that there is a cost" (165, 166). This research takes as its purpose "not a delineation of the social and political implications of error and correctness but an investigation of those mental processes involved in making errors and correcting them" (167).[1] Note that researchers pursuing such matters do not deny the social controversy "surrounding" errors. But they assume that those matters surround without, as it were, infiltrating or impinging upon error, that the controversy exists outside the perimeter of the site where error is produced and corrected. And if the "mental processes" responsible for producing and correcting error are indeed distinct from the social and political "implications" of what is produced, then one may justifiably dismiss questions about the social constitution of error as immaterial to research on error, questions belonging to the province of sociolinguists and social activists but not writing teachers.

In what follows, I want to call that distinction into question. My intent is not to call composition researchers and teachers to ethical account, nor to deny the necessity of teaching conventions of writing (though I have some recommendations for how we might better teach them). Rather, I argue that the distinction between "error" and its social implications is false, and that, consequently, to the extent that any research and teaching is based on that distinction, it is flawed. The "sociality" of error has much to do with both its production and correction, and if we are properly to understand and respond to written error, we need to attend to that sociality in our research and teaching. Such attention need not and should not override our attention to matters of cognition and perception but inform it. In short, the split between social approaches and cognitive approaches to error, like the sociocognitive divide compositionists generally have recently been attempting to cross, is a problematic split which hampers our research and teaching.[2] I begin by considering in some detail how errors might be viewed as social in their production and correction, rather than only in their implications. I then examine two ways in which this is elided in some of the literature on error, and the problematic results of such elisions. Finally, I examine how a more fully "social" view of error might inform our teaching of editing.

I: Errors as Social "Achievements"

In a critique of literacy studies, Sylvia Scribner notes that although literacy is most often defined as "an attribute of *individuals*," "the single most compelling fact about literacy is that it is a *social* achievement" (emphasis in original). For, as she explains,

> Individuals in societies without writing systems do not become lit-
> erate. . . . the individual child or adult does not extract the meaning
> of written symbols through personal interaction with the physical
> objects that embody them. Literacy abilities are acquired by indi-
> viduals only in the course of participation in socially organized ac-
> tivities with written language. . . . It follows that individual literacy
> is relative to social literacy. . . .
>
> The enterprise of defining literacy, therefore, becomes one of as-
> sessing what counts as literacy . . . in some given social context. (72)

But if, as Scribner urges us to do, we acknowledge literacy to be a social
rather than an individual achievement and thus an achievement that
varies from time to time and place to place, we must simultaneously
also acknowledge "errors" in writing as social achievements, though of
a peculiar kind. For if definitions of literacy must involve "what counts
as literacy . . . in some given social context," then definitions of error in
writing must similarly involve what counts as an "error" in some given
social context.[3]

We can get a sense of how errors might represent social "achievements" by recalling the social interaction in and by which they are produced, recognized, and corrected. Errors in writing are usually described
as the failure of writing to conform to *conventions* in language or notation. But a convention, as Raymond Williams reminds us, carries from
its roots the sense of meeting—like an annual "convention"—and, by
derivation, agreement. In writing, Williams observes, a convention functions as "an established relationship, or ground of a relationship, through
which a specific shared practice—the making of actual works—can be
realized" (*Marxism* 173). Through specific notations, Williams observes,
such relationships are "expressed, offered, tested, and amended in a
whole social process, in which device, expression, and the substance of
expression are in the end inseparable" (*Marxism* 171–72). Any failure in
conventions thus represents a failure of the parties involved to reach
agreement, the rejection by one party of the relationship expressed and/
or offered by the other.

We can thus understand errors as representing flawed social transactions, instances of a failure on the part of *both* the writer and reader to
negotiate an agreement (the process of offering, testing, and amending)
as to the kind of relationship that should exist between them and as to
the kind of significance to be attributed to the written notations offered,
a failure which makes impossible the realization of a certain kind of
"work."[4] This view of error helps to explain the difficulty of determining whether a given notation—e.g., the "fragmented" free modifier—
represents an error or, say, an effective stylistic device. The status of the
form as an error depends largely on the relationship between a particu-

lar writer and a particular reader at a particular time—the status and authority which, in a particular time, the writer claims and which the reader agrees to accord the writer. It is a matter re-negotiated at each writing and at each reading. Quarrels between publishing writers and their editors or critics concerning the acceptability and significance of particular usages attest to the negotiated status of given notations as errors.

If we can distinguish basic writers from others on the basis of their errors, we may say that what distinguishes them is not so much that they make more errors than do other writers or that their errors are more severe but that (1) on their own, basic writers don't recognize the same particular notations their intended readers do for what those readers recognize them as (errors) and (2) they are not aware of, or do not know how to reach an agreement with these readers through the process of offering, testing, and amending notations. We may say that, in Scribner's sense, many of *their* errors remain at least partially *un*achieved, for if errors are social achievements, then they can't fully exist until both reader and writer agree on their existence. Whereas the more successful student writers will frequently recognize and agree with their readers that particular notations are "errors," basic writers, though they may believe in the sincerity of teachers who mark their papers as full of errors, are seldom in agreement with them. When I first ask students in my basic writing classes to correct errors in their writing, individually or in groups, their "corrections" often leave untouched the errors I have in mind and alter what I fail to see as originally in error. Paradoxically, at least one of my goals may well be to help them to produce—i.e., achieve or recognize—more of the kind of errors I recognize in their writing.

But such an achievement can be reached only through a process of negotiation. And in negotiation, the parties operate in a relation of power that inevitably changes both. As P. H. Gulliver observes, negotiation is "a dynamic process of exploration in which change is intrinsic: changes in each party's assessment of his requirements, in his expectations of what is possible, preferable, and acceptable, and changes in his understanding of the opponent's assessments and expectations" (*Disputes and Negotiations* xvii). It is a process of "learning and adjustment by the parties" (Gulliver 81). If the negotiation results in agreement, "the position of each [party] has been subtly changed not only by the terms offered, but by its experience of the other and exposure to the other's persuasion" (Vickers 151; qtd. in Gulliver 81). Negotiation is not a matter of one party persuading a second to adopt the position of the first, nor a process of exchange (barter) between two parties, but a process of joint change and learning in which power operates dialectically.

To teach students to "achieve" errors through negotiation, it thus will not do simply for me to bully students into confessing the status of certain notations as errors. For the errors to be "achieved" as errors, the achievement must represent an agreement reached between the writer and reader to attribute a certain kind of significance to specific notations, and that agreement must be the result of a relationship in which *both* writer and reader hold a degree of power and authority. But what especially marks much present-day basic writing as such—as a type of writing and as an institution—is a very different social relationship inherent in the activity of the writing and its teaching, a relationship in which authority is imagined to reside with the teacher/reader alone, but in which no one, including the teacher, has power. Rather, the teacher becomes the instrument of a power operating through her upon the student. The writer assumes no authority for the specific notations offered, and the teacher/reader refuses to ascribe any power or authority to the writer. When confronted with certain usages in the writing of basic writers, teachers are either not willing or unprepared to participate in the kinds of relationships with the writer and the text which do ascribe power and authority to the writers and their writing. In Elaine Lees's example, readers laugh at the student sentence "People nowadays are using sex to sell things all the time (such as in movies, TV, and pubic advertising)" because of the kind of writer they imagine the student to be, one without any authority as a writer ("Proofreading as Reading" 225). Given different assumptions about the writer, the word "pubic" might well be read as fully appropriate, not an "error" at all. Joseph Williams similarly points to the role which readers' sense of writers plays in producing error when he wryly observes that "if we [teachers] could read those [error-ridden] student essays unreflexively, if we could make the ordinary kind of *contract* with those texts that we make with other kinds of texts, then we could find many fewer errors" (159; quoted in Lees, "Proofreading" 217; my emphasis).

That teachers seldom make such contracts with students results from treating the asymmetry of power relations between teachers and students as necessarily denying students *any* agency or power. Because students have less power, they are imagined to have none. But as social theorist Anthony Giddens observes, "Power relations . . . are always *two-way*, even if the power of one actor or party in a social relation is minimal compared to another. Power relations are relations of autonomy and dependence, but even the most autonomous agent is in some degree dependent, and the most dependent actor or party in a relationship retains some autonomy" (93; see also Isaac 79–95). Power itself is best conceived not so much as a resource but as a capability (Giddens 68, 91).

Students who fail to exercise power or authority do not deny the possibility of their own agency but simply reject it. As Giddens observes, "*An agent who does not participate in the dialectic of control, in a minimal fashion, ceases to be an agent* [sic]" (149). Similarly, teachers who fail to acknowledge the power of their students likewise reject the opportunity of negotiating with them, and so, however indirectly, reject their own power and agency as well.

But if we accept the view that errors are the product of social relationships, and that editing is a matter of negotiating those relationships, then our teaching of error and editing will have to engage issues of power, authority, and conflict. What counts as an error will have to be taught as negotiable and thus variable, dependent on the specific historical and social context in which a notation occurs, its status as an error varying from reader to reader, even from reading to reading, as agreements as to relationships of power and authority are renegotiated. In the last decade of error research, however, it is just these issues that have been dismissed from consideration.

II: Errors as Linguistic Confusion

Hull's observation that researchers have chosen to walk a "middle ground in the controversy [over error], neither despairing that students must learn a privileged language nor grieving overlong that there is a cost" ("Research" 166) hints at why compositionists have tended to dismiss issues of conflicts in power and authority from consideration. The issues, however real, are assumed to be long-settled, "dead," the controversy something about which one can do little but despair and grieve. There are two interdependent assumptions governing this view: (1) that the conventions constituting standard written English are largely fixed and (2) that the social order which has determined the appropriateness or nonappropriateness of certain conventions is largely fixed. The language of privilege is settled, and students must, if they are to have access to privilege, learn it. The strategies for responding to students' errors adopted by those accepting the validity of these assumptions are thus necessarily strategies of accommodation. Those adopting such strategies make two additional assumptions: (3) that it is counterproductive to remind students of what cannot be changed (a "dead" issue, after all) and (4) that students are at a significant remove from the conventions of standard Edited American English. Evidence of these assumptions appears in the models and metaphors governing descriptions of basic writers and their difficulties. The changes in student writing hoped for are described using metaphors of travel from one fixed location to another, whether from one fixed linguistic territory to another, one cognitive stage or state to another, one discourse community to another, or from an outside to an inside. In some of these, the problems of basic writers are reconceptualized as being not primarily social but cognitive and/or linguistic. Improvement in writing is identified with models adapted from theories of cognitive development or second-language acquisition. In the process, what might otherwise be termed conflicts of power or agreement get redefined as linguistic or cognitive problems, and pedagogical implications are drawn that ignore the social dimension of the problems.

We can see this process operating in Mina Shaughnessy's characterization of the difficulties of basic writers in her highly influential *Errors and Expectations*:

> *Confusion,* rather than *conflict,* seems to paralyze the writer at this *level. Language learners* at any level appear to seek out, either consciously or unconsciously, the underlying patterns that govern the language they are learning. They *are pressed by their language-learning faculties* to increase the degree of predictability and efficiency in their use of language. This is *less a choice they make than an urge they have* to move across the territory of language as if they had a map and not as if they were being forced to make their way across a mine field. What has been so damaging about the experience of BW students with written English is that it has been so confusing, and worse, that they have become resigned to this confusion, to not knowing, to the substitution of protective tactics or private systems or makeshift strategies for *genuine mastery* of written English in any form. (10, my emphases)

In this passage, Shaughnessy establishes a "middle ground" by describing the problems of basic writers as those of anyone learning a new language. Using the evidence of what error analysts would call an "intermediate language" in students' writing, she argues that basic writers' problems are best understood in terms of inevitable cognitive growth— a matter of "confusion," not "conflict," evidence of their "level" of "language learning," the pursuit of an "urge they have," not a "choice they make." Learning to write conventionally correct prose is equated with learning a new language, and learning a new language is presented as involving purely cognitive demands. For the terms of "conflict," "choice," and negotiation inherent in that practice of learning and using the conventions of Standard EAE Shaughnessy substitutes a restricted set of terms drawn from models of second-language acquisition.[5]

That Shaughnessy should choose to make such a substitution seems to result from her sense that attention to the sociality of errors constitutes a damaging evasion of error rather than a focus on one of its intrinsic elements. In a passage following the one quoted above, she argues, "To try to persuade a student who makes these errors that the problems with his writing are all on the outside, or that he has no problems, may well be to perpetuate his confusion and deny him the ultimate freedom of deciding how and when and where he will use which language" (11). Shaughnessy likens the transactions of writers and readers to bargaining, but a bargaining in which errors represent so much static interference, not disagreements:

> [Errors] demand energy [from the reader] without giving any return in meaning; they shift the reader's attention from where he is going (meaning) to how he is getting there (code). In a better world, it is true, readers might be more generous with their energies, . . . but it would be foolhardy to bank on that kind of persistence except perhaps in English teachers or good friends. (12)

Shaughnessy acknowledges that what counts as an error continues to vary and that this is socially determined. "This is not to say," she reminds us, "that the boundaries of error do not shift nor to suggest that certain battles along those borderlines are not worth waging" (13). But such battles are "battles," not negotiations.[6] As such, they have no place in the immediate work of the basic writing classroom:

> [W]hen we move out of the centuries and into Monday morning, into the life of the young man or woman sitting in a BW class, our linguistic contemplations are likely to hover over a more immediate reality—namely, the fact that a person who does not control the dominant code of literacy in a society that generates more writing than any society in history is likely to be pitched against more obstacles than are apparent to those who have already mastered that code. (13)

In a critique of Shaughnessy, Min-Zhan Lu, adopting a perspective afforded by Marxist and poststructuralist theories of language, has identified in Shaughnessy's work a "politics of 'linguistic' innocence," a politics constituting a part of Shaughnessy's "legacy" to later researchers on error which Lu would have us resist. Lu argues that we cannot view writers in any writing as operating within any single linguistic sphere—either controlling or not controlling the "dominant code of literacy," for example—nor as ever being politically innocent. Rather, as these theories suggest,

> language is best understood not as a neutral vehicle of communication but as a site of struggle among competing discourses. Each discourse puts specific constraints on the construction of one's stance—how one makes sense of oneself and gives meaning to the world. . . .

> Each time one writes, even and especially when one is attempting
> to use one of these discourses, one experiences the need to respond
> to the dissonance among the various discourses of one's daily life.
> Because different discourses do not enjoy equal political power in
> current-day America, decisions on how to respond to such disso-
> nance are never politically innocent. ("Redefining" 27)

Lu argues that students' attention needs to be drawn to the politics of
those decisions, not to decry their implication in politics, but so that
students may make those decisions from a position of being more fully
informed. To overlook those implications is to oversimplify, and thus to
confuse, the task that our students, like all writers, face when writing.
The task is not one of moving from one fixed sphere or stage or community of language use to another, or of choosing one over another, but of
responding to the dissonance among these for particular, often conflicting purposes to which one would like to align oneself at a particular
time in a particular writing (Lu, "Redefining" 35).

To illustrate the sort of confusion to which silencing such dissonance
can lead both students and researchers, I want to discuss Mary Epes's
1985 study of the socially charged issue of the influence of spoken dialect on basic writers' errors. Epes's study is worth considering in detail
because the care with which Epes builds her case and the pedagogical
implications she draws show how easily issues of power, status, and
class associated with learning writing conventions can be sidestepped
by even the best work of researchers and also, and more important, the
highly problematic "middle ground" to which such sidesteps lead them.

In her study, Epes provides an elaborate comparison between the
number and types of errors produced by two groups of adult basic writers, one composed of thirteen speakers of standard dialect, whom she
parenthetically describes as "all native speakers [of English], mostly
middle class, and mostly white," the other composed of thirteen speakers of nonstandard dialect, whom she parenthetically describes as "all
native speakers [of English] and all black except one" ("Tracing" 8).[7] She
reports that "differences in cognitive, composing, and reading skills do
not seem to account for the differences in the error rates of the two
groups" (the second group makes many more errors, and more errors of
certain types, than the first) and so concludes that dialect differences are
to blame (15). In reporting her conclusions, she explicitly dismisses the
influence of nonlinguistic factors on students' performance: "[T]here are
peculiarly linguistic (as distinct from sociological and psychological)
reasons for the severe problems with the written language almost universally experienced by nonstandard dialect speakers" (29). The *terms*
of her explanation would seem to suggest otherwise:

> Because NSD speakers must write a language which is in certain
> ways in *conflict* with the language they speak, they are more subject
> than SD speakers to an *insecurity* which can have a highly adverse
> effect on their development as learners and writers. . . . For a variety
> of reasons traceable to nonstandard speech patterns, NSD speakers
> do not develop the perceptual skills necessary to control some as-
> pects of the written code at the same pace that SD speakers gener-
> ally do. (29–30; my emphases)

But though to readers unfamiliar with Epes's article, "conflict" and "insecurity" might suggest social, political, and affective psychological factors for students' difficulties with writing, Epes has already earlier redefined such terms as bearing purely linguistic significance, the conflict
and insecurity which, say, a native speaker of French might encounter
in attempting to speak English purely for purposes of recreation (if one
can imagine such an attempt). We can see this redefining of "linguistic"
as a category encompassing all sorts of difficulties in Epes's earlier commentary on the multiple hypercorrect forms which the speakers of NSD
produce in their writing. Epes describes such forms as signs

> both of [NSD speakers'] struggle to resolve the conflict between their
> spoken language and the one they're trying to write, as well as of
> the *linguistic insecurity* which grips them as soon as they pick up a
> pen. Over the years when they should and could be growing in lit-
> eracy skills, *this insecurity* apparently becomes for many a *general-
> ized malaise* which affects every aspect of their experience as writers,
> and, unfortunately, their overall *self-image* as learners. (22, my em-
> phases)

An initial "insecurity" and "conflict" described as purely "linguistic"
are identified as the source of students' later experience of "general
malaise" and lousy "overall self-image."[8]

Epes transforms the problem of NSD speakers' written errors into a
linguistic and perceptual problem by maintaining a distinction between
composing and encoding, between norms that are optional and those
that are givens (by whom to whom? we might ask), a distinction that is
basic to the design and method of analysis of her study—indeed, a distinction she makes early on in order to "head off confusion about the
goals and design" of her study. She explains:

> As a skill, encoding includes control over all the norms of the writ-
> ten language—the norms relating both to its visual forms (spelling,
> punctuation, capitalization, indentation, etc.) and to its linguistic
> forms (denoting tense, number, case, word-class, etc.). Encoding is
> distinct from composing inasmuch as it is concerned with the giv-
> ens of the written code, whereas composing is concerned with the
> options of the written language which that code represents. . . .

> For the purposes of this investigation, I define error narrowly as any clear deviation from the norms of standard written English. This definition places error in the domain of right/wrong, not of better/worse. So defined, errors manifest weaknesses in encoding skills, not in composing skills. (6, emphases in original)

Epes finds "[difficulties in objectifying the code] to be particularly severe among the NSD speakers" (27), difficulties which Epes links to differences between NSD and the "norms" of the written code. The fact that "their natural language forms happen to be unacceptable in writing does not make it any easier for NSD speakers to see, much less to avoid them [i.e., NSD forms in writing]" when looking for errors (21). When asked to "detect" errors when reading a passage "encoded" with NSD forms, they have trouble "seeing" the NSD forms *as* errors (21). What Epes sees as a clear matter of right and wrong, they can't see. And finding themselves unable to "objectify" the code, they experience "conflict," "general malaise," and end up with poor "overall self-image as learners." In Epes's argument, the conventions of writing—matters of agreement as to what is and isn't acceptable or optional—are treated as matters of physical, visual facts, "facts" which NSD speakers can't see. The students' experience of conflict concerning the "factuality" of these conventions and their difficulty seeing their own forms as errors thus appear to indicate their lack of perceptual skills. Whereas Shaughnessy rejects the possibility that basic writers experience "conflict" by re-naming it the experience of "confusion," Epes redefines conflict *as* confusion, a confusion explained as resulting from a lack of ability to see what, or in the ways that, some others see.

I don't mean to deny the cognitive or linguistic dimensions to learning writing or, for that matter, other dimensions, such as the physical demands of typing or handwriting, to which Epes, Shaughnessy, and other writers attend in their studies of error. But I do deny the distinction Shaughnessy and Epes make between confusion and conflict, and between the cognitive or linguistic, on the one hand, and the social. By adopting a desocialized, depoliticized model for their understanding of writing problems, presenting the learning of writing as an individual's journey across the "territory of language" to "genuine mastery of written English," these writers misrepresent the conventions of writing as "givens" and the academic success of some with those conventions as natural, the possession of "genuine" mastery. Effective editing, or the production of conventionally "correct" writing, comes to be seen as ordinarily an inevitable part of an *individual's* cognitive or linguistic development, something which one's "language-learning faculties" press one to learn, an ability which every college student ought to have already acquired but which basic writers haven't. And for those accepting these views, basic writers come to be labeled unnatural, stuck in an earlier stage of cognitive development (Lunsford, "Cognitive Development"), unable to see words "as they are" (Laurence, "Errors' Endless Train" 30), trapped by cognitive barriers which prevent them from real learning in which they can see "the reality behind the symbol" (Goldberg 40).[9]

In short, such studies misrepresent the conventions of writing as fixed rather than inevitably shifting, renegotiated throughout history and in each act of writing; in so doing, they misrepresent the inevitable and recurring confrontation with conflict which any "mastery" of written English in fact entails and the difficulties which basic writers face in attempting to achieve such "mastery." Finally and perhaps most important, in sidestepping the conflict inherent in academic (and any other type of) writing, such studies result in pedagogies which can contribute to the very confusion and malaise from which students suffer. For they reinforce basic writers' sense that their position as writers is one of powerlessness. The teacher/reader remains in control of, and the authority on, what counts as mature writing, the target language, what is "right," even "reality." In a sense Epes likely is accurate in identifying her students' feelings as ones of "generalized malaise," "insecurity," or poor "overall self-image." She reports that the students she interviewed complained themselves that "when they were involved in composing, they tended uncontrollably to 'slip back' and use 'bad English' in their writing." One, Epes reports, chastizes herself, "'There I go again. I don't say that ["there was several patients"] no more. It's out of my past' (28). Students who are repeatedly told they are not seeing what's there, getting it wrong instead of right, not being "objective," may well believe such usages to be "slips," "bad English," instances of once again not using the "right word." By locating written error in the "domain of right/wrong," we encourage student writers to position themselves as having no control over or authority on their writing, a position, by the way, which students may find all too tempting, since in denying them power, it also relieves them of responsibility.

This is not to say that those studies sidestepping social dimensions to writing have yielded no insights. The claims of those who see basic writers' problems as showing cognitive or perceptual inabilities or those who see such problems as evidence of stages akin to those in second-language acquisition are based on studies conducted too carefully to be simply false. Epes, for example, demonstrates convincingly a correlation between the primary spoken dialect of the students in her study and specific types of errors in their writing, a correlation much debated in prior studies. I am arguing, however, that the cognitive and perceptual demands of writing that researchers like Epes have described are intrinsically social in ways the writers fail to acknowledge or confront, ways which radically qualify both the significance of their claims and the kinds of utility their pedagogies possess. The "cognitive" and "linguistic" intersect with the "political" and the "social." Epes's argument, for example, needs significant qualification: Though she does demonstrate a correlation between her students' spoken dialect and specific errors in their writing, it is not at all clear that the differences between the spoken dialect and the written "code" alone as purely linguistic phenomena account for NSD speakers' difficulties. Rather, as I have shown her own language suggesting, the attributes of class, power, and identity associated historically with that dialect and that code in the United States seem to have much to do with their difficulties.[10] In understanding basic writers' problems with error and especially in devising pedagogies to address those problems, we need to take the intersections of their political, social, linguistic, and cognitive dimensions into account. For example, though NSD speakers' difficulties in producing or identifying specific forms may make it seem necessary and useful to assign them some kind of grammar lessons on those forms and exercises in improving "perception skills," as Epes recommends (30–31), we need to consider how such teaching practices risk reinforcing the distress which such students experience insofar as they present as inarguable "givens" what students have neither received nor decided fully to accept.

III: Errors as Cultural Difference

In "Proofreading as Reading, Errors as Embarrassments," Elaine Lees suggests one model for understanding errors which begins to take into account how the production of errors might itself have social and political dimensions. Drawing from Joseph Williams, the work of Stanley Fish, and her own research on writing and reading behavior, Lees argues,

> Students who proofread their own work unsuccessfully may be viewed not so much as "missing what's there" on the surface of their texts as constructing . . . those texts differently from the way other, powerful readers do. Though a student may compose a text in which a teacher finds errors, we cannot assume that the student constructs, or can construct, a text that reveals those errors as he or she reads. (220)

For Lees, this is not, it bears emphasizing, a "perceptual" problem, at least not in the sense of physical visual impairment, something to be fixed by eye exercises. Rather, for Lees, the problem basic writers have with error is one of not yet belonging to the interpretive community of proofreaders, with its shared goals, procedures, assumptions, and values. It is a problem of social identity, a lack not simply of skill or knowledge but of agreement. Lees suggests that this may account for why some basic writers have so much difficulty learning to see their errors, for to do so may require that they not only move into a new "interpretive community" but move out of another ("Proofreading" 226–27).

The model Lees offers, by redefining perception in social terms, eliminates some of the reductiveness of responding to students' difficulties with proofreading as purely cognitive or perceptual by reconceiving perception and cognition themselves as social. However, in place of the distinction between seeing what's on the page and what isn't, this model substitutes a distinction between cultural communities presented as largely fixed—the community of proofreaders versus the others. This fixing of communities thus risks reinscribing the task of basic writers as moving from one community to another, but now with all the attendant ethical questions to which such moves, described in such terms, give rise. If proofreading is not a matter of improved perception or advanced cognition, what justification can we offer for teaching it? Why should students exchange their goals, procedures, assumptions, and values for those of their teachers? And why should teachers themselves encourage such an exchange?

In short, in place of viewing students as moving up the stages of linguistic maturity, in this model basic writers' difficulties are seen as those of acculturation. And in line with this second view, teaching writing can come to be seen as a matter of cultural imperialism, of asking students to move from an "oral" to a "literate" culture, to exchange the language of home and family (with its attendant goals, procedures, assumptions, and values) for the language of the academy (with all *its* cultural baggage). And what might otherwise be thought of as a continuum, or at least a cacophony, of goals, procedures, assumptions, and values is imagined as a choice between two distinct alternatives.

We can see this way of distinguishing basic writers operating in descriptions of them as members of an "oral" rather than a "literate" culture (Farrell, "Literacy, the Basics"; Ong 51; Sloan) or as lacking a "textual" orientation, reading only for "gist" or "meaning" but not for "code" (Lees, "Proofreading" 227; Epes 26), as evidenced by their failure to attend to or see the need for citing passages from a text—their own or another's—when discussing its meaning; by the physical distance students often maintain between themselves and (written) texts; and by their apparent failure, when reading aloud from their own texts, to see any difference between the words they speak and the marks on the page.[11]

A number of pedagogies based on this distinction have been developed to produce a "textual" orientation in students. Donna Gorrell, for example, recommends having students engage in "controlled" composition—that is, exact copying of passages or copying them and then altering specified lexical or syntactic forms—to combat what she describes as students' "lack of attention to written forms." Such practices require what she describes as "accuracy in both transcription and manipulation," thereby focusing "student attention on lexical and syntactic forms in the written language" (308). Exercises which have students infer understandings of syntactic forms and rules of punctuation from examples similarly give students practice in attending to particular syntactic forms and marks of punctuation. (For examples, see D'Eloia, "Uses"; Lunsford, "Cognitive Development"; *The Comp-Lab Exercises; Connections.*) In so doing, students are to develop a "textual" orientation—a tendency to pay attention to the "codes" of writing.

Aside from the ethical dilemmas it raises, there are at least three problems with viewing errors as signs of cultural difference. First, those making a distinction between a textual versus an oral orientation, or between "code" and meaning (like Epes's distinction between "encoding" and "composing"), often fail to take into account the socially produced sense of what "reading for code" involves, and so fail to honor the "textual" orientations students do bring to their reading. The distinction between a "textual" (or "literate") and an "oral" orientation can thus easily slide back into the distinction between accurate versus faulty perception which Lees is at pains to dismantle (see quotations from Gorrell, above). The distinction can in fact better be described as a difference in the practice of constructing, or composing, meaning out of "code." If I "depart from my text" in delivering a speech, this is not a sign of my illiteracy or lack of textual orientation but a sign of a different orientation to my text, a different use I am making of it no less sophisticated, perhaps more, than that of a speaker reading verbatim. The problem many basic writers may have is not that they lack textual orientation but that they frequently adopt kinds of textual orientation unaligned to the kinds of orientations their teachers sometimes want them to take.

This points to the second problem with viewing basic writers and their teachers as belonging to separate interpretive communities: it ignores the degree to which neither basic writers nor their teachers are so simply identified or distinguished from one another.[12] Basic writers are not strangers to the land of proofreading (they have, after all, heard of and pay attention to the sentence, commas, grammar, etc.), any more than English teachers lack approaches to writing and reading that basic writers regularly adopt. Basic writers regularly employ most of the marks of punctuation common in English writing, try to follow regularized spelling, and so on. English teachers often ignore nonstandard punctuation and syntactic patterns. We can get a sense both of the differences that exist between the kinds of textual orientations teachers and students take toward texts and of the overlap between those orientations in some of the literature describing the editing processes of basic writers. Hull, analyzing a protocol of an editing session between a tutor and a student, has remarked

> how unswervingly the student and tutor talk past one another. . . .
> The tutor brings to her reading a particular kind of understanding
> of texts, where it makes sense to pay attention to the structural logic
> of sentences, and she tries to explain the errors in terms of that understanding. And in so doing, she loses the student, who just isn't
> able to participate in her discussion, not yet being a party to her
> notions of error and editing. He, on the other hand, seems to have
> his own agenda for improving his text, an agenda which turns upon
> a concern, not so much for how individual sentences are put together, but for what is appropriate semantically and stylistically.
> ("Acts of Wonderment" 216)

The student described clearly has a particular orientation to his text. In the editing session Hull describes, the student makes a number of changes in his text in order to clarify his meaning and improve his style. However, his kind of orientation to his text doesn't allow him to see the problems the tutor sees, problems of blurred syntax and punctuation. As Hull puts it, he is "not yet . . . a party to her notions of error and editing." Hull describes a successful editing tutorial as one in which "[the student] finally sees enough instances of the error and gets sufficient feedback on his attempts to correct it that he is able to think about punctuating sentences in his tutor's terms rather than his own" ("Acts of Wonderment" 219). This shift in perspectives, Hull notes at the beginning of her essay, like the shift in perspective that enables a teacher to understand the logic of a student's errors, can lead to a sense of "wonderment," which she describes as "the apprehension and appreciation of another's way of thinking; a kind of insight, often sudden, at times marvelous, that allows one to see from another's vantage; an epiphany, if you will" (199). We should not dismiss either the real pleasures of such shifts in perspective or their substantial value for both teachers and students. At the same time, however, we need to acknowledge two qualifications to what such shifts represent. First, we need to recall that such shifts are not purely cognitive or perceptual ones, as the visual metaphor of "perspective" might suggest. As Patricia Bizzell explains,

> [S]tudents who struggle to write Standard English need knowledge
> beyond the rules of grammar, spelling, and so on. They need to know:

> the habitual attitudes of Standard English users toward this pre-
> ferred form; the linguistic features that most strongly mark group
> identity; the conventions that can sometimes be ignored; and so on.
> Students who do know the rules of Standard English may still seem
> to academics to be writing "incorrectly" if the students are insensi-
> tive to all these other features of language use in the community—
> then the students are using academic language in unacademic ways.
> ("Cognition" 224)

Second, however, we also need to acknowledge that such shifts are not
so simple, so binary, as the metaphor of perspective shifting would suggest. For however full of wonderment, such shifts are not instances of
students encountering the previously unimaginable. In the editing protocol Hull analyzes, though the student is not initially party to the perspective of his tutor, neither is he wholly a stranger to it. When the tutor
mentions terms like *sentence, comma,* and *period,* the student doesn't ask
for definitions, as he might if he were a foreigner (see "Acts of Wonderment" 216–18). Rather, he learns, or seems to learn, a new concept for
how sentences and periods and commas, about all of which he has some
previous knowledge, might relate to one another. And the tutor, though
frustrated initially by the failure of the student's focus to correspond to
her own, can understand, recognize, and respond meaningfully to his
earlier focus on matters of style, rhetorical strategy, semantics: whether
or not, for example, the student ought to admit in his paper that he
doesn't like a story his teacher has assigned (215).

Viewing errors as signs of cultural difference, then, can perpetuate
the false sense of each cultural orientation as unified and distinct from
the other. A final problem with this view is related to this last. Not only
is there overlap between the perspectives of basic writers and their teachers. Each of those perspectives is itself constantly shifting. The ground
of the "new" territory to which teachers might see themselves as attempting to lead students is not only not entirely new to students, it is
not firm; the perspective which we would presumably have them adopt
itself shifts. Though the metaphor of "perspective shifting" would suggest that teaching students to edit represents a kind of "conversion" process whereby students come to abandon what is imagined to be "their"
ways of seeing texts and adopt "ours," and though the metaphor of "ter-
ritories" of language would suggest teaching editing as involving a kind
of growth, or "expansion" of, by addition to, the repertoire of perspectives students can adopt towards texts, the fact is that neither "our" perspective—the attitudes, goals, assumptions and practices of the "academic discourse community"—nor "theirs" is itself (and I am questioning the identification of it as singular) fixed but is constantly shifting,
renegotiated in every instance of language use.[13] There is no utopian

promised land either to which or from which we might lead students. The lack of agreement among teachers as to labels for errors, what does and doesn't count as an error, and the relative importance of particular kinds of errors illustrates the shifting perspectives of the "academic discourse community" (see Connors and Lunsford, Greenbaum and Taylor, Wall and Hull). We might, as Sidney Greenbaum and John Taylor do, attempt to enforce agreement as to what does and doesn't count as an error, joining their call for increased training so that teachers will "be capable of identifying and correctly labeling errors for themselves" (174), assuming, as they do, that "[i]t is reasonable to expect that teachers should be able to identify and correct errors that are relevant to their discipline" (169). But this assumption, with all due respect for the English profession, is not reasonable but rather a plea for a utopian condition. Susan Wall and Glynda Hull, though they too call for the development of what sounds like a kind of utopian "common language" for teachers and students to use to talk about error, also admit that, in the long meanwhile,

> Students must . . . understand that for particular teachers errors may have several different and interchangeable names; that different teachers may name the same kinds of errors differently; that certain jargon terms like "usage" have different meanings depending upon the teacher; that what teachers consider an error in writing may vary considerably; that a teacher's labels may be imprecise or even missing, so that they must be attentive to other cues such as boundary markings or questions to infer the kind of error the teacher perceives; that suggested revisions or comments like "wrong word" imply a version of the text that the teacher is constructing, not exactly the one they wrote or intended; and that even if all errors are identified with labels, some require consulting a rule or convention to be corrected while others involve revisions that are more negotiable. (286–87)

This is a tall order for students but, unlike the call for universal agreement on error, not, I would argue, an unreasonable one, provided teachers, particularly English teachers, participate in helping students achieve such an understanding.

IV: Teaching Editing as Negotiation

I have argued above that the most serious risk of any pedagogy designed to teach editing is that it may reinforce students' sense of themselves as powerless in their writing, for the powerless cannot negotiate. Precisely for this reason, I am not advocating that teachers simply offer students a new "presentation" of errors as "social," lecturing them on the historicity of specific notions of "correctness" in writing and mocking inconsistencies in style handbooks, especially if the effect of this would be to persuade students to dismiss the real significance of error, however construed, for writers and readers. To do so would simply reinforce students' sense of their position as powerless receivers of the wisdom of others, adding to their bewilderment and confusion in the face of different notions of error while failing to honor that confusion as an appropriate response to the confusing situation Wall and Hull describe. Rather than attempting to sell students a new theory of error, we need to find ways to engage them in negotiations with readers about error in their writing and in theorizing about error. Teaching the history of the negotiation of particular conventions as "correct" can have value only to the extent that it encourages students to take active roles in continuing such negotiations in their own writing. For it is only by doing so that their notational practice as writers will represent a "choice they make."

Such choices will not, of course, be made "freely," if by "freely" we mean divorced from issues of power and authority. Teachers, the academy, larger social institutions wield far more power than do individual students. It would be misleading to pretend to ourselves or to our students that this is not the case. I have been arguing, however, that it is equally misleading and damaging to pretend to ourselves or to our students that they lack any power. Indeed, the changes students make to their texts to correct errors can represent what Giddens terms the "instantiation" of students' power in action (91), in the context of negotiations with particular readers concerning meaning. For a basic writer to change an idiosyncratic spelling of a word to a socially sanctioned spelling or to "unblur" the syntax of her sentence at the request of a reader should not be seen as an instance of the power of the institution operating on the powerless but as the student's exercise of her power as a student and writer (see Isaac 81). Students do have the power to refuse to make such changes, to insist on idiosyncratic spellings and nonstandard syntactic patterns. That they seldom choose to do so signals not their lack of power but their use of it in a negotiating strategy by which they attempt as writers to communicate particular meanings to particular readers. Just as basic writing students *choose* enrollment (see Shaughnessy, *Errors* 3; D'Eloia, "Teaching Standard" 9), so, not very surprisingly, those students frequently choose to attempt to employ standard spellings, uses of punctuation, and syntactic patterns. As Giddens observes, "Every instance of the use of language is a potential modification of that language at the same time as it acts to reproduce it" (220). To deny students any attributes of agency in making such choices is to deny them any right or responsibility for such choices, and so to discourage their investment in their writing. We can acknowledge the play of hegemonic forces in constructing possible choices for students without denying the operation of agency in students' alignment with one or the other of those choices in their negotiations.[14]

How might we teach editing as such a process of negotiation? My suggestions fall into two categories: practices in conferences or small groups with individual students, and more general practices in writing assignments and class discussions. Hull advocates ideally using individual tutorials to teach editing because such tutorials enable teachers to tailor instruction to the specific problems an individual student has with error and editing and, unlike workbooks, to keep attention focused on the student's own writing ("Acts of Wonderment" 219–22). Class instruction, she argues, is most useful for addressing "those things that the majority of students don't do in their writing [but need to learn how to]," like using quotation marks, and for teaching general strategies for the detection and correction of mistakes, but not for calling attention to the particular mistakes which individual students make (222).

Yet class discussions can also be used to provide an important social context for the work conducted in individualized editing tutorials, so that such work would be perceived as individual negotiations between different ways to "read" the student's texts rather than as the elimination of "individual" problems, occasions for dealing with the individual student's failure to "get it right," "right" being what the teacher or group or peers or a particular handbook, as authority, says goes. In class discussions, we might pose some questions to students about the varying notions of "error" they have already learned. We can present students with the conflicting evidence on "correctness" provided by examples of printing from earlier and later times or by different style handbooks or by different genres, and ask them, in class discussions and perhaps in writing assignments, what they make of such conflicts and how they resolve them in their own practice as writers. Or we might ask them to consider how they would classify kinds of errors: what do they make, for example, of such annoyances as smeared ink, illegible handwriting, or putting the wrong date down? If these are "errors," how would they describe the relationship of these sorts of "errors" to things like misspellings, or missing or repeated words, or homonym confusion, or blurred sentence structure? Or missing deadlines? Or use of the first-person pronoun? In what sense would they say any of these constitute "errors"? How would they rank (and define) the seriousness or significance of such different types of errors as misspellings, blurred syntax, comma splices, omitted words? To whom? Under what conditions? (in notes to oneself? in a "speech text"? a letter home?) By what criteria? Such questions would present the issue of error as something about which they as writers must theorize and make choices, not something they need simply learn about and acquiesce to, though in their theorizing and in their writing they must also confront the theories, rankings, definitions of other readers (including teachers) as well. For such questions would put students in the position to negotiate and renegotiate the concept of "correctness," including, importantly, the concept of its negotiability. In a particular semester, teachers and students might well negotiate, as a class, the relative acceptability of particular types of errors for particular writings produced for that course, thus bringing out the degree to which errors are contextual—and ways to respond to them, e.g., agree that the teacher would circle all misspellings, or write in the correct spellings, or ignore misspellings completely, or adopt different markings at different stages of the course. (Rankings would of course vary not only in ordering but in the categories devised—for example, writing "hte" might be considered a far more serious error by a given class than writing "then" for "than" or writing "definately," and a failure to proofread at all could be considered more serious than either.) And such negotiations need not be exercises in humiliation for students confronting the greater power and authority of the teacher, either. Teachers can serve as mediators, offering informed guidance to what might well be acceptable outside the course, in different writings or in various contexts. And students invested in college are unlikely to desire, let alone attempt to bargain for, the ignoring of all errors. Making marking practices negotiable would have the added bonus of demystifying those practices, making their meanings explicit through the process of negotiation, and thus offering another example of how conventions of notation come to be conventions (in the sense of "agreements"). And it will render the meaning of those practices something which teachers and students alike must learn anew through the process of negotiation undergone in a particular course.

Individual conferences could provide the occasion for negotiations between the writer and the teacher/reader about specific writings. But if editing is to be taught as a matter of negotiation, of agreeing on specific meanings for given notations rather than being a matter of eliminating static from the transmission of meaning, then these conferences would have to involve questions of meaning, purpose, and relationship as much as they involve "code." Especially when students' writing seems to show clear problems of "form," as in garbled syntax, teachers will have to resist the temptation to define the problem as merely "formal," for in doing so, they risk changing the meaning the student intended. As Elizabeth Tricomi observes, simply asking writers of garbled sentences what they mean by them frequently elicits from the students an ungarbled version which clarifies the meaning (64). But, she warns, "Often I have thought I understood a garbled sentence, only to discover through conversation with its student-writer that I did not at all. If I had merely inserted my revised version, I would not have helped since my grammatically correct sentence would not have expressed the student's intended meaning" (64). Rather than teaching editing as a matter of dressing meaning up or eliminating static, conversations like the one Tricomi describes can teach editing as a process of negotiation between reader and writer, negotiation as to competing ways of making meaning of the same text. Here Hull's advice to teach editing using the student's own text has particular force, since it allows for the push and tug of negotiation between a writer and a reader about what to make of a given text, not unlike the negotiation that occurs between professional writers and editors about texts. Often enough, to be sure, that editing will result in "conformity" to certain conventions, to the reproduction of established relationships between reader and writer, because of the acknowledged currency of those conventions and the choice of the writer to align herself with the power of that currency. But sometimes, too, editing can involve resisting or at least contesting those conventions, manipulating conventions for what, for the moment, can be unconventional effects, as interviews with students about their breaks with convention will sometimes reveal. With each act of writing, students, like all writers, have the choice of reproducing or working to alter or oppose hegemonic writing practices (Raymond Williams, *Marxism* 112–13). A teacher (or a student reader) can offer his reading of a particular notation and argue for the currency of that reading (that a lack of notation leads to ambiguity or suggests a meaning that surprises or confuses him), but the writer can argue as well for her reading of that notation. The conversation Tricomi describes would ideally to my mind continue with the student and teacher analyzing the differences between the "garbled" and several possible "ungarbled" versions, noting the differences in meaning that result, attempting to account for the production of the different versions, and working out how to choose from among them.

How we structure those conferences will help to determine whether they become sites of negotiation or of domination and accommodation. Tricomi recommends that we ask students about the ambiguity which sentences create for us or ask simply what the student means by a particular sentence or passage, explaining what troubles us, or that we read aloud to the student those sentences that make us stumble (63–64). The value of such practices, it seems to me, lies in the relationship they establish between the student, the teacher, and the text. Students maintain authority over and responsibility for their notations; teachers adopt the roles of readers who want to understand but may read those notations differently. In my own experience, I have found it useful to foreground the difference between my reading of a student's text and her own by providing each of us a photocopy of the text. I read my copy aloud to the student as she reads silently, illustrating to the student my reading of her text and the difficulties which that reading leads me to have with it without denying her own reading. This practice also provides imme- diate and appropriate occasions for me to ask the sorts of questions Tricomi recommends. In conferences, I have asked students to type their papers into the computer from their handwritten copies as I look on. As they type, they frequently ask questions themselves about how they origi- nally notated their papers, change their notation as they go, and dis- cover ambiguities in the meaning of particular sentences or passages (frequently ones which gave me no trouble) and attempt to explain them to themselves and me simultaneously, trying revisions out on me with "Would it make better sense to say . . . ?" or "What do you think that means?" Putting them to work on their own texts by putting them in control of the computer keyboard positions them materially as in con- trol of and responsible for deciding what will be entered and how. My role, as the questions quoted above suggest, then becomes that of either the curious draft reader or mediator between their handwritten version and the version they are entering, raising questions that occur to me about differences I perceive between the two but without authority to alter the writing.

A similar sort of structuring might be adopted using peer groups com- prised of one student whose writing was under consideration, with the other group members responding as readers to that writing, each pro- vided with his or her own copy of the original. The argument against peer editing groups has been that basic writers are not competent edi- tors and so cannot provide appropriate advice to their peers. But this argument holds only if we see the purpose of such groups to be the production of a set of error-free papers. On the other hand, if teachers take as their aim teaching the dynamics of negotiation inherent in any editing, then peer groups can provide a valuable site for practice in such dynamics.[15] The point of such group meetings would be not to arrive at a consensus, with teacher as final arbiter.[16] Instead, disagreements among group members as to the "correctness" or appropriateness of particular forms, common enough in my experience, would provide occasions to investigate the negotiable and clearly variable acceptability of such forms. That a teacher's response to some of those forms might vary signifi- cantly from a group of student readers' responses could be used to high- light further how questions of different sorts of power and authority enter into the making of conventions. This does not, or should not, mean that a student writer would learn to deny the particular authority of student readers by submitting instead to the teacher's authority (or vice versa). But students can attend to how contexts and readers need to be taken into account, if not always submitted to, in choosing one form over another. A student's confrontation with differences between those forms which one or more of his peers will accept and/or a particular teacher finds acceptable, or between what different student readers take a particular form to mean, will prepare him for confronting and understanding differences between the responses of different teachers and other readers to his writing as one of the normal conditions of writing and reading, rather than as yet another proof that English is an alien, confusing world.

But structuring conferences and small group work in such ways, through such practices, must be part of a larger structuring of course design if these are to be sites for negotiation rather than a coy type of domination. It is sometimes recommended that editing be taught as a separate, final stage in the writing process, so that students may focus their attention primarily on the production of meaning, not blocked by concerns about conventions. But a pedagogy which views errors as themselves bearing meaning rather than interfering with its transmission cannot distinguish editing from composing. Though such a pedagogy might still ask students to defer attention to editing, it cannot distinguish between composing and encoding. All parts of the "composing process," including editing, must be taught as involving negotiation about meaning. Class discussions and writing assignments must reinforce students' sense of their position as negotiators of meaning construction in their writing at every stage.

Elaine Lees, calling the ability of literate readers to produce more than one reading of a text "heterotextuality," suggests that we may need to artificially reduce such heterotextuality for basic writers so that when editing, they can concentrate on constructing meanings appropriate for proofreading ("Proofreading" 227, 228). But I have been arguing that it is not such students' heterotextuality but their false sense that such heterotextuality is wrong that confuses them. Therefore, I would encourage class discussions and writing assignments which have students develop and reflect upon multiple ways of constructing meaning out of texts, including "academic" ways of reading in which those issues raised by what is called "proofreading" matter.

For example, we can give our students writing assignments in which distinctions between, say, direct or indirect quotations, or the notation of exact wording or restrictive versus nonrestrictive modifiers, can matter in the way they often do for academics, assignments which in all likelihood will encourage them to respond in "academic" ways to texts they have read, to attempt to establish "academic" relationships in their writing to the texts on which they comment and to their imagined audience and to reflect on such relationships.[17] Requiring students to respond in their own writings to other texts, ideally writing responses to the same text, allows class (or small group) discussion of their writing to focus on and attempt to account for the kinds of value of "academic" and other "textual orientations" resulting in the different responses of different students, or in succeeding responses of the same student given several assignments on the same text.[18] In such discussions, we can point to the negotiation of meaning and relationship in students' own notational practices, through analysis of the texts they produce and the relationship of those texts to the texts they have read. Such discussions can involve students in the practice of the kind of myopic—i.e., "close"—reading in which academics sometimes engage in order to show them the valuable kinds of meanings that such reading yields and the kinds of relationships between readers, writers, and texts which it establishes. And those meanings and relationships associated with "close" readings can and should be compared with the kinds of meanings and relationships associated with other kinds of reading which often compete for readers' attention—readings which, for example, take a writer's political identity as a crucial determinant of the significance of his writing ("John Berger is a Marxist, and so his arguments should be dismissed"), or which rely on the authority of a specific reader or a majority of readers to determine meaning ("As the review said, this book is about. . . ."; "As everyone has said, the writer means. . . ."), or which take a reading as a kind of springboard for the student to offer up commonplaces on a general topic ("This story shows that you shouldn't judge a book by its cover.") Though such readings may seem outrageous, they are entirely appropriate for certain purposes under certain conditions, just not (or not always) for purposes honored in classrooms. To engage students more directly with questions of "error," we can ask them to explore the relationships in meaning and authority between texts (ideally their own) which might be described as transcribing, summarizing, or interpreting a second text and how those differences play out in their own writing practice, so that while they are learning "controlled composition" they are also considering who and what is being controlled in such a practice, and to what purpose.

I'll use an assignment from David Bartholomae and Anthony Petrosky's anthology *Ways of Reading* to illustrate how teachers can position their students as writers negotiating different ways of reading a text. The assignment, which follows a reprint of Chapter Two of Richard Rodriguez's *Hunger of Memory*, "The Achievement of Desire," asks students to consider the relationship between Richard Rodriguez and Richard Hoggart (from whose book *The Uses of Literacy* Rodriguez draws the concept of the "scholarship boy" to make sense of his own experience) as it is suggested by Rodriguez's references to Hoggart's text (*Ways of Reading* 520–21). The question for students is in what ways Rodriguez's use of Hoggart in the writing of his essay resembles the use a "scholarship boy" might make of the sayings of his teacher. Is Rodriguez being "an imitative and unoriginal pupil" in relying as he does on Hoggart?

I like the way this assignment first of all engages students in exploring how writers can establish relationships differing in authority by how they incorporate the texts of others into their own. The appropriateness of direct quotations, indirect quotations, and terms is explored not in terms of "right/wrong" but in terms of kinds of textual authority. In analyzing Rodriguez's use of Hoggart, students discover how a writer negotiates—in the sense of both navigating and bargaining—the authority he grants to another and that which he transfers to or assumes himself. That analysis itself involves students in the kind of "close" reading of texts which I encourage for the kind of authority it allows them to establish for themselves as writers. Discussion of students' written responses can focus on the students' own negotiation of such authority: using the term and concept of the "scholarship boy" which they have taken second-hand from Rodriguez, how do they establish their own authority on the relationship between Rodriguez and Hoggart? The challenge of the assignment for students lies precisely in how they can position themselves as authorities in relationship to not one but two prior texts. It is that challenge which makes questions about the appropriateness of such "mechanics" as quotation marks, quotations of quotations, even the "exactness" of transcriptions, seem anything but mechanical. Indeed, such questions address issues subtler than, but also co-extensive with, such "larger" rhetorical concerns as the construction and interplay of voice, audience, and representation of subject matter which students presumably also have been addressing in their writing practice.

And negotiating. When I asked students in a basic writing class who had just read Rodriguez's *Hunger of Memory* to write an essay in which they tried to make sense of Rodriguez's statement that "education is a long, unglamorous, even demeaning process—a nurturing never natural to the person one was before one entered a classroom" (*Hunger of Memory* 68), and reminded them to "use references to specific incidents and statements Rodriguez makes throughout his book to help us understand what leads you to interpret his book and the quoted passage as you do," a student wrote as part of his response:

> After reading Rodriguez's autobiography, I too get the feeling of disappointment, a feeling of disrespect towards his education and what it has done to him. I think that his education has separated him from his past. When he first started school, he would shy away from learning experiences and interacting with other kids. His bond with his mother and father was extremely close (Aria). His Hispanic culture was all that he knew and what he really loved. The outside world, that of the gringos, was far away, distant and unfriendly. *I have nothing to back up my thoughts of it being unfriendly; it is just the feeling I got when I read the book* [my emphasis]. His Spanish made him feel at home, comfortable, and most of all intimate with his family. On page 18, he says, "Family language: my family's sounds. The voices insisting: You belong here, we are family members. Related. Special to one another. Listen!"

What strikes me about this passage is that the student demonstrates not only his awareness that some readers would demand something to "back up" the feeling he has (and his ability to offer kinds of "back up") but also his own unwillingness to deny responses not "authorized" by such practices. In stating that he has no "back up" but still feels the way he does, he is in effect negotiating with readers, explaining the conditions under which he's arrived at his response and under which they will have to consider its validity. He has moved from perceiving his role as a writer being a person trapped in a set of arbitrary but unquestionable rules to that of someone making deals, negotiating with readers about what he thinks they might want, what he's willing to give, and what he's looking for in return.

For students to imagine the kind of relationship between reader and writer in which such "mechanical" notational practices as quotations matter in more than "pedantic" ways is of course difficult. For them to imagine that they can participate in such a relationship is daring. For them to attempt to establish and alter such relationships through their writing is both. But we can encourage our students to make such attempts by teaching all aspects of writing, including editing, as negotiations in which they can play a role and in which they have a stake.

7 Professing Multiculturalism: The Politics of Style in the Contact Zone

Min-Zhan Lu

In her 1991 essay "Arts of the Contact Zone," Mary Louise Pratt points out that while colleges and universities have increasingly deployed a rhetoric of diversity in response to the insistence of nonmainstream groups for fuller participation, the "import" of "multiculturalism" remains "up for grabs across the ideological spectrum" (39). I begin with Pratt's reminder because I want to call attention to the images of "grabbing" and "import." These depict "multiculturalism" as a construct whose "import"—meanings, implications, and consequences—is available only to those willing to expend the energy to "grab" it: to search, envision, grasp, articulate, and enact it. And these images conjure up the act of importing—of bringing in—perspectives and methods formerly excluded by dominant institutions. I want to articulate one "import" of multiculturalism here by exploring the question of how to conceive and practice teaching methods which invite a multicultural approach to style, particularly those styles of student writing which appear to be ridden with "errors." And I situate this question in the context of English Studies, a discipline which, on the one hand, has often proclaimed its concern to profess multiculturalism but, on the other hand, has done little to combat the ghettoization of two of its own cultures, namely composition teaching and student writing.

My inquiry is motivated by two concerns which I believe I share with a significant number of composition teachers. The first results from a sense of division between the ways in which many of us approach style in theory and in our teaching practice. I have in mind teachers who are aligned in theory with a view of composition which contests the separation of form and meaning and which also argues against a conception of "academic discourse" as discrete, fixed, and unified. This alignment, while generating a critical perspective toward traditional methods of teaching style through drills in "correct usage," does not always result in any immediate revision of such methods in classroom practice. Some of us tend to resolve this gap between theory and practice in one of two ways: (1) we set aside a few weeks to teach "usage" or "copyediting" in the traditional way while spending the rest of the term helping students to revise their work on a more conceptual level; or, (2) we send students who have "problems" with "usage" to the writing workshop. Such "resolutions" often leave the teacher frustrated. Because she recognizes the burden on those at the fringe of having to "prove" themselves to those at the center by meeting the standards set by the latter, she cannot but take seriously students' anxiety to master "correct" usage. Nevertheless, she is aware that instead of helping them to overcome such an anxiety, her teaching strategies risk increasing it, as they may reinforce students' sense of the discrepancy between their inability to produce "error-free" prose and their ability to come up with "good ideas," and they may confirm these students' impression that only those who make "errors" need to worry about issues of "usage" and "editing." My second concern has to do with a division many of us feel between our role as composition teachers and the role we play as students, teachers, or scholars in other, supposedly more central areas of English Studies. As our interest in composition teaching, theory, and research evolves, we are increasingly interested in contesting the second-class status of work in composition. At the same time, we are often all too aware that we ourselves are guilty of perpetuating the divisions between composition and other areas of English Studies by approaching the writings of "beginners" or "outsiders" in a manner different from the approach we take to the writings of "experts."

Two stories, both of which took place around the turn of this century, illustrate part of the historical power of that kind of division. The first story comes from Gertrude Stein's *The Autobiography of Alice B. Toklas*. According to Stein, right after she had made arrangements to have her book *Three Lives* printed by Grafton Press of New York, "a very nice American young man" was sent by the press to Paris to check on her:

> You see, [the young man] said slightly hesitant, the director of the Grafton Press is under the impression that perhaps your knowledge of english. But I am an american, said Gertrude Stein indignantly. Yes yes I understand that perfectly now, he said, but perhaps you have not had much experience in writing. I suppose, said [Stein] laughing, you were under the impression that I was imperfectly educated. He blushed, why no, he said, but you might not have had much experience in writing. Oh yes, she said, oh yes. . . . and you might as well tell [the director] . . . that everything that is written in the manuscript is written with the intention of its being so written and all he has to do is to print it and I will take the responsibility. The young man bowed himself out. (68)

This exchange between an indignant Stein and an embarrassed "young man" reveals some of the criteria used by "educated America" when dealing with an idiosyncratic style. These criteria are: (a) the writer's "knowledge of English," which is seen as somehow dependent on whether she is a native speaker, and (b) the writer's "experience in writing," which is seen as related to whether she has been "[im]perfectly educated." Stein, an "American" bearing certification of a "perfect" education from Radcliffe and Johns Hopkins Medical School, knew she had the authority to maintain that everything in her manuscript was "written with the intention of its being so written." Stein's indignation and the embarrassment she elicited from the "young man" suggest that in the early 1900s, ethnic and educational backgrounds were two common denominators for determining whether style represented self-conscious and innovative experimentation or blundering "errors."

The second story took place a few years prior to the Stein event, when the style of another writer, Theodore Dreiser, was also questioned by a publisher to whom he had submitted his first novel, *Sister Carrie*. The rejection letter from Harper faults Dreiser for his "uneven" style which, according to the editors, was "disfigured by colloquialisms" (*Sister Carrie* 519). Existing manuscripts of the book's revision indicate that Dreiser did not defend his style with the kind of authority Stein exhibited. Instead he sought editorial help from his wife Jug and friend Henry because he deemed both to have been better educated than himself. There is evidence in the revised manuscript that Dreiser adopted nearly all of Jug's corrections of grammar and Henry's rewording of his Germanic rhythms and cumulative sentence structures (*Sister Carrie* 580–81). Read in the context of Stein's story, Dreiser's willingness to have all aspects of his style "corrected" might be attributed to his acute awareness of the criteria used by "educated America" when dealing with the writing of the son of an impoverished German immigrant with extremely sporadic formal education. The early reception of *Sister Carrie* proves the validity of Dreiser's concern, as even its defenders attributed its "crude" style to his ethnic background and lack of formal education.[1]

Almost a century after these events, more and more English courses are now informed by a view of language as a site of struggle among conflicting discourses with unequal sociopolitical power. Students in these courses are beginning to approach the style of what they call "real" writers like Stein and Dreiser very differently. Interest in multiculturalism has also shifted the attention of some teachers to writers' success at what Bakhtin calls "dialogically coordinating" a varied and profound "heteroglossia" (295–96). Analysis of style in these classrooms often centers on the politics of the writer's stylistic decisions: (a) mapping the "heteroglossia" on the internal and external scenes of writing, (b) attending to the writer's effort to look at one discourse through the eyes of another, and (c) considering the writer's willingness to resist the centripetal forces of "official" discourses. Viewed from this multicultural perspective on style, the writings of both Dreiser and Stein could be considered in terms of the efforts of each to dialogically coordinate the profound heteroglossia within and outside official "educated" discourses. For readers adopting this perspective, neither Dreiser's ethnic background nor his "imperfect" educational background would be used to dismiss his "uneven" style solely as evidence of "error"—that is, to conclude that his style merely reflects his lack of knowledge or experience in writing. In fact, given the frequency with which writings from what Gloria Anzaldúa has called the "borderlands" are being currently assigned in some English courses and the praise this type of writing receives for its hybridization of "official" discourses, Dreiser's readiness to yield to the authority of the "better educated" now appears "conservative"—indicating a passive stance toward the hegemony of ethnocentrism and linguistic imperialism. In fact, the publication of the Pennsylvania edition of *Sister Carrie* in 1987 indicates that such a critical view privileging resistance was in operation when the editors decided to delete many of the changes made by the "better educated" Jug and Henry in the hope of preserving the "power and forcefulness" of Dreiser's original prose (*Sister Carrie* 581).

However, Dreiser's reaction still haunts me, especially when I move from teaching students to analyze the idiosyncratic style of "real" writers to helping them to work on their own styles. In my "literature" courses for junior- or senior-level college students or "writing" courses for first-year students, students learn to talk with considerable eloquence about the politics of stylistic decisions made by "real" writers, especially those writing from the borderlands by choice and/or necessity. Most of the readings I assign for these classes call attention to writers' need and right to contest the unifying force of hegemonic discourses, and thus make Dreiser's submission to the authority of the "better" educated appear dated and passive. Yet the meaning of Dreiser's submissiveness changes for me and most of my students as soon as we move to work on the style of a student writer, especially when we tinker with what we call the writer's "discursive voice": that is, when dealing with deviations in diction, tone, voice, structure and so on (which we loosely call the "rhetorical register" of the writer's voice), or with punctuation, syntax, sentence structure and so on (which we refer to as the "grammatical register" of the writer's voice). On those occasions, how to sound "right" suddenly becomes a "real" concern for my students: pervasive, immediate, and difficult for me to dismiss. My students' apparent anxiety to reproduce the conventions of "educated" English poses a challenge for my teaching and research. Why is it that in spite of our developing ability to acknowledge the political need and right of "real" writers to experiment with "style," we continue to cling to the belief that such a need and right does not belong to "student writers"? Another way of putting the question would be, why do we assume—as Dreiser did—that until one can prove one's ability to produce "error-free" prose, one has not earned the right to innovative "style"?

Again, I believe Dreiser's account of his own educational experience might shed some light on the question. In *Dawn*, Dreiser writes about his opportunity to attend the University of Indiana, Bloomington, for two short terms. A former teacher made arrangements to exempt Dreiser from the preliminary examinations because, Dreiser points out, these exams would have quickly "debarred" him (342). Life as what we might today call an open admissions student at Indiana made Dreiser feel "reduced." He "grieved" at his "inability to grasp . . . such a commonplace as grammar" (378). Even though he knew he was able to apprehend many things and to demonstrate his apprehensions "quite satisfactorily" to himself, he found the curriculum "oppressive," leaving him "mute" with "a feeling of inadequacy" (425). The events surrounding the efforts of Dreiser and Stein to publish their first books indicate that the common approach of the editors, publishers, and critics to their idiosyncratic styles was not coincidental. Dreiser's experience at Indiana, his willingness to have his "uneven" style "corrected," and Stein's quick rebuttal to the "young man" all point to the institutional source of this approach. A common view of "style" as belonging only to those who are beyond "error," and a certain type of college curriculum treating matters of grammar or usage as the prerequisites to higher education, seem mutually reinforcing. It is this belief that pushes students identified as having "problems" to meet such "prerequisites" and assigns teachers trained to deal with such "problems" to the periphery or borderlands of higher education.

Dreiser's memories of Indiana seem symptomatic of the feelings of a significant number of college students I encounter. I have in mind particularly students who seem quick to admit that they are "not good" at writing because they have been identified at some point in their education as needing special—remedial, laboratory, or intensive—instruction in the "basics." Like Dreiser, they are frustrated at their inability to grasp "grammar" because they have been encouraged to view it as "such a commonplace"—something everyone who aspires to become anyone ought to be able to master. And they feel muted and reduced by the curriculum because it does not seem to recognize that they are quite able to grasp subjects other than "grammar" and demonstrate their understanding of such subjects satisfactorily to themselves, if perhaps not in writing to others. It seems to me that one way of helping students to deal with this frustration would be to connect their "difficulties" with the refusal of "real" writers to reproduce the hegemonic conventions of written English. And it seems to me that this will not take place until teachers like myself contest the distinction between "real" and "student" writers and stop treating the idiosyncratic style of the not-yet "perfectly educated" solely in terms of "error." One form of contestation could be to apply to student writing the same multicultural approach we have been promoting when analyzing the work of "real" writers. Susan Miller has argued in *Textual Carnivals* that the tendency to treat student writers as "emerging, or as failed, but never as actually responsible 'authors'" has served to maintain the low status of composition studies in its relations to those "outside it, and its self-images and ways of working out its new professionalization" (196, 195). An approach to student writing that treats students as real writers would undo such binaries and thus assert the right and ability of writing teachers and students to fully participate in a truly "multi-cultural" curriculum.

My aim here is to discuss a teaching method formulated out of my attempt to apply a multicultural approach to student writing. The classroom I envision intersects with various models of teaching writing as "repositioning" or models that treat the writing classroom as a "borderland."[2] One central aspect of this type of "border pedagogy" is its concern to treat meaning as resulting from the writer's effort to negotiate a position in response to multiple and often conflicting forces, discursive as well as social and historical. Border pedagogy contests a before/after frame of mind, the belief that until a writer has proven her competency in English—i.e., learned to produce "error-free" prose—she has not earned the right to experiment with critical thinking or innovative style. It critiques the ethnocentric cast to such a belief, viewing it as speaking more to the anxiety of those in power to control who has the right to tamper with something called "our" culture than to some kind of "essence" in student writing.[3] To various degrees, border pedagogies present the classroom as a potential "contact zone." Border pedagogies contest an either/or approach to the individual's relationship with conflicting cultures. Instead, they foreground students' needs, rights, and abilities to approximate, negotiate, and revise "official" cultural rules.

In arguing for a multicultural approach to styles traditionally displaced to the realm of "error," I align my teaching with a tradition in "error" analysis which views even "error-ridden" student writings as texts relevant to critical approaches available to English Studies. I have in mind here research using theories of the production of meaning to conceptualize the action of a student/writer in the process of composing an idiosyncratic style and reception theories to map the action of a teacher or student reader in the process of speculating on the causes and revisions of nonconventional style(s).[4] I am particularly interested in explicitly foregrounding the category of "resistance" and "change" when helping students to conceptualize the processes of producing and interpreting an idiosyncratic style in students' own writings. In the classroom I envision, the notion of "intention" is presented as the decision of a writer who understands not only the "central role of human agency" but also that such agency is often "enacted under circumstances not of one's choosing" (West 31). I define the writer's attempt to "reproduce" the norms of academic discourses as necessarily involving the re-production—approximating, negotiating, and revising—of these norms. And I do so by asking students to explore the full range of choices and options, including those excluded by the conventions of academic discourses.

These aspects in the classroom I envision inevitably distance it from classrooms influenced by one belief prevalent in ESL courses or courses in "Basic Writing": namely, that a monolingual environment is the most conducive to the learning of "beginners" or "outsiders." This belief overlooks the dialogical nature of students' "inner voices" as well as the multicultural context of students' lives. The classroom I envision also differs from approaches to students' ambivalence toward the effects of education exemplified by Mina Shaughnessy's *Errors and Expectations.* Shaughnessy convincingly shows the relevance to error analysis of a range of feelings common to students likely to be identified as basic writers: their anxiety to "sound academic" and to self-consciously emulate the formal style (194), their low self-esteem as learners and writers, and their sense of ambivalence toward academic discourse. But as I have argued in "Conflict and Struggle," Shaughnessy's goal in acknowledging students' ambivalence is only to help them dissolve it (904–6). Because this ambivalence arises from sources well beyond the classroom— coming from the unequal power relationships pervading the history, culture, and society my students live in—not all students can or even want to get rid of all types of ambivalence. On the contrary, the experiences of writers like Gloria Anzaldúa, bell hooks, and Mike Rose suggest that, appropriately mobilized, a sense of ambivalence might be put to constructive uses in writing.

At the same time, the sort of resistance I want to promote differs from the kind underlying romantic celebrations of students' "right to their own language," celebrations that operate on a view of students as "free agents." Unlike such celebrations, resistance in border pedagogy rejects both the notion of social and historical determinism that would enforce a particular style as the inevitable, only possible style for students to pursue, on the one hand, and, on the other, the notion of the free will of a freely choosing subject. It instead encourages student writers to challenge the either/or positions to conflicting cultures promoted by the hegemonic in the current-day United States and it insists, in the words of Cornel West, that "openness to others—including the mainstream—does not entail wholesale co-optation, and group autonomy is not group insularity" (33).

To foreground the concepts of "resistance" and "change" when analyzing the styles of a student or "real" writer, I ask students to read deviations from the official codes of academic discourses not only in relation to the writer's knowledge of these codes but also in terms of her efforts to negotiate and modify them. Aside from increasing the student's knowledge of and experience in reproducing these official forms, I am most interested in doing three things: (1) enabling students to hear discursive voices which conflict with and struggle against the voices of academic authority; (2) urging them to negotiate a position in response to these colliding voices; and (3) asking them to consider their choice of position in the context of the sociopolitical power relationships within and among diverse discourses and in the context of their personal life, history, culture, and society.

Because of the tendency in English Studies to ghettoize the culture of composition, I will use some student writing produced in writing courses for first-year students to illustrate how I would actually go about teaching a multicultural approach to style. And I am going to focus on features of writing styles which are commonly displaced to the realm of "error" and thus viewed as peripheral to college English teaching. In using these rather than other types of examples, I hope to illustrate as well the need to view composition as a site which might inform as well as be informed by our effort to profess multiculturalism in other, supposedly more "advanced" and "central" areas of English Studies. Bartholomae has recently reminded us that there is no need "to import 'multiple cultures' [into the classroom, via anthologies]. They are there, in the classroom, once the institution becomes willing to pay that kind of attention to student writing" ("Tidy House" 14–15). Such attention, he explains, could produce composition courses in multiculturalism "that worked with the various cultures represented in the practice of its students" ("Tidy House" 14). My second reason for using these examples is related to the ways in which conflict and struggle—important aspects of life in the contact zone—have been perceived by teachers specializing in error analysis. These teachers tend to hear arguments foregrounding conflict and struggle in the classroom as sloganeering "students' right to their own language" in order to eliminate attention to error, or as evidence of a "PC" attack on the "back to basics" movement (see, for example, Traub). The examples I use here, I hope, will demonstrate a way of teaching which *neither* overlooks the students' potential lack of knowledge and experience in reproducing the dominant codes of academic discourses *nor* dismisses the writer's potential social, political, and linguistic interest in modifying these codes, with emphasis on the word "potential."

When teaching first-year writing classes, I usually introduce the multicultural approach to student writing style around the mid-point of the term, when I feel that students are beginning to apply to their actual practices a view of writing as a process of re-seeing. To present the writer's experimentation with style (including what is generally called "copyediting" or the "correction of error") as an integral part of the revision process, I look for sample student writings with two characteristics. First, I am interested in writings with the kinds of "error" a majority of the class would feel they can easily "spot" and "fix." This type of writing allows me to acknowledge some potential causes of nonconventional styles and effective methods of revising them which are more widely disseminated in traditional writing classrooms and workshops and more familiar to most students. Second, I look for styles which are also more conducive to my attempt to help the writer to negotiate a new position in relation to the colliding voices active in the scenes of writing.[5]

Following is a handout I have used when teaching first-year composition classes. The two segments on the handout are from the papers one student wrote in response to two assignments, one asking her to discuss an essay, "From a Native Daughter," by Haunani-Kay Trask, and another asking her to comment on the kind of "critical thinking" defined in the "Introduction" to an anthology called *Rereading America*. For the convenience of discussion in this essay, I have added emphasis to the handout:

> Segment One:
>
> As a Hawaiian native historian, Trask *can able to* argue for her people. As a Hawaiian native, she was exposed to two totally different viewpoints about her people. She was brought up in Hawaii. During this time, she heard the stories about her people from her parents. Later on she was send to America mainland to pursue higher education, in which she learnt a different stories about her people. Therefore, she understood that the interpretation of land was different

between the "haole" and the native. To prove that the "haole" were wrong, she went back to Hawaii and work on the land with other native, so she *can* feel the strong bond with land her people have which the "haole" *could* not feel. The "haole" historians never bother to do so as they were more interested in looking for written evidence. That was why Trask, as a native Hawaiian historian, argued that these "haole" historians were being ignorant and ethnocentric. That is also why Trask suggested the "haole" historians learn the native tongue.

***

Segment Two:

Elements like perceiving things from different perspective, finding and validating each alternative solutions, questioning the unknown and breaking the nutshell of cultural norms are important for developing the ability of "critical thinking." . . .

Most of the new universities' students are facing new challenges like staying away from family, peer pressure, culture shock, heavy college work etc. I *can* say that these are the "obstacles" to success. If a student *can able to* approach each situation with different perspectives than the one he brought from high school, I *may* conclude that this particular student has climbed his first step to become a "critical thinker." . . .

However, there is one particular obstacle that is really difficult for almost everyone to overcome, that is the cultural rules. From the textbook, I found that cultural rules are deep rooted in our mind and cause us to view things from our respective cultural viewpoint. Even though cultural values lead the way of life of a particular group of people, they blind us as well. I relate to this because I truly believe that the cultural rules of my country, Malaysia, make my life here difficult. In order to achieve a "critical mind," one should try to break from his own cultural rules.

***

"can," verb:
1. to be able to; have the ability, power, or skill to. 2. to know how to. 3. to have the power or means to. 4. to have the right or qualifications to. 5. *may; have permission to.* (*The Random House Dictionary*)

" able," adjective:
1. having necessary power, skill, resources, or qualifications; qualified: *able to lift a trunk;* . . . *able to vote.* (*The Random House Dictionary*)

When using this handout to initiate a multicultural reading/writing, I am most concerned to give students a sense of how to go about mapping a contact zone—using a piece of writing to generate diverse interpretations, each viewed as a socially constructed form of reading enacting discursive stances or voices endorsed by particular cultural sites, and revising that text in the context of that contact zone—enacting a process of re-writing in which each student negotiates with the diverse stances or voices the class has constructed during the discussion.

I usually begin by asking students what particularly about the two segments might be said to make the voice of the writer idiosyncratic. My students in both writing and literature classes have been fairly quick in tracing it to the "can able to" structure in the two segments. Then I ask the class to speculate on potential causes of that idiosyncrasy. Students' responses to this question usually go something like this: here is a "foreign" speaker, a student from Malaysia, trying to use the English idiom "to be able to" and ending up with an "error." So we usually talk a little bit about the difference in grammatical function between the verb "can" and the verb "to be" in relation to the adjective "able." And I describe the writer's own initial interpretation of the cause of this "error": her native language is Chinese. With the help of a workshop tutor, she had realized that the Chinese translation for both "can" and "be able to" is the same. When using the expression "be able to," she would be thinking in Chinese. As a result, she often ended up writing "can able to." I would refer to her own initial reading because I am interested in complicating but not denying the relationship between style and the writer's knowledge of and experience with the conventions of written English. So I try to acknowledge first that exposure to and practice in reproducing the "be able to" structure could be one of the ways to revise these segments.

I then go on to complicate this approach by also calling attention to the relationship between form and meaning. What might be the difference in meaning between "can," "be able to," and "can able to"? Most of the students I have encountered tend to see "can" as interchangeable with "be able to." To them, "can able to" appears redundant, like a double negative. To problematize this reading, I usually call attention to the two dictionary entries included in the handout, especially to definition 5 under "can." Definition 5 opens up a new reading by presenting the word "can" as having one more meaning than "to be able to." Rather than approaching the issue of ability from the perspective of what an individual possesses, definition 5 approaches it from the perspective of the external forces *permitting* something, as in the verb "may."

Most native English speakers among my students tend to argue that in actual usage, only grandmas and schoolteachers make the distinction between "can" and "may." *Everyone* uses "can" and "be able to" interchangeably nowadays. In response, I tell them the writer's position on the issue. She was aware of the distinction—she was the one who first called my attention to definition 5. At this point, a "contact zone" would begin to take shape with three conflicting positions on the meanings of "can" and "able to": the position of a speaker of idiomatic English, the position of the dictionary, and the position of a "foreign" student writer. Since the "foreign" student writer is here being cast as that of someone lacking knowledge and expertise in formal and idiomatic English and thus the least powerful of the three, I am most interested in furthering the students' existing construction of that position so it is not so easily silenced.

To that end, I pose the question of whether, read in the context of the two segments in the handout, one might argue that the "can" in the two "can able to" structures does not take on the same meaning as the other uses of "can" in the rest of the segments. This line of inquiry usually leads us to compare the meaning of the "can" in the first sentence in Segment One to the two "can's" in the seventh sentence and to the meaning of the "can" in the "can able to" in Segment Two as well as the "can" in the previous sentence or the "may" in the second half of the same sentence. My aim here is to get students to re-construct the voice of the writer by focusing on the various uses of the word "can" in the two segments. When exploring the question, I also try to direct attention to the passive voice (Trask was "brought up in Hawaii" and "send to America mainland to pursue higher education") in the sentences following the statement "Trask can able to argue for her people." I explore with the class how and why this passive voice might be read as indicating that the student writer is approaching Trask's ability from the perspective of the external circumstances of Trask's life—using "can" in the sense of her having the "permission to" become a native Hawaiian historian—as well as from the perspective of her having the qualifications to argue as an historian. The two uses of "can" in sentence seven, however, present Trask's and the "haole" historians' (in)ability to "feel" the Hawaiian's bond with the land as more related to a person's will and attitude rather than to whether each "may"—has the permission to— learn the Hawaiian language or work with the people. ("The 'haole' historians never bother to do so.") Similarly, in the second segment, the "can" in "a student can able to adopt different perspectives," when read in the context of the writer's discussion of the difficulties for "everyone to overcome" the "obstacle" of cultural rules and of her own experience of that difficulty, again foregrounds the role of external conditions and their effect on one's ability to do something. In that sense, this "can" is closer in meaning to the "may" in "I may conclude," a conclusion presented as depending more on the action of someone else than on the ability of the "I" drawing the conclusion. At the same time, this "can" is different from the "can" in the "I can say . . ." since the latter seems to depend on the ability of the speaker to name the situations as "obstacles" rather than on whether or not the speaker has permission to so name them.

In getting the class to enact a "close reading" of the two segments, I aim to shift attention to the relationship between a discursive form, "can able to," and the particular meanings it might be said to create in particular contexts. As a result, a new question often surfaces: What kind of approach to "ability" is enacted by a speaker of idiomatic English who sees "can" and "be able to" as completely interchangeable in meaning? In exploring this question, students have mentioned popular sayings such as "if there is a will, there is a way"; TV shows such as *Mr. Rogers' Neighborhood* which teach viewers to believe "everyone is special," possessing unique qualities; and various discourses promoting the power of positive thinking. Students begin to perceive the way in which a common treatment of "can" and "to be able to" as interchangeable in meaning might be seen as contributing to a popular American attitude toward the transcendental power of the individual. Once we locate these conflicting approaches to the notion of ability, it becomes clear that the revision or "correction" of the "can able to" in these two segments can no longer take place simply at the level of linguistic form. It must also involve a writer's negotiating a position in relation to value systems with unequal social power in the United States: one "popular" and the others "alien," "dated," or "formal" but critical. Once this structural "error" is contextualized in conflicting attitudes toward a belief in the transcendental power of the individual, the issue can no longer be merely one's knowledge of or respect for the authorities of a dictionary English versus colloquial English, or one's competency in a particular language, but also one's alignment with competing discursive positions.

At this point, we will have mapped a contact zone with a range of choices and options both among linguistic forms and discursive alignments. As we move on to the question of how each of us might revise these two segments, I would make sure that each student further enlarges this contact zone by taking into consideration the specific conditions of her or his life. I would have already introduced my definition of the "conditions of life" in previous assignments and class discussions, a definition that includes a whole range of discursive sites, including that of race, ethnicity, gender, sex, economic class, education, religion, region, recreation, and work. I also encourage each student to think about "life" in terms of the life she has lived in the past, is living in the present, and envisions for the future. Furthermore, I stress that decisions on how to revise should also be related to each student's interpretation(s) of the two texts discussed in the segments. To summarize, the contact zone in which the revision takes place would encompass the collision of at least the following voices: the voice of a "foreign" student writer (as constructed by the class at the beginning of the discussion), the voice(s) of the writer of the two segments (as constructed by the class discussion resulting from a "close reading" of the various uses of "can"), the voice of a dictionary, of a speaker of idiomatic English, the voices important to the specific conditions of each student's life, the voice of a teacher, and the voice emerging from each student's interpretation of the two texts discussed in the two segments.

Since decisions on how to revise the "can able to" structure depend on who is present, the particular ways in which the discussion unfolds, and who is doing the revision, such decisions vary from class to class and student to student. To illustrate the unpredictability of the outcome, let me use two decisions made in two different courses, one by the original writer of the two segments and one by another student whose native language is also Chinese. Like all other students in my class, during the process of a "close reading" of the uses of "can" in these two segments, the original writer encountered a construction of her "voices" which she may not have fully considered before the discussion. Therefore, when revising the two segments, she too had to negotiate with these forms of reading and constructions of voices. Upon reflecting on the conditions of her life, she reviewed the attitude toward "ability" promoted in the particular neighborhood in Malaysia where she grew up. In view of that as well as of her own experience as a "daughter" (especially her difficulties persuading her parents to let her rather than only the "sons" go abroad for college), her current "difficulty" in adjusting to the kind of "critical thinking" promoted in my classroom (which she felt was the direct opposite of what she was told to do in her schooling back home), and her admiration of Trask's courage to "argue for her people," the writer decided to foreground the relationship between individual ability and the conditions in which that ability "may" be realized. With the help of her classmates, she came up with several options. One was to add an "if" clause to a sentence using "be able to." Another was to change "can able to" to "may be able to." One student suggested that she use "can able to" and then tag a sentence to explain her reasoning—her view of "ability." Among the suggestions, the writer picked "may be able to" because, as she put it, it was clearly "grammatically correct" and "says what I want to say." As the term progressed, one of the students in the class used "can able to" playfully in a class discussion, and others caught on. It became a newly coined phrase we shared throughout the term.

However, a Vietnamese American student whose home language is also Chinese took a very different stance toward the hegemonic attitude toward "ability" and for a quite different reason from what led some of my American-born students to identify with the voice of an idiomatic speaker. Using examples from his immigrant community, he argued for the importance of believing in the capacity of the individual. He pointed out that the emphasis on external conditions had made some people in his community fatalistic and afraid to take up the responsibility to make changes. According to him, there is a saying in classic Chinese similar to "if there is a will, there is a way." His parents used it repeatedly when lecturing him. So he was all for using "can" and "be able to" interchangeably to foreground the power of the individual. He hoped more people in his community would adopt this outlook. Accordingly, his revision changed "can able to" to "be able to." At the same time, he also changed the passive voice in the sentences referring to Trask's childhood and education in the first segment to the active voice, arguing that there is enough basis in the essays to sustain that reading.

Given the frequency with which students opt for the voices of academic authority, I used to wonder if this kind of teaching is driven more by my view of language as a site of struggle than by the needs of students eager to internalize and reproduce the conventions of academic discourse. My conclusion is: No, this process of negotiation is particularly meaningful for students anxious to master the codes of academic discourse, especially because their discursive practices are most likely to have to take place in the kind of postmodern capitalist world critics such as Fredric Jameson have characterized. Although the product, their decision to reproduce the code, might remain the same whether it is made with or without a process of negotiation, the activities leading to that decision, and thus its significance, are completely different. Without the negotiation, their choice would be resulting from an attempt to passively absorb and automatically reproduce a predetermined form. In such cases, the student would perceive different discourses, to borrow from Bakhtin, as belonging to different, fixed, and indisputable "chambers" in her consciousness and in society. And she would evaluate her progress by the automatism with which she was able to move in and out of these "chambers." If and when this student experienced some difficulty mastering a particular code, she would view it as a sign of her failure as a learner and writer.

On the other hand, if the student's decision to reproduce a code results from a process of negotiation, then she would have examined the conflict between the codes of Standard English and other discourses. And she would have deliberated not only on the social power of these colliding discourses but also on who she was, is, and aspires to be when making this decision. If the occasion arises in the future when she experiences difficulty in reproducing a particular code, as it very likely will, her reaction would be much more positive and constructive. Aside from tracing it to her knowledge and experience, she would also contextualize her difficulty in the power struggle within and among cultures important to her life. To borrow from my Malaysian student, she would be thinking in terms of not only whether she is able to but also whether she "can able to" reproduce it. Furthermore, having participated in processes of negotiation in class, she would have some idea of how to go about coping with her difficulty.

Learning to work on style in the contact zone is also useful for those students interested in exploring ways of resisting the unifying force of "official" discourse. First, it can help students hear a range of choices and options beyond the confines of their immediate life. Second, negotiating as a group gives them the distance they need but might not have when dealing with their own writing in isolation. Therefore, devoting a few class periods to familiarizing students with this approach to style can be fruitful, especially if students are asked to theorize their action afterward by reflecting on its strengths and limitations. Once I feel that the students have a sense of how to go about enacting such a process, I encourage them to practice the method on their own, and I use conferencing and workshops to help individual students further that line of exploration.

Obviously, one of the challenges for such a teaching method is that one can only project but not predict a class discussion on the basis of the chosen sample. In fact, life in the contact zone is by definition dynamic, heterogeneous, and volatile. Bewilderment and suffering as well as revelation and exhilaration are experienced by everyone, teacher and students, at different moments. No one is excluded, no one is safe (Pratt, "Arts" 39). Therefore, learning to become comfortable in making blunders is central to this type of teaching. In fact, there is no better way to teach students the importance of negotiation than by allowing them the opportunity to watch a teacher work her way through a chancy and volatile dialogue. Seemingly simple markers such as skin color, native tongue, ethnic heritage or nationality can neither prescribe nor pre-script the range of voices likely to surface. How to voice and talk to rather than speaking for or about the voices of the "other" within and among cultures is thus not a question which can be resolved prior to or outside of the process of negotiation. Rather, it must remain a concern guiding our action as we take part in it.

At the same time, the teacher's willingness to enter a process of dynamic negotiation does not mean she cannot explore ahead of time the kind of voices she might want to introduce into the dialogue or the type of discursive sites in which she might want the student to situate the act of re-vision. Neither does it mean that she would not have to take it upon herself to urge and guide the student writer to engage in dialogue with the voices emerging from that site or to take a socially responsible position in relation to these conflicting voices. I'll use two more examples to illustrate how I would plan a tutorial with a student. The following are segments from a student's folder:

Segment One

Rodriguez father was a working man. From the passage it seems like his father had a very good paying job, else how could they afford to live in the neighborhood the did. Rodriguez also attended a catholic school. Since *this a private school* it takes a little bit of money to attend *these types schools.* So I feel his family was financially stable.

Segment Two

Education played a large part in Rodriguez life. Rodriguez couldn't get enough education. . . .

Rodriguez urge to learn so despertly he became a scholarship boy. Always looking for new things to read. He practically shut his parents off. . . . He would come home after school and just read all day.

Rodriguez wanted to be so much like his teachers. He thought if he read and took notes, memorized *the books major themes,* he would becme as smart as his teachers.

When reviewing this student's writing, I noticed the recurrence of several patterns, such as his way of indicating the possessive case and a tendency to drop the copulae, as illustrated by the parts I have highlighted in the two segments above. I would enter these segments (without the emphasis) on the computer screen to focus the tutorial with this student. Using these segments, I would plan to help him see copyediting as an integral part of the revision process and to revise these in a contact zone which I would help him construct by asking him to recall and then re-view what he is trying to say in the original. Because there are enough references in one of his papers to suggest that this writer is an African American who grew up speaking a version of English very different from the kind of written English he encountered at school, I would be concerned to familiarize this writer with the conventions of academic English. To that end, I would spend a part of the tutorial finding out his knowledge of the difference between the conventions of his home dialect and written English and the levels of identification he habitually enacts with these discourses when speaking and when writing both inside and outside college classrooms. In the process, I would hope to help him map out a contact zone that would include the voices of a dialect speaker as he constructs it when examining the discourse of home, the voices of a speaker of Standard English as I project it and as he depicts it, the voices of a writer of Standard English (as envisioned by him and by me), and the voices of the "I" of these two segments (as we construct it through re-reading the segments).

More specifically, as Bartholomae recommends, I would help him create an "oral reconstruction of the written text" by asking him to read the segments aloud ("Study" 266). I would call attention to the potential difference between the voice "reading for meaning," from "top down" ("Study" 263) and the voice of a reader/writer of Standard English, as enacted by me when reading the segments. If doing so suggests that his ways of handling the possessive case and the copulae might be related to "dialect interference," then we would spend some time talking about the difference in the use of copulae and structure of the possessive cases in the spoken languages he uses and in the written English I practice. And we would spend some time experimenting with ways of revising Segment One by negotiating with the forms we have located in these discourses.

But to complicate this reading of his style, I'd then turn his attention to the sentence in Segment Two: "*Rodriguez urge to learn so despertly* he became a scholarship boy." Mary Epes has suggested that students need to treat the process of "encoding" as completely different from the process of "composing" (31). However, I would choose to focus on this sentence precisely because revision of its "form," its "encoding," cannot be separated from its "content." I would first ask the writer to recall what he was trying to say when writing the sentence. I would type into the computer what he says so we might later come back to it. Then I would provide him with two sentences I came up with when trying to "translate" his sentence into the kind of English I use when writing:

> (1) Rodriguez's urge to learn was so desperate that he became a scholarship boy.

> (2) Rodriguez was urged to learn so desperately that he became a scholarship boy.

And I would ask him which of my interpretations of what he might be trying to say seemed more acceptable to him at this point, if either. Given what he wrote in his paper, which he pretty much summarized with the sentences I have included here, I suspect he would choose the first one. If so, we would use it to construct the voice of a writing teacher and explore how its structure and meaning were different from and/or intersected with the other voices we had mapped out so far. These would include the voice of the writer he has constructed when recalling his "intention" and the voices I would also have him construct with the question of how he might put it if he were saying or writing about the same thing to a family member, a peer in his neighborhood, or a fellow student close to him. And I'd urge him to experiment with different ways of revising the original text by taking different positions in relation to these voices.

Finally, I would also explain to him my reasons for coming up with the second sentence. One of the benefits of doing so is to familiarize him with the ways in which a reader like myself goes about "seeing" a sentence: the attention I give to the adverb form of the word "desperately," which led me to speculate that he may be using the word "urge" as a verb. This approach brings up the question of whether Rodriguez is the subject or the object of the "urge." This question, I would add, leads me to think that although in the context of his paper, neither possibility makes sense, in the context of Rodriguez's book, at least as I read it, the passive voice might actually make sense. So our discussion might turn to certain aspects of the book and his interpretations of these aspects, which he might not have considered so far in his writings. The purpose here would be to help him see experimentation with style as a way of generating meaning in a process of rereading and rewriting. Throughout the tutorial, I would also be focusing my energy on urging him to contest the boundaries set by the sentences I offered and by the versions he has come up with while also making sure that he does not lose sight of the politics of his decision in the context of the conditions of his life.

Here is another sentence I have selected from the writing of a student who has a tendency to use a "there are could be" structure:

> There are could be many students who could claim that they remember how education had changed their family life.

When working on this feature in his style, I'd begin by asking the student to read the sentence aloud. If he stumbles over the "are could be" or edits out the "could be" in orally reconstructing the sentence, I would ask him to talk about why he decided to do so, both in terms of meaning and form. Then I would ask him to consider the extent to which his "reading" speaks for or deviates from what he had in mind in writing in order to acknowledge, as Tricomi has argued, that reading aloud is one method for revision (264). But unlike Tricomi, who is mainly concerned that the revision "conforms" to the student's "intended meaning," I would also be interested in using the voice established in the first revision as a point of departure to initiate a process of negotiation. That is, I'd then proceed to introduce new voices by asking the student to experiment with new ways of revising the sentence. For example, I could ask him to consider the possibility of deleting the word "are" instead of the phrase "could be." We would then discuss the change in form by comparing the third version with the first and second, and we'd move on to consider the change in meaning between the second and third. To help him imagine more voices, I might suggest we try ways of retaining both "are" and "could be" in the sentence, leading him to come up with sentences such as "There are (could be?) many students who would. . . ." or "There could be/have been many students who would. . . ." And I would discuss with him the potential change in form and meaning in each case. Having located a range of voices, I would encourage the student to take a position among these diverse possibilities, taking into consideration the arguments he has made in the rest of the paper, his reading of Rodriguez's book, and especially the complex contexts of the student's personal and social life. For example, I might ask him to consider the following questions: how might his being a male, white, over thirty, a full-time employee in "business," the first one in his family to attend college, and a father of two children constrain his choice among this range of voices? Why and how might he want to contest such constraints? (For instance, would his choice change if he were to look at the issue from the point of view of his children rather than that of himself and his parents? Would the gender of his children make any difference to his choice?) In choosing a particular form of identification, which aspect of his life might be most affected? In what way?

On the other hand, I would be aware when planning for this tutorial that it is also possible that when asked to read the sentence aloud, the student would skip the "could be" (or "are") without showing any evidence of being aware that he had done so (see Bartholomae, "Study" 261–63). Then the tutorial would take quite a different turn than the scenario I have just projected. I could show him the sentence I'd jotted down from the sentence he read and ask him to compare it with his original sentence. Or I might ask him to listen to me read his original sentence while silently comparing what I say with the sentence I'd jotted down from his reading. One way or another, I'd be getting him to locate the difference between his reading and mine so we could then discuss why he skipped the phrase "could be" (or "are") but put it down when writing. And we'd explore the potential change in form and meaning resulting from each reading. To avoid overpowering his reading with mine, I might also point to other sentences with "there are" or "could" constructions in his papers and ask him to talk about why he did not put down both in those cases. And I might ask him to experiment with ways of cueing readers how they are supposed to consider only one of the forms on the page when reading, even though both are on the page, such as coming up with a sentence like "There are (could be?). . . ." In short, I would keep in mind that the actual negotiation would depend on the particular responses this student writer put forward as well as by my concerns as a teacher.

Needless to say, this type of teaching would work better when students are also asked to try the same method when analyzing the style of "real" writers so they understand that the "problems" they have with style are shared by all writers. For example, when students in a first-year writing course were reading Trask's essay "From a Native Daughter," I asked them to discuss or write about aspects of her style which seemed to deviate from the style of other historians they had encountered. Several students observed that the paragraphs in Trask's essay are shorter, including a series of one-sentence paragraphs with parallel structures of "And when they wrote . . . , they meant . . ." (123–24). Others were struck by the opening of Trask's essay, where she addresses her audience directly and asks that they "greet each other in friendship and love." She tells many more personal stories and uses fewer references for support, and she uses the imagery of a lover to depict the role of language. I urged them to examine these stylistic features in relation to the particular stance Trask seems to have taken toward the conflict between "haole" (white) culture and the native Hawaiian culture. Having approached the writing of a "real" writer from the perspective of the relationship between meaning, form, and social identifications, students are likely to be more motivated in applying this perspective to their own style and its revision.

At the same time, using a student paper to enact a negotiation in the contact zone can create a sense of immediacy and a new level of meaningfulness about abstract concepts discussed or enacted in the assigned readings for students in "literature" and "critical theory" classes. For example, the handout with the "can able to" construction can be used in senior-level critical theory courses when discussing Bakhtin's notion of "internal dialogism," Raymond Williams's concept of "structures of feeling," Cornel West's "prophetic critics and artists of color," and "dense" critiques of colonial discourse by such writers as Edward Said or Homi K. Bhabha. In the process of re-vising the "can able to" structure in the handout, in actively negotiating conflict in a contact zone, students in literature and cultural critical theory courses can gain a concrete opportunity to test the theories of various critics against their own efforts to practice them. This type of activity reduces the "alienation" undergraduate students often experience when asked to "do" theory. Testing theories against their own writing practices can also enable students to become more aware of the specific challenges such theories pose as well as the possibilities they open up for the individual writers committed to practicing these viewpoints. This method can also be used in upper-level literature courses when teaching such "borderland" literature as Sandra Cisneros's short story "Little Miracles, Kept Promises" or *Breaking Bread* by Cornel West and bell hooks. Reading and revising a student text, students can become more sensitive to the ways in which a "real" writer negotiates her way through contending discourses. At the same time, such reading and revision of their own writing allows students to enter into dialogue with "real" writers as "fellow travellers," active learners eager to compare and contrast one another's trials and triumphs.

One of the reactions to teaching style on the contact zone is fear that it will keep students from wanting to learn the conventions of academic discourse. My experience so far suggests that the unequal sociopolitical power of diverse discourses exerts real pressures on students' stylistic choices. After all, students choose to come to college, the choice of which speaks volumes on that power. The need to write for professors who grade with red pens circling all "errors" is also real for a majority of our students in most classrooms outside English departments. Therefore, although the process of negotiation encourages students to struggle with such unifying forces, it does not and cannot lead them to ignore and forget them. It acknowledges the writer's right and ability to experiment with innovative ways of deploying the codes taught in the classroom. It broadens students' sense of the range of options and choices facing a writer. But it does not choose for the students. Rather, it leaves them to choose in the context of the history, culture, and society in which they live.

Another reservation toward this type of teaching is that students who cannot write a "coherent" sentence are not ready psychologically and intellectually to participate in the kind of intricate reading/writing required by such a pedagogy. When addressing this concern, I believe we ought to focus our attention more on the teacher's potential hesitance to meet the challenge of living in the borderlands than on whether it truthfully reflects the ability of students to live there. Bartholomae has recently made the grim observation that "Basic writers may be ready for a different curriculum, for the contact zone and the writing it will produce, but the institution is not. . . . because of those of us who work in basic writing, who preserve rather than question the existing order of things" ("Tidy House" 15). Horner, discussing "border" approaches to teaching Basic Writing, warns that the approach I am advocating "assumes the shifting identity of both teachers and students, an assumption with which few teachers or students are comfortable" ("Mapping" 47). But one might argue that life in the contact zone puts the teacher more than the students at a disadvantage, for it has always been the privilege of the more powerful but never the right of those with "lower," "foreign," and/or "beginning" status to avoid the need to negotiate conflicts in their day-to-day existence. It seems to me that the feasibility of a multicultural approach to style rests on the willingness of "us" to yield the protection of "our" power provided by the code of the "objective," "civilized," "rational," "sophisticated" tone of voice.

At the same time, I am not suggesting that moments of consensus, or time spent sharing our knowledge and experience in employing a particular voice, have no place in the sort of classroom I am promoting. As Pratt cautions, to foreground the fact that no one is safe in the contact zone does not necessarily mean we displace the use of "safe houses," social spaces where groups can constitute themselves as communities with high degrees of trust and understanding ("Arts" 40). My main argument with teachers who claim that life in the contact zone is too confusing and traumatic for our students is that classrooms which avoid any sign of conflict and struggle turn themselves into nothing but "safe houses" where "comfort" belies the complexity, instability, and volatility of life within and outside the classroom.

The question of how to articulate a multicultural approach to style when analyzing the writings of student writers is particularly urgent for those of us committed to professing a multicultural English Studies. English Studies as a discipline has continually been energized by the intrusion of "aliens." To borrow a metaphor from Stuart Hall in his reading of the heritage of cultural studies, the house of English has been broken into by "thiefs" on many nights (282). "Thiefs" as diverse as African Americanists, feminists, and post-colonialists have managed not only to interrupt but significantly transform the lifeway of the residents of English. On the other hand (and I find this very disturbing), in spite of such self-renewing changes, English has largely remained a site where only its peripheral members—graduate students, adjuncts, part-timers, and junior faculty—are regularly assigned to deal with the idiosyncratic style of student writers. For those of us committed to a multicultural lifeway who stand on the periphery of our discipline by choice and necessity, it is especially important to break the divisions between "errors" and "style" and between approaches to the writings of "real" and student writers. In turning the teaching of style when dealing with student writing into a site where the pedagogical arts of the contact zone can be explored, practiced, and theorized, we might claim for students and teachers of what are called "basic skills" the right to actively participate in constructing a truly multicultural curriculum.

However, to approach the struggle over the import of multiculturalism solely in terms of a conflict among critical and pedagogical theories without taking into consideration the actual working conditions surrounding the effort of teachers to produce and implement such theories would be grossly reducing both the complexity and contentiousness of life in the contact zone. One of the "common sense" notions among teachers of writing, especially those assigned to deal with the "basics," is that "reasonable loads" ensuring "adequate time to fulfill" the multiple responsibilities of a writing teacher are still far from being a given where most of us work, in spite of repeated position statements on these issues from professional organizations like the Conference on College Composition and Communication and the National Council of Teachers of English ("Guidelines," "Statement"). Furthermore, our interest in and commitment to theories of language and teaching are heavily constrained by our sense of what "works" in the classroom on Monday morning, which is itself inevitably related to conditions such as teaching loads, course assignments, class size, assessment procedures, and the institutional status of individual teachers. I point to these specific constraints to emphasize what narratives of pedagogical theory such as this one both can and cannot do. The actual conditions in which most of us work, if we take them as givens, make teaching style as a process of negotiation appear highly "irrelevant." The sheer demands on time and energy such a pedagogy makes and the kind of one-on-one contact with students it requires suggest that for a lot of us, it is not a pedagogy which would "work" if not accompanied by drastic changes in our working conditions. At the same time, from the perspective of theory and research, it could also appear highly "relevant" if we consider the ways in which it implicitly points to the need for "adequate time" and "reasonable loads"—changes in our existing working conditions to meet professional guidelines. That is, this pedagogy could function as a relevant voice in our negotiation with colleagues and administrators over the conditions of our work because of its potential ability to mobilize the institutional authority of "theory." Our sense of what "works" is always related to our view of what is "realistic." Unfortunately, as Raymond Williams points out, being "realistic" "probably more often means 'let us accept the limits of this situation' (*limits* meaning *hard facts*, often of power or money in their existing and established forms) than 'let us look at the whole truth of this situation' (which can allow that an existing *reality* is changeable or is changing)" (*Keywords* 218). I take Williams to be saying here that our sense of reality often fails to attend to the dialectical relationship between the conceptual and the actual or between theory and practice. Rather, we tend to adopt a before-after frame of mind, driven by our sense of the "hard facts." The overwhelming pervasiveness of the "limits" confronting our work often leads us to assume that such "hard facts" form a stable and seamless net, a "thing" existing independently of our thoughts and actions rather than dialectically related to them. It is in the interests of hegemonic forces that we accept these "limits" as the preconditions of how we think and act and thus that we occlude our attention from the changeable and changing. For the same reason, it can only be in the interests of teachers and students labeled "basic" by such hegemonic forces to explore and formulate theories which demand changes in existing limits to our working conditions as well as to our thinking and action. To do so might often mean self-consciously looking for institutional cracks and gaps where such exploration is possible. It is important to keep in mind that the emergence of a critical discourse alone cannot bring about the change it promotes. However, it is also imperative that we recognize it as one of the potential forces for envisioning and constructing the changeable and changing. The two are not mutually exclusive from the perspective of dialectics. I offer my narrative of why and how to teach style as a process of negotiation in the hope that it serves as a comment on the need for change in not only existing approaches to the style of "real" and "basic" writers but also existing working conditions which "limit" our interest in and commitment to approaches which question all "hard facts."

Some Afterwords: Intersections and Divergences

Bruce Horner

In various ways, the writings collected in this volume pose the question of how a cultural materialist approach would operate in current debates in basic writing and college composition generally: the possibility of eliminating basic writing through "mainstreaming" or other strategies; the relevance of contact zone pedagogies and feminist and post-colonial critiques of the politics of representation to basic writing; the relation between basic writing and the "author-function"; challenging the continuing separation between matters of "style" and matters of "content"; and the perduring textual bias of research in composition.

Debate on basic writing in the mid-1990s sometimes echoes in troublesome ways the polarized debate during Basic Writing's "birth," seeming to allow for only two positions, for or against. This "re-polarization" of debate on basic writing results in part from recent New Right cutbacks to funding public higher (and other) education and simultaneous and consequent increasing reliance on part-timers and other non-tenure-line faculty, heavier teaching loads (more courses with more students per section), less student financial aid, less support staff and materials (paper, computers, workshop tutoring) for students and teachers, and the decay of schools' physical plants: in other words, the continuation of or, in some cases, return to working conditions suffered as "temporary" in the 1970s. In that context, any work, including the work collected in this volume, that calls into question the politics of discursive practices may well be slotted into the "against" position. Certainly our insistence on the historicity of Basic Writing challenges the construction of "basic writing" into an objective, unified, and stable entity, represented as a "course," "student," or "writing." To teachers concerned with their own and their students' immediate institutional survival, however, any suggestion that "basic writing" is a construct may seem an elitist gesture from those situated to afford engagement in fine theoretical distinctions, at best an irresponsible admission, but in any event likely to provide additional fodder to those on the New Right attacking basic writing programs, teachers, and students. For if "basic writing" does not signify a "real" phenomenon, a concrete body of students with self-evident needs that must be met, then one may legitimately question whether or not to preserve basic writing programs. Similarly, given existing power relations in the United States, any emphasis on the political import of the teaching of basic writing may well seem to threaten to encourage those in positions of dominance to exercise that dominance more conclusively by putting an end to basic writing programs. Even teachers who agree that representations of basic writing are constructs that have functioned strategically but problematically may well argue that such theoretical critiques are not worth the immediate, perhaps long-term, and significant material losses that such critiques may cost. Responding to the keynote speech given by David Bartholomae at the 1992 Conference on Basic Writing in which Bartholomae questions the usefulness of "more talk of basic writing" ("The Tidy House"), Karen Greenberg, for example, worries, "If reactionary political academics and budget-minded administrators and legislators join forces with composition 'stars' like David Bartholomae to attack basic writing programs, then these programs are doomed" ("Politics" 66).

On the other hand, attention to issues of difference and power in the production and reception of all representations of students through historicizing those representations can contribute practically in two ways. First, it can equip those concerned with students' welfare to combat powerful but damaging representations of students and teachers also being offered as the "objective facts" about them. Locating current representations of students in the ongoing history of conflicting representations of such students can enable us to benefit from that history. "Basic writing" itself, we need always to remember, was invoked as a term to combat dominant representations of students as "other": "illiterate," "boneheads," "barbarians," "not college material." While one may get the sense that current debate over basic writing is entirely *new,* in fact there has never been agreement about the definition of basic writing: it has since its inception been a contested term, and was itself introduced as part of a longer ongoing debate on how best to represent students.

The specific debate between Bartholomae and Greenberg alludes to this history of competing representations. Bartholomae's critique of the term "basic writing" notwithstanding, he does not call for ending basic writing programs, for, as he explains, he fears "what would happen to the students who are protected, served in its name," suspecting it would allow "the return of a way of speaking that was made suspect by the hard work and diligence of those associated with basic writing" ("Tidy House" 20–21). His challenge for basic writing, instead, is to take basic writing as the name for "a contested area. . . , a contact zone, a place of competing positions and interests" (21). And Greenberg, while worried that "if enough people subscribe to David Bartholomae's views on basic writing, there won't be any basic writing instruction in college much longer," insists that basic writing programs based on deficit or remedial models "deserve to be eliminated" (66, 67). Thus both Greenberg and Bartholomae engage in the ongoing struggle over how best to represent students and writing now commonly represented as "basic," calling attention to the material consequences of such representations in specific social historical locations.

Further, attention to issues of difference and power in the production and reception of diverse stances on how best to represent students can promote alternative representations by variously situated teachers, program administrators, and students by locating any representations in those situations. For example, Bartholomae's critique of basic writing needs to be accompanied by consideration of the specific material constraints experienced by teachers, students, and institutions and the implications of his critique for them. And the "success" that Greenberg describes students achieving through certain programs needs to be understood and defined in terms of the social and historical location of those students and programs. Further, both arguments need to be located more specifically in the constraints shaping and allowing for those arguments to be heard, so that we can be attuned as well to what is silenced in those arguments, and what arguments are not heard at all.

It is encouraging to note attempts to locate programs for basic writing in terms of just such constraints, as occurs, for example, in Rhonda Grego and Nancy Thompson's "Repositioning Remediation" and Mary Soliday's "From the Margins to the Mainstream," both of which appear in the February 1996 issue of *College Composition and Communication* along with an accompanying Interchange on "Rethinking Basic Writing" in responses from Akua Duku Anokye, Suellynn Duffey, and Judith Rodby: "Housewives and Compositionists," "Mapping the Terrain of Tracks and Streams," and "What's It Worth and What's It For? Revisions to Basic Writing Revisited." As these titles suggest, all the writers challenge the inevitability and naturalness of basic writing, instead, like Bartholomae, seeing the term as strategic, preserving an institutional "slot," however problematically, for certain students and teachers. But all of them also imagine any strategy in the context of historical and social and material pressures on those students and teachers: the historical "feminization" of work in composition, especially basic writing; the absence of credit granted for student's work and tuition paid for "remedial" courses; the pervasive "downsizing" of funding for education; the "remedial" function of composition historically. Moreover, by locating their own work in the specifics of their own institutions, they reject the application of their arguments universally to all institutions. Grego and Thompson report on the strategy of a writing "studio" program they developed in response to a state-mandated elimination of credit for basic writing, but caution, "The Studio is not a destination which we urge others to pursue simply as some latest trend" (82). Soliday, while describing what appears to be an effective FIPSE-funded project at CUNY in which basic writing students are placed in "mainstream" courses, warns that "institutional politics contextualize a mainstreamed course, and once the new course is no longer protected by the prestige and funding of a special grant, politics can redefine the course's original goals"; consequently, "we have to be acutely aware of our role in a potential struggle over redefining the considerable territory which constitutes remedial education within an institution" ("From the Margins" 96). In particular, Soliday notes the danger that administrators might well view mainstreaming not "as a method of enhancing instruction for open admissions students, [but] for cutting costs by eliminating remedial courses and the students these courses traditionally have served" (97). Suellyn Duffey echoes such cautions in her response, stating "neither [article] should convince us to mainstream basic writing students at our own institutions" (104). Rather, while she sees Grego and Thompson's article illustrating that "mainstreaming can work, [it] should not be seen as evidence that mainstreaming is a desirable alternative to tracking. Instead, it describes several adaptations to enforced mainstreaming, but those adaptations argue neither for nor against it" (105). And Judith Rodby ends her response by calling for more talk and writing to each other "comparing and developing a *variety* of political strategies, private and covert, deliberate and public, to preserve the integrity of our work with students and their writing" (111, emphasis mine). Rodby's call is especially important in confirming both the value and the dynamics of such discourse: while rejecting any reified notions of basic writing, she insists on the sharing of strategies to address it precisely because it is problematic—variously constituted and re-constituted and inherently strategic—rather than a problem susceptible to merely technical solution, and she calls for hearing a greater number of strategies, thus bringing out the different constraints that tend to muffle some voices while amplifying others.

Such accounts demonstrate the cogency of understanding basic writing as indeed a "contact zone," Mary Louise Pratt's evocative image for one of the "social spaces where cultures meet, clash, and grapple with each other, often in contexts of highly asymmetrical relations of power"

("Arts" 34). Many compositionists concerned to address issues of differences and power in the teaching of writing both institutionally and pedagogically have been attracted to Pratt's image, for it both foregrounds
the operation of power relations in constructing and erasing difference
and gives a positive valuation to the unleashing and play of difference.
Indeed, one could argue that even critiques of the problematics of the
"contact zone" in some ways offer additional support for the cogency of
understanding composition and basic writing as a site of such contact.
By foregrounding questions of power and difference, those problematics
offer useful directions for teaching and research countering hegemonic
discourse on basic and other writing. The question raised by the image
of the contact zone is how one responds, institutionally and pedagogically, to the dynamic heterogeneity to which the image points. Does one
respond, as Pratt describes is historically typical, by eliminating, ignoring, or silencing evidence of such heterogeneity? Or, if one decides to
embrace and encourage it, how does one go about doing so, given existing power relations and the real dangers to which such clashing and
grappling may lead? Related to this question is the more general issue
of the role teacherly "authority" plays in a politicized understanding of
the teaching of writing. Given asymmetrical relations of power within
the classroom, how can a teacher enact his commitments to the ideals of
democracy and social justice toward which contact zone pedagogies are
intended to work without betraying them through the exercise of his
position of power? And how do asymmetrical relations of power within
institutions impinge on those teachers and their students, especially the
dominated and their need for "safe" space and communal support? Such
questions fall with particular force on teachers of basic writing as the
dominated of the dominant, perpetually negotiating both *with* and *as*
the dominant for themselves, their programs, and their students.

What is highlighted by these questions is the need to view the "arts
of the contact zone" as a historically specific strategic response, a representation of education put forth in competition with dominant representations of education as the site for (re)producing social homogeneity.
In decontextualized conceptualizations of "contact zones," not only individual students and cultures but power and the contact zone itself are
all essentialized, imagined as reified, uniform entities neither produced
by nor susceptible to change. Thus reappropriated, contact zone pedagogy can seem at best, as Joseph Harris has complained, "a kind of
multicultural bazaar, where [students] are not so much brought into
conflict with opposing views as placed in a kind of harmless connection
with a series of exotic others" ("Negotiating" 33). The "harmless connection" or "contact" thus achieved is likely to be "superficial," for it

assumes both the essential immutability of the individuals' cultural identities and cultural tourism as its sole motive. What is needed, Harris
goes on to say, is "how competing perspectives can be made to intersect
with and inform each other. . . . how (or why) individuals might decide
to change or revise their own positions (rather than simply to defend
them) when brought into contact with differing views" (33). Otherwise,
the contact zone as a strategy of articulating oppositional or alternative
discourse in order to make resistance to hegemonic discourse possible
is contained, rendered into the liberal pluralist ideal of conversation:
once all voices have been heard, class can be dismissed.[1] "Contact" becomes itself reified as a process in and for itself rather than being understood as a response to and with consequences in specific social and historical conditions. Thus Harris argues that the contact zone be seen not
so much as a "social space" in which different groups are heard but a
"forum," "process" or "event" constituted by and making possible "a
local and shifting series of interactions," "negotiations, interventions,
and compromises" ("Negotiating" 37). Both contact zones themselves
and the taking of positions will have to be imagined in dynamic rather
than static terms, as strategies to address debate on social justice.

Given the asymmetrical relations of power among students and between students and teachers, many will understandably be suspicious
of the utopian overtones of such aims. From one position, such aims
will seem to be an abuse of teachers' authority, the politicization of what
should be an occasion for the neutral acquisition of writing skills. Others might see a teacher's use of her authority over students to pursue an
ideal of social justice as contradicting that ideal. Despite their differences, however, both such positions are linked by a reliance on a
decontextualization of teaching and a monolithic, essentialized conception of power and of individual students and teachers. Concerns about
the "politicization" of teaching falsely assume that courses exist outside
relations of power in society, forgetting the array of social historical pressures leading to the very presence of teachers, courses, and students. In
fact, power operates in classrooms whether or not teachers or students
choose to acknowledge or intervene in its operation. As a corollary,
whatever authority teachers possess, power is not restricted to or controlled by teachers. Those concerned that teachers may "impose" on students falsely assume that teacher authority renders students powerless
to resist teachers' ideas and efforts, forgetting that teacher authority is
more appropriately seen as something negotiated rather than exercised
by fiat (see Bizzell, "Power" 54–58). Further, students and teachers represent a heterogeneous array of intersecting and divergent identifications, interests, pressures, and circumstances. Indeed, any individual

student or teacher, rather than representing a single, monolithic set of interests, beliefs, and affinities, exhibits traits of both instability and continuity in her interests, positions, identifications, and circumstances. The question is then how to engage students in constructing bases for positions of alignment in the context of social and historical differences. Imagined thus, the "contact zone" is less a space one "enters" than a type of activity in which people explicitly negotiate such differences and alignments.

The heterogeneity of interests both within and among students and teachers combats the likelihood of any course serving a single political agenda. That likelihood is further thrown into question if we challenge assumptions about power underlying concerns about such a course. Patricia Bizzell notes that critical pedagogues' suspicions about any exercise of power result from "an insufficiently differentiated conception of power . . . as a unitary force with uniform effects" ("Power" 54–55). Teachers sympathetic to critical pedagogy have attempted to engage in persuasion because of the appeal of its egalitarianism: no party is imagined as having the right to impose her views on others, not even a teacher; all are equal in the "dialogue." In practice, however, teachers' attempts to disengage from power, imagined as inherently coercive, have resulted either in leaving the classroom open to the exercise of power by others (say, particular groups of students already in positions of dominance over other students), in suspicions that this disengagement is one way or another a ruse or cheat, or, at best, to a general retreat by all from any engagement of any kind with others. The problem with such disengagement, Bizzell notes, results from a failure to recognize the context in which teaching takes place: existing power relations in society are far from the egalitarian ideal in which true "collaboration" and persuasion might occur; positing such an ideal as already existing within the classroom simply allows those relations to operate unchecked ("Power" 59). Indeed, such disengagement among critical pedagogues represents what Bizzell elsewhere identifies as a nostalgic dream of transcending ideology: aware that ethical commitments are "just another ideological construct" and that there is no escape from ideology into "reality," teachers nonetheless desire to "transcend" ideology by disavowing their commitments ("Marxist" 55). To this recognition of the inevitability of the play of ideological commitments should be added a corollary: that teachers are in some ways more powerful than students does not mean that students have no power. Thus teachers, suspicious of coercive power, who therefore refuse to exercise any power falsely assume that attempts at coercion will meet with no resistance. While it is important to acknowledge the hegemonic role schools play, it is crucial, as Raymond

Williams warns, to resist seeing hegemony "as more uniform, more static, and more abstract than in practice, . . . it can ever actually be." Instead we need to recall that "a lived hegemony is always a process . . . . [that] has continually to be renewed, recreated, defended, and modified . . . . [and that] is also continually resisted, limited, altered, challenged by pressures not at all its own" (*Marxism* 112).

If recognition of the heterogeneity of students' and teachers' positions and identifications may combat concerns about the dangers of political coercion, the dynamics of the hegemonic process obviate them: no position is free of power relations or political commitments: all teaching participates either to reinforce, reproduce, or work against the hegemonic, which itself inevitably meets with resistance. The question for teachers then becomes whether or not to acknowledge the operation of that process and actively intervene in it. This would involve ideological critique of, rather than mere liberal tolerance for, diverse positions, including critique of the ideology underlying one's own pedagogy. From the perspective of an Althusserian understanding of ideology, such demystification must be understood as both ongoing and multidirectional. But such demystification must be accompanied by attention to not only what is but what might be, what is emergent, potentially generated by the contradictions revealed through demystification (see Bizzell, "Marxist Ideas," and Jameson, "Conclusion"). The kinds of tensions resulting from investigating contradictions through a contact zone pedagogy can have constructive as well as deconstructive effects (Bizzell, "Marxist Ideas" 64–67). The kind of pedagogy we would argue for, in other words, sees the pursuit of hope and of critique related dialectically rather than in simple opposition: conflict and struggle can be generative and productive in its aims and effects. It is thus that we might achieve a contact zone pedagogy where differences are negotiated to change existing relations of domination, rather than being invoked only to produce either a pluralist "multicultural bazaar" or a battle between enemies. The idea of the contact zone, like "multiculturalism," has arisen as a strategy aimed at confronting existing injustice to achieve yet unrealized justice.[2] In place of conservative appeals to find a "common ground" positing an essentialized humanity—appeals which historically have silenced difference and pushed some to the periphery to affirm the right of others to the center—the idea of the contact zone rejects proprietary claims and fixed identities, asking instead how identities and social spaces are formed and reformed and the role of power relations in such formations.

This emphasis on both the fluidity of teachers' and students' subject positions and the role of power in forming those positions is aligned to

the work of composition teachers and researchers interested in contesting representations of students and teachers as inhabiting discrete cognitive, social, and/or discursive locations (Rose, "Narrowing"; Hull,
Rose, Fraser, Castellano; Hull and Rose, "'This Wooden Shack Place'"
and "Rethinking Remediation"). The challenges to dominant ways of
demarcating basic writers from other writers and from teachers that have
resulted from such work is necessary for a truly productive contact zone
pedagogy and also important in combating the reductive understandings of cognition, social identity, experience, and discourse such representations support. Most recently such work has challenged the distinction between basic writers and Authors, demonstrating the implication
of the "author function" in maintaining the hierarchical organization of
English studies—most notably the position of literary study in relation
to composition—and the authority of teachers over students (Miller;
Crowley; Stygall; Grego and Thompson 68–70).[3] Mainstreaming represents one response to increasing awareness of the role institutional processes have played in marginalizing basic writers, eliminating those processes by eliminating institutional mechanisms which maintain the distinction between "basic" and other writers.

The distinction between Authors and students represents part of a
chain of binaries distinguishing not only Authors from writers but art
from mechanics, (unalienated) work from labor, and the individual will
from social demands, binaries that serve to maintain the prestige of one
set of writers, and the study of that set, and the low status of other writers and those studying their writing. Because basic writing teachers occupy the most marginal, precarious place in college and university English departments, they have historically felt the pressures of these binaries most keenly and have therefore responded to them most sharply.
Moreover, aside from the institutional interest basic writing has in contesting the denigration of its students, basic writing teachers' own experience with their students and the now increasing body of research on
the history of literacy and on canon formation support radical challenges
to those binaries. However, precisely because of the marginal position
of basic writing students, teachers, and programs both within English
studies and within educational institutions generally to which the au-
thor/student binary is based and which it maintains, teachers may well
be tempted to erase the distinction between Authors and basic writers
by positing basic writers as Authors. While erasures of the differences
between authors and student writers might in some instances represent
a radical overhauling of dominant approaches, in some versions it can
represent a reactionary return to the bourgeois individualism of
expressivism. In such versions the Author/student writer binary would

remain intact: the "other" would simply be moved to the side of the dominant, the legitimacy of the norms constructing Authors remaining unchallenged.

But if we re-define "authors" as "writers" with a lowercase "w"—that is, as social historical agents working in relations of power with others, such as readers—we and our students can then draw on the rich example of the actual work that all practicing published and unpublished writers and editors and critics engage in as they negotiate the meaning and acceptability of specific writings (as Lu shows in "Professing Multiculturalism"). To do this requires that we accept a more dynamic conception of power relations; that we acknowledge the instability of authors, texts, meanings, and canons; and that we contextualize differences established among writers socially and historically rather than essentializing them. Given the present implication of many English teachers in maintaining the stability of authors, texts, meanings, and canons, this is a difficult requirement to meet. However, by historicizing the establishment of the binary differentiation between Authors and basic (and other) writers, we can transform our traditional approaches to that differentiation—commonly a source of ambivalence and embarrassment among teachers and students—into an occasion for classroom inquiry. Most directly, the ongoing negotiation of such differences would be acknowledged as a substantive issue for the profession as a profession and as a "basic" issue for teachers and students in individual courses. In this way students' and teachers' "personal" experiences with writing would be connected to the social and institutional forces shaping that writing and to which that writing itself responds. For example, efforts are being made to demystify for students the standards and institutional processes by which their placement and exit tests are evaluated, presenting those as negotiated and negotiable historical agreements rather than unalterable "givens," so that students might be in a position to work both toward meeting those standards and toward changing them through renegotiation. The issue for such courses is thus not simply accommodating such standards but learning how to negotiate the operation of such pressures which have already constructed students as writers. This means recognizing the operation of the material, social, and historical within the classroom and within the student.[4]

Historicizing the linguistic, institutional, and pedagogical mechanisms maintaining the distinction between Authors and student writers in this way would not so much erase the differences in discursive interests, material circumstances, and performances as contextualize them. Doing so would enable teachers both to address and contest what are often seen as conflicting demands: what Grego and Thompson distinguish as the "material" vs. the "psychic" needs of students or, more broadly, matters of "thought" vs. "feeling," "conceptualization" vs. "experience," style vs. matters of content, or error vs. ideas. For some, any attention to the former can seem to be capitulation to unjust social pressures on basic writers, the ignoring of students' psychic needs as writers and their ideas and experiences that would be highly inappropriate in a response to the writings of established authors. Others argue in turn that refusing to attend to such matters is to abandon basic writers to the force of those pressures. Both positions, however, maintain the distinction between the "social" and the "individual" in writing; what is needed instead is a pursuit of what Williams calls for as the "reciprocal discovery of the truly social in the individual, and the truly individual in the social" (*Marxism* 197). Such discovery, a not unrealistic goal for teaching, involves examining both the ways in which the materiality of writing is malleable and the continuing process by which "the contents of [the individual writer's] consciousness are socially produced" (193). Thus the interests of the "social" and of the "individual" writer, a writer's "psychic" and "material" needs, rather than being in competition, are instead investigated as irrevocably, radically intertwined.

To investigate the "social production" of individual consciousness is not, of course, to belabor the presence and pressure of the dominant but to bring into dynamic play potentially oppositional emergent and/or residual pressures also operating on individual consciousness. Williams notes that

> no mode of production and therefore no dominant social order and therefore no dominant culture ever in reality includes or exhausts all human practice, human energy, and human intention. . . . . [what modes of domination] select from and consequently exclude . . . may often be seen as the personal or the private, or as the natural or even the metaphysical . . . since what the dominant has effectively seized is indeed the ruling definition of the social. . . . there is always . . . practical consciousness . . . that is unquestionably social and that a specifically dominant social order neglects, excludes, represses, or simply fails to recognize. (*Marxism* 125)

Compositionists drawing on feminist and post-colonial theory have worked to recuperate "personal experience" and other categories traditionally excluded from academic discourse to capture the heterogeneity and instability of "individual" consciousness or subjectivity by situating the "individual" at the intersection of class, race, gender, and other social categories as a site of power struggle among and within cultures and discourses, in alignment with the attempts of contact zone pedagogy to make possible the articulation of oppositional discourse. In teaching, this involves making productive use of what Williams identifies as

the "tension between the received interpretation and practical experience." This tension arises precisely because "there are the experiences to
which the fixed forms do not speak at all, which indeed they do not
recognize" (*Marxism* 130).

However, recuperating the oppositional potential of such experiences
is complicated. One's "practical consciousness" of experience differs from
"official consciousness" by being "what is actually being lived, and not
only what it is thought is being lived. . . . a kind of feeling and thinking
which is indeed social and material, but each in an embryonic phase
before it can become fully articulate and defined exchange" (130–31).
Compositionists hoping to draw on students' practical consciousness to
elicit oppositional thoughts and feelings must thus confront the complex mediation of those thoughts and feelings by official consciousness,
one's learned sense of "what it is *thought* is being lived." Further, they
must simultaneously resist the dominant's identification of such consciousness *as* "personal," "private," "feelings" distinct from the social,
even as they attempt to invoke what has been relegated by the dominant to such categories. As Williams warns, the relations of practical
consciousness "with the already articulate and defined are . . . exceptionally complex" (131).

Work that is successful in addressing that complexity must avoid two
seemingly opposed tendencies both of which, albeit in different ways,
essentialize personal experience. First, experience can be read as the
passive "carrier" of determinate social structures—nothing more than,
say, one's racial, ethnic, gender, or class identity. Alternatively, and sometimes in reaction to this tendency, there is the tendency to return to the
bourgeois individualism of old-style expressivist pedagogy, in which
students are encouraged to tell of their "true, personal experience" purified of "outside influence." Both tendencies, however, suppress what
Williams describes as the "living and reciprocal relationships of the individual and the social" (*Marxism* 194). As a result, as in weaker versions of contact zone pedagogy, what begins as an attempt to make productive use of difference becomes a reification of difference, whether in
terms of social identity or in distinctions between the "personal" and
the "social." Those combatting such tendencies do so by both invoking
and problematizing the "personal" in its relations to the social. Mary
Soliday, for example, describes a basic writing course in which, as students read and write autobiographical literacy narratives, they learn to
locate their own experiences with literacy and those described in others' accounts of literacy learning as participating in the clash and transformation of identities, cultures, and languages. In the process, they learn
that "their experience is, in fact, interpretable" ("Translating" 512) and

therefore something in which they can intervene critically. Thus Alisha, one of the students described, theorizes her own experience and others' experience with differences of language, identity, and culture to develop a "new sense of self" that can negotiate the various pressures these exert on her (518–20). Her writing comes to evince a "skillful intermingling of life writing and exposition of other texts" intertwining the "personal" and the "social" (519). And in "Reading and Writing Differences," Min-Zhan Lu has described her use of a sequence of reading and writing assignments to enable students to use experience both "experientially" and analytically through revising their responses to readings. Drawing on feminist critics on the margin who have critiqued the erasure of difference resulting from unreflective uses of "personal" experience, Lu argues for a pedagogy in which students analyze their experience "not only for what it allows [them] to reach towards but also what it might prevent [them] from reaching" in order to open a perspective in which they "conceive of transforming [themselves] with the aid of others." Such a pedagogy encourages students to examine the ways in which their experiences with discrimination serve to enable them to make certain gendered meanings out of elements of a story while blinding them to issues of class, ethnicity, nationality, race, and sexual preference. They thus come both to revise their readings of the story and their sense of their own experience. In such courses, personal experience is taken not as the discrete residence of the individual immune to the play of the social nor as yet another passive register of the social but as a site of and for contesting meanings, building on, responding to, and revising those meanings. Newly emergent meanings of both the self and society arise in and through that process of contestation.

The emphasis in such work on the operation of the material, social, and historical in the teaching, learning, production and reception of writing intersects with recent feminist and postcolonial critiques of work in composition and literacy education which re-locate that work as gendered, raced, and classed, challenging the universality and politics of the "norms" in the styles of writing taught, who teaches whom how, under what material and institutional conditions, and the interests served by such practices.[5] That work also intersects with ethnographic research in composition taking as its aim the elucidation of how cultural conflict gets inscribed in students' writing, classroom discourse, and composition research.[6] Such intersections, however, are suggestive for revealing points of divergence as well as of alignment. Two related points of divergence seem particularly salient in helping to delineate significant gaps in and thus future directions for the work represented by the writings

collected in this volume: what may be termed its "macro-textual" bias
and a resulting absence in it of "thick" accounts. In a review essay on
"Composition in the 90s," Tom Fox notes,

> though our theory is social, composition's focus on the classroom
> pulls us the other way, towards idiosyncrasy, individual students
> and their successes, "good" days in single classrooms. . . . No doubt
> we experience our classrooms this way because of the fact that we
> teach in these time periods and we grade individual students. But
> the institutional shape of our experience and the political theories
> that we admire thus may work against each other—the former to-
> wards atomistic and individualist views and the latter towards
> multiple, social frameworks.
>
> The conceptual and rhetorical challenge of writing about peda-
> gogy in the age of politics is how to weave these two perspectives
> together. (569)

In calling for such a weaving, Fox echoes Hull, Rose, Fraser, and
Castellano's conclusions from their analysis of classroom discourse. Hull
et al. observe that much research on reading and writing consists of "either fine-grained analyses of texts or of the cognitive processes involved
in text comprehension and production *or* . . . studies of wider focus on
the social and political contexts of reading, writing, and schooling" (321).
Citing critics from a variety of disciplines, they warn that what is needed,
in fact, is a constant

> moving between micro-level, close examination of oral or written
> discourse and macro-level investigations of society and culture—
> seeking connections between language, cognition, and context. . . .
> Without the microperspective, one runs the risk of losing sight of
> the particulars of behavior; without the macroperspective, one runs
> the risk of missing the social and cultural logic of that behavior.
> (321–22)

Hull et al. thus argue that we need the kind of "weaving" for which Fox
calls, and Fox offers an account of how institutional segmentation of
teachers' experience constrains their attempts to engage in the sort of
weaving movement Hull et al. deem necessary. In a corollary critique,
Judith Rodby has noted that "Research on texts rather than people, a
bias promoted by the literature departments of which we are a part,
deflects our attention from theoretical frameworks that could help us
see and then explain literacy development and interpersonal relationships," and so she calls for more case study and participant-observer
research to produce "more thick description, more information about
how the physical and conceptual context and the purpose and the social
milieu influence student writing" (111). I take Rodby to be calling not
for a rejection of the textualization of experience brought on by structur-

alist and poststructuralist theory but for an expansion of the "texts" studied. The "texts" on which our own research focuses, while in many ways expansively defined, do not incorporate those typically addressed in case study and participant-observer research, and thus our work offers primarily "macro" perspectives on basic writing. Our analyses of specific writings by students and teachers and classroom discussions serve primarily to illustrate what we see as the logic and implications of our theoretical positions for understanding the production and reception of "basic writing" as a type of student, text, program, and discourse. Our hope is such "thin" analyses may contribute to the collaborative "thickening" of the field's account of itself and to the problematizing as well of experience in ethnographic research.[7] Similarly, while our analyses intersect with feminist and post-colonial critiques of literacy education, and while we hope that they may contribute to such critiques, they do not take up the specific ways in which work in basic writing is inscribed by class, race, gender, and other social categories, as do Stygall and Brodkey, for example. We look to further pursuit of such specificities in understanding practices in basic writing. Finally, we look as well to delineations of the specific relations between basic writing and literacy education both at more "advanced" and "lower" levels of schooling and at non-institutional sites of literacy learning, in the United States and elsewhere, at present and in the past, not to erase differences between the various literacy practices but to bring such differences into contact, further revealing the operation of the material, social, and historical in the teaching, learning, production and reception of all writing.

Notes

Introduction

1. We take Raymond Williams's term "cultural materialism" to designate the materiality of discursive practices—that is, interpreting historical materialism as treating "superstructural" practices as constitutive of as well as constituted by the structures of the "material base."

2. These assumptions draw on Louis Althusser's notion of ideology, Antonio Gramsci's notion of hegemony, Raymond Williams's notion of the materiality of culture, Jacques Derrida's critique of the metaphysics of presence, Fredric Jameson's notion of the political unconscious, and Michel Foucault's theory of discourse and power. For a more detailed account of the Foucauldian impress on our work, see Lu's discussion in her response included in the December 1993 *College English* "Symposium on Basic Writing: Conflict and Struggle, and the Legacy of Mina Shaughnessy," (55.8: 894–901). Jameson's concept of the political unconscious informs Horner's reading of dominant discourse on Open Admissions ("'Birth'" 15–23). Horner discusses Althusser's notion of ideology in "Some Afterwords" and Williams's notion of the materiality of culture in "Some Afterwords" and "Re-thinking the 'Sociality' of Error."

3. Compare, for example, Wagner, Heller, and Kriegel's *Working Through*, Shaughnessy's *Errors*, and Ira Shor's *Culture Wars*.

4. See, for example, accounts by Patricia Bizzell and David Bartholomae of their first experiences with basic writing programs, and Shaughnessy's observation near the end of *Errors and Expectations* that teachers are beginning to see the difficulties of basic writers as those of every writer "writ large" (Bartholomae, "The Tidy House"; Bizzell, Introduction; Shaughnessy, *Errors* 293).

Chapter 1

1. Basic Writing is used to name the canonized field as it exists and is institutionally reinforced through various means; basic writing (not capitalized) indicates a more open vision of the field as material practice and that which escapes institutionalization, a more open field of possibilities.

2. For a sense of the precarious conditions for faculty at CUNY during its mid-seventies retrenchment, see Kapsis and Murtha.

Chapter 3

1. To acknowledge the exclusion involved in the institutionalization of a field and discourse, I use the capitalized form, Basic Writing, to refer to the dominant ways basic writing has been represented and to call attention to the fact that the work actually performed by teachers and students placed in classrooms labeled as basic, which I identify as "basic writing," is always much more heterogeneous and dynamic.

2. For a discussion of such differences, see Lyons (1985) 184–85.

3. See Lu, "Redefining" for an account of a similar move in *Errors and Expectations*.

4. For analysis of Bernstein's "structuralism," see also R. Gibson's *Structuralism and Education*.

Chapter 4

1. My view of language has been informed by Louis Althusser's notion of ideology, Antonio Gramsci's analysis of hegemony, Jacques Derrida's critique of the metaphysics of presence, Michel Foucault's theory of discourse and power, and the distinction Raymond Williams makes between practical and official consciousness.

2. For discussion of Shaughnessy's pedagogy in relation to her democratic aspirations, see Robert Lyons and rebuttals to John Rouse's "The Politics of Shaughnessy" by Michael Allen, Gerald Graff, and William Lawlor.

3. In arguing for the need to show "interest in and respect for language variety," Shaughnessy cites William Labov's analysis of the inner logic, grammar, and ritual forms in Black English Vernacular (Shaughnessy, *Errors* 17, 237, 304). Shaughnessy also cites theories in contrastive analysis (156), first-language interference (93), and transformational grammar (77–78) to support her speculations on the logic of basic writers' errors.

4. For a critique of the way modern linguistics of language, code, and competence (such as Labov's study of Black English Vernacular) tend to treat discourses as discrete and autonomous entities, see Mary Louise Pratt's "Linguistic Utopias."

Chapter 6

1. Hull ends her review by calling for research attending to the larger social setting of basic writing, research which "will pay respectful attention to a student's position as an outsider" (183–84). In "Rethinking Remediation," she and Mike Rose report on a research project they are conducting which takes as its focus the social setting of remedial writers, and in "'This Wooden Shack Place,'" she and Rose present an analysis of the social bases of the kinds of readings basic writers and their teachers perform.

2. On the distinction between social and cognitive approaches, see Bizzell, "Cognition." For attempts to bridge these approaches, see Berkenkotter and Flower.

3. Cf. Kenneth Bruffee's discussion of Richard Rorty's concept of "normal discourse" ("Collaborative Learning and the 'Conversation of Mankind,'" 642–43).

4. Cf. Martin Nystrand's description of written errors as representing occasions when readers and writers are "OUT OF TUNE WITH EACH OTHER [sic]" (65–66).

5. This is not to suggest that second-language acquisition does not itself possess social dimensions of power, status, and class (witness Richard Rodriguez's *Hunger of Memory* and recent debates between the Canadian provinces) or that theorists of second-language acquisition attribute no importance to the social dimensions of language learning (see, for example, Stephen Krashen's discussions of the roles which the "affective filter" and "acculturation" play in second-language acquisition, 30–32, 45–50). Such dimensions, however, have often been ignored by teachers adopting models of second-language acquisition to understand written error.

6. See Anatol Rapaport's distinction between "fights," on the one hand, and what he calls "games" and "debates" (1–12).

7. Epes explains that she selected members for each group from a pool of speakers representing a "spectrum of spoken dialect," from either end of which she chose members. She determined dialect primarily on the basis of grammatical features (8, n. 8).

8. Barbara Mellix's essay "From Outside, In" provides an account of an NSD speaker's experience learning to write "standard" English which illuminates social and political dimensions of that experience not addressed by Epes, though suggested by concerns expressed by the NSD speakers Epes studies about speaking "right" and using "bad English" (Epes 28).

9. For a general critique of applications of theories of cognition to basic writers' problems, see Rose, "Narrowing the Mind and Page."

10. For an articulation of this argument, see Patterson 154–56.

11. By "text" I refer here to printed words, not the broader sense which this term has come to signify in critical theory and cultural studies.

12. See Bartholomae, "Writing," for a different examination of the difficulty of distinguishing between basic writers and teachers.

13. For a useful general critique of the utopian overtones invoked by the term *community* in studies of writing, see Joseph Harris's "The Idea of Community in the Study of Writing." Harris critiques the appropriateness of both "growth" and "conversion" as metaphors for describing the changes the basic writers undergo in "Three Metaphors."

14. See Giddens's critique of what he terms the "derogation of the lay actor" implicit in theories which deny the validity of reasons members of a society give for their actions (71–72).

15. For a similar argument regarding peer groups generally, see Bruffee, "Collaborative Learning and the 'Conversation of Mankind,'" 646–67.

16. See Ede and Lunsford's cautions on collaborative writing pedagogies as technologies of institutional power (112–16, 120) and their discussion of hierarchical and dialogic modes of collaboration (133–35).

17. One of the problems with workbooks is that the context they establish *as* workbooks is at odds with encouraging students to adopt "academic" attitudes toward their contents.

18. Cf. Hull and Rose's discussion of the value of eliciting the "mismatch" between remedial writers' ways of reading and those encouraged by their teachers ("'This Wooden Shack Place'" 296–97).

Chapter 7

1. See, for example, Anderson, "An Apology for Style"; Kazin, *On Native Grounds;* and Mencken, "The Dreiser Bugaboo."

2. See Lu, "Writing as Repositioning." For a discussion of "border" pedagogy in teaching Basic Writing, see Horner, "Mapping."

3. See, for example, Rose, "Language of Exclusion."

4. See, for example, Bartholomae, "The Study of Error"; Elaine Lees, "Proofreading as Reading," "The Exceptable Way"; Horner, "Rethinking."

5. For an extended discussion of teaching editing as negotiation that informs my own, see Horner, "Rethinking," especially pages 188–96.

Some Afterwords

1. On the limitations of this sort of approach, see Frank Walters 828.

2. See, in this regard, Pratt, "Daring to Dream" 8–12, and Lu, "Representing and Negotiating Differences in the Contact Zone."

3. I have more to say about the challenges to the distinction between students and authors in composition pedagogy in "Students, Authorship, and the Work of Composition."

4. For a similar argument from a somewhat different perspective, see Walters, especially pages 825, 827.

5. See, for example, Brody; Delpit; Fox, *Social Uses;* Gilyard; Jarratt; Miller; Royster; Stuckey; Villanueva.

6. See, for example, such studies as Stygall; Hull and Rose, "'This Wooden Shack Place'" and "Rethinking Remediation"; Hull, Rose, Fraser, and Castellano; Brodkey; and Ewald and Wallace.

7. We have subsequently pursued this line of inquiry in Lu and Horner, "The Problematic of Experience: Redefining Critical Work in Ethnography and Pedagogy."

Works Cited

Adams, Peter Dow. *Connections: A Guide to the Basics of Writing.* Boston: Little, Brown, 1987.

Agnew, Spiro T. "Toward a 'Middle Way' in College Admissions." *Educational Record* 51 (Spring 1970): 106–11.

Allen, Michael. "Writing Away from Fear: Mina Shaughnessy and the Uses of Authority." *College English* 41 (1980): 857–67.

Anderson, Sherwood. "An Apology for Crudity." *The Stature of Theodore Dreiser: A Critical Survey of the Man and His Work.* Ed. Alfred Kazin and Charles Shapiro. Bloomington: Indiana UP, 1965.

Anokye, Akua Duku. "Housewives and Compositionists." *College Composition and Communication* 47 (1996): 101–3.

Anzaldúa, Gloria. *Borderlands/La Frontera: The New Mestiza.* San Francisco: Aunt Lute, 1987.

Armstrong, Paul, B. "Pluralistic Literacy." *Profession* 88: 29–32.

Aronowitz, Stanley. "Paulo Freire's Radical Democratic Humanism." McLaren and Leonard 8–24.

Bakhtin, Mikhail. *The Dialogic Imagination.* Ed. Michael Holquist. Trans. Caryl Emerson and Michael Holquist. Austin: U of Texas P, 1981.

Baldwin, James. *Conversations with James Baldwin.* Ed. Fred L. Standley and Louis H. Pratt. Jackson: UP of Mississippi, 1989.

———. *The Price of the Ticket.* New York: St. Martin's, 1985.

Barasch, F. K. "Collective Bargaining at CUNY." *Change* Summer 1973: 14–16.

Bartholomae, David. "A Reply to Stephen North." *PRE/TEXT* 11 (1990): 121–30.

———. "Inventing the University." *When a Writer Can't Write: Studies in Writer's Block and Other Composing Process Problems.* Ed. Mike Rose. New York: Guilford, 1985. 134–65.

———. "Released into Language: Errors, Expectations, and the Legacy of Mina Shaughnessy." *The Territory of Language: Linguistics, Stylistics, and the Teaching of Composition.* Ed. Donald A. McQuade. Carbondale: Southern Illinois UP, 1986. 65–88.

———. "The Study of Error." *College Composition and Communication* 31 (1980): 253–69.

———. "The Tidy House: Basic Writing in the American Curriculum." *Journal of Basic Writing* 12.1 (Spring 1993): 4–21.

———. "Writing on the Margins: The Concept of Literacy in Higher Education." *Sourcebook* 66–83.

Bartholomae, David, and Anthony Petrosky. *Facts, Artifacts, and Counterfacts: Theory and Method for a Reading and Writing Course.* Upper Montclair, NJ: Boynton/Cook, 1986.

Belsey, Catherine. *Critical Practice.* London: Methuen, 1980.

Bennett, William. *To Reclaim a Legacy: A Report on the Humanities in Higher Education.* National Endowment for the Humanities, 1984.

Berg, Anna, and Gerald Coleman. "A Cognitive Approach to Teaching the Developmental Student." *Journal of Basic Writing* 4.2 (Fall 1985): 4–23.

Berkenkotter, Carol. "Paradigm Debates, Turf Wars, and the Conduct of Sociocognitive Inquiry in Composition." *College Composition and Communication* 42 (1991): 151–69.

Berlin, James A. *Rhetoric and Reality: Writing Instruction in American Colleges, 1900–1985.* Carbondale: Southern Illinois UP, 1987.

Bernstein, Basil. *Class, Codes and Control.* 4 vols. London: Routledge, 1971, 1973, 1975, 1990.

———. "Elaborated and Restricted Codes: Overview and Criticisms." *Class, Codes and Control* 4: 94–132.

Berthoff, Ann E. "Is Teaching Still Possible? Writing, Meaning, and Higher Order Reasoning." *College English* 46 (1984): 743–54.

Bizzell, Patricia. "Arguing about Literacy." *College English* 50 (1988): 141–53.

———. "Beyond Anti-Foundationalism to Rhetorical Authority: Problems Defining 'Cultural Literacy.'" *College English* 52 (1990): 661–75.

———. "Cognition, Convention, and Certainty: What We Need to Know about Writing." *PRE/TEXT* 3 (1982): 213–43.

———. "Foundationalism and Anti-Foundationalism in Composition Studies." *PRE/TEXT* 7 (1986): 47–56.

———. Introduction. *Academic Discourse and Critical Consciousness.* U of Pittsburgh P, 1992. 3–30.

———. "Marxist Ideas in Composition Studies." *Contending with Words* 52–68.

———. "Power, Authority, and Critical Pedagogy." *Journal of Basic Writing* 10.2 (Fall 1991): 54–70.

———. "What Happens When Basic Writers Come to College?" *College Composition and Communication* 37 (1986): 294–301.

———. "William Perry and Liberal Education." *College English* 46 (1984): 447–54.

Board of Higher Education, The City of New York. Statement of Policy by the Board of Higher Education. 9 July 1969.

Boomer, Garth. "How to Make a Teacher." *English Education* 25 (1993): 3–18.

Boomer, Garth, Nancy Lester, Cynthia Onore, and Jonathan Cook, eds. *Negotiating the Curriculum: Educating for the 21st Century.* London: Falmer, 1992.

Bourdieu, Pierre. *Homo Academicus.* Trans. Peter Collier. Stanford: Stanford UP, 1988.

———. *Language and Symbolic Power.* Ed. John B. Thompson. Trans. Gino Raymond and Matthew Adamson. Cambridge, MA: Harvard UP, 1991.

Brodkey, Linda. "On the Subjects of Class and Gender in the 'Literacy Letters.'" *College English* 51 (1989): 125–41.

Brody, Miriam. *Manly Writing: Gender, Rhetoric, and the Rise of Composition.* Carbondale: Southern Illinois UP, 1993.

"Brooklyn College Graduates First Group of Open Admissions Students June 6." Office of College Relations, Brooklyn College of the City University of New York. 6 June 1974.

Brown, Rexford G. "Schooling and Thoughtfulness." *Journal of Basic Writing* 10.1 (Spring 1991): 3–15.

Bruffee, Kenneth A. "Collaborative Learning and the 'Conversation of Mankind.'" *College English* 46 (1984): 635–52.

———. "Collaborative Learning: Some Practical Models." *College English* 34 (1973): 634–43.

———. "On Not Listening in Order to Hear: Collaborative Learning and the Rewards of Classroom Research." *Journal of Basic Writing* 7.1 (Spring 1988): 3–12.

Bruner, Jerome. Introduction. Vygotsky, *Thought and Language* (1962). v–x.

Buckley, William F. Jr. "Among the Illiterate at CUNY." *Rochester Times-Union* 8 June 1976.

Burke, Kenneth. *Attitudes Towards History.* Boston: Beacon, 1961.

———. "Questions and Answers about the Pentad." *College Composition and Communication* 29 (1978): 33–35.

———. "Rhetoric—Old and New." *Journal of General Education* 5 (1950): 202–9.

Cameron, Deborah. *Feminism and Linguistic Theory.* London: Macmillan, 1985.

"Case for Open Admissions." Editorial. *Change* Summer 1973: 9–10.

Cisneros, Sandra. "Little Miracles, Kept Promises." *Woman Hollering Creek and Other Stories.* New York: Vintage, 1991. 116–29.

"City U. Gets Braced for 35,000 Frosh." *Daily News* 14 September 1970.

"City U. in a Crusher." *Daily News* 18 November 1971.

Cole, Michael, and Sylvia Scribner. Introduction. Vygotsky, *Mind in Society* 1–14.

Connors, Robert J. "Basic Writing Textbooks: History and Current Avatars." *Sourcebook* 259–74.

Connors, Robert J., and Andrea A. Lunsford. "Frequency of Formal Errors in Current College Writing, or Ma and Pa Kettle Do Research." *College Composition and Communication* 39 (1988): 395–409.

Contending with Words: Composition and Rhetoric in a Postmodern Age. Ed. Patricia Harkin and John Schilb. New York: Modern Language Association, 1991.

Courage, Richard. "Basic Writing: End of a Frontier?" *Journal of Teaching Writing* 9.2 (Fall/Winter 1990): 247–60.

Crowley, Sharon. "writing and Writing." *Writing and Reading Differently: Deconstruction and the Teaching of Composition and Literature.* Ed. Douglas Atkins and Michael L. Johnson. Lawrence: UP of Kansas, 1985. 93–100.

"CUNY Open-Admissions Plan Found Benefiting Whites Most." *Chronicle of Higher Education* 2 October 1978.

"CUNY Opening Doors to All HS Graduates." *New York Post* 10 July 1969.

D'Angelo, Frank J. *A Conceptual Theory of Rhetoric.* Cambridge, MA: Winthrop, 1975.

D'Eloia, Sarah G. "Teaching Standard Written English." *Journal of Basic Writing* 1.1 (Spring 1975): 5–13.

———. "The Uses—and Limits—of Grammar." *Journal of Basic Writing* 3 (1977): 1–48. Rpt. *Sourcebook* 373–416.

Davidson, Carl. "Toward a Student Syndicalist Movement, or University Reform Revisited." Position Paper, Students for a Democratic Society National Convention. August 1966. Rpt. *The New Radicals in the Multiversity and other SDS Writings on Student Syndicalism* (1966–67). Sixties Series No. 2. Chicago: Kerr, 1990.

Delpit, Lisa D. "The Silenced Dialogue: Power and Pedagogy in Educating Other People's Children." *Harvard Educational Review* 58 (1988): 280–98.

Dreiser, Theodore. *Dawn.* New York: Fawcett, 1931.

———. *Sister Carrie: The Pennsylvania Edition.* Philadelphia: U of Pennsylvania P, 1981.

Du Bois, W. E. B. *The Autobiography of W. E. B. Du Bois: A Soliloquy on Viewing My Life from the Last Decade of Its First Century.* International, 1968.

———. *The Education of Black People: Ten Critiques 1906–1960.* Ed. Herbert Aptheker. Amherst: U of Massachusetts P, 1973.

Duffey, Suellynn. "Mapping the Terrain of Tracks and Streams." *College Composition and Communication* 47 (1996): 103–7.

Ede, Lisa, and Andrea Lunsford. *Singular Texts/Plural Authors: Perspectives on Collaborative Writing.* Carbondale: Southern Illinois UP, 1990.

Elbow, Peter. *Writing Without Teachers.* London: Oxford UP, 1973.

Elifson, Joan M., and Katharine R. Stone. "Integrating Social, Moral, and Cognitive Developmental Theory: Implications of James Fowler's Epistemological Paradigm for Basic Writers." *Journal of Basic Writing* 4.2 (Fall 1985): 24–37.

Emig, Janet. *The Composing Processes of Twelfth Graders.* Urbana, IL: National Council of Teachers of English Research Report No. 13, 1971.

———. *The Web of Meaning: Essays on Writing, Teaching, Learning, and Thinking.* Ed. Dixie Goswami and Maureen Butler. Upper Montclair, NJ: Boynton/Cook, 1983.

Epes, Mary. "Tracing Errors to their Sources: A Study of the Encoding Processes of Adult Basic Writers." *Journal of Basic Writing* 4 (1985): 4–33.

Epes, Mary, Carolyn Kirkpatrick, and Michael Southwell. *The Comp-Lab Exercises.* Englewood Cliffs, NJ: Prentice-Hall, 1980.

———. "The COMP-LAB Project: An Experimental Basic Writing Course." *Journal of Basic Writing* 2.2 (Spring/Summer 1979): 19–37.

Eskey, David E. "Standard/Nonstandard English: Toward a Balanced View." *English Journal* December 1976: 29–31.

Evans, Rowland, and Robert Novak. "The Wrecking of a College." Editorial. *Washington Post* 24 December 1974.

Ewald, Helen Rothschild, and David L. Wallace. "Exploring Agency in Classroom Discourse or, Should David Have Told His Story?" *College Composition and Communication* 45 (1994): 342–68.

Faculty, English Department, City College. Letter. 15 December 1971. Archives, City College of New York.

Faigley, Lester. "Competing Theories of Process." *College English* 48 (1986): 527–42.

———. *Fragments of Rationality: Postmodernity and the Subject of Composition.* U of Pittsburgh P, 1992.

Farrell, Thomas J. "Developing Literacy: Walter J. Ong and Basic Writing." *Journal of Basic Writing* 2.1 (Fall/Winter 1978): 30–51.

———. "Literacy, the Basics, and All That Jazz." *College English* 38 (1977): 443–59. Rpt. *Sourcebook* 27–44.

———. "Open Admissions, Orality, and Literacy." *Journal of Youth and Adolescence* 3 (1974): 247–60.

Fish, Stanley. *Is There a Text in This Class? The Authority of Interpretive Communities.* Cambridge, MA: Harvard UP, 1980.

Fiske, Edward B. "City College Quality Still Debated after Eight Years of Open Admission." *New York Times* 19 June 1978: A1.

Flower, Linda. "Cognition, Context, and Theory Building." *College Composition and Communication* 40 (1989): 282–311.

Flynn, Elizabeth A. "Composing as a Woman." *College Composition and Communication* 39 (1988): 423–35.

———. "Feminism and Scientism." *College Composition and Communication* 46 (1995): 353–68.

Fox, Tom. "Basic Writing as Cultural Conflict." *Journal of Education* 172.1 (1990): 65–83.

———. "Proceeding with Caution: Composition in the 90s." *College Composition and Communication* 46 (1995): 566–78.

———. "Standards and Access." *Journal of Basic Writing* 12.1 (Spring 1993): 37–45.

———. *The Social Uses of Writing.* Norwood, NJ: Ablex, 1990.

Freire, Paulo. Foreword. McLaren and Leonard ix–xii.

———. *Pedagogy of the Oppressed.* Trans. Myra Bergman Ramos. New York: Continuum, 1970.

Fulkerson, Richard. "Composition Theory in the Eighties: Axiological Consensus and Paradigmatic Diversity." *College Composition and Communication* 41 (1990): 409–29.

Gibson, R. *Structuralism and Education.* London, Methuen, 1984.

Giddens, Anthony. *Central Problems in Social Theory: Action, Structure and Contradiction in Social Analysis.* Berkeley: U of California P, 1979.

Gilyard, Keith. *Voices of the Self: A Study of Language Competence.* Detroit: Wayne State UP, 1991.

Giroux, Henry. *Border Crossings: Cultural Workers and the Politics of Education.* New York: Routledge, 1992.

———. "Paulo Freire and the Politics of Postcolonialism." McLaren and Leonard 177–88.

Goldberg, Marilyn K. "Overfamiliarity: A Cognitive Barrier in Teaching Composition." *Journal of Basic Writing* 4 (1985): 34–43.

Gorrell, Donna. "Controlled Composition for Basic Writers." *College Composition and Communication* 32 (1981): 308–16.

Gould, Christopher, and John Heyda. "Literacy Education and the Basic Writer: A Survey of College Composition Courses." *Journal of Basic Writing* 5.2 (Fall 1986): 8–27.

Graff, Gerald. "The Politics of Composition: A Reply to John Rouse." *College English* 41 (1980): 851–56.

Graff, Harvey J. "The Legacies of Literacy: Continuities and Contradictions in Western Society and Culture." *Literacy, Society, and Schooling: A Reader.* Ed. Suzanne de Castell, Allan Luke, and Kieran Egan. Cambridge UP, 1986. 61–86.

Gray, Barbara Quint. Introduction. *Journal of Basic Writing* 2.2 (Spring/Summer 1979): 3–5.

Greenbaum, Sidney, and John Taylor. "The Recognition of Usage Errors by Instructors of Freshman Composition." *College Composition and Communication* 32 (1981): 169–74.

Greenberg, Karen L. "The Politics of Basic Writing." *Journal of Basic Writing* 12.1 (Spring 1993): 64–71.

Grego, Rhonda, and Nancy Thompson. "Repositioning Remediation: Renegotiating Composition's Work in the Academy." *College Composition and Communication* 47 (1996): 62–84.

Gross, Theodore L. Letter to City College Provost Egon Brenner. 3 October 1975. Archives, City College of New York.

———. Letter to City College Provost Egon Brenner. 16 October 1975. Archives, City College of New York.

———. Letter to City College Provost Egon Brenner. 27 October 1975. Archives, City College of New York.

"Guidelines for the Workload of the College English Teacher." College Section, National Council of Teachers of English, 1987. *College English* 49 (1987): 560A–D.

Gulliver, P. H. *Disputes and Negotiations: A Cross-Cultural Perspective.* New York: Academic, 1979.

Hall, Stuart. "Cultural Studies and Its Theoretical Legacies." *Cultural Studies.* Ed. Lawrence Grossberg, Cary Nelson, and Paula Treichler. London: Routledge, 1992.

Hamalian, Leo, and James V. Hatch. "The City College Rebellion Revisited." *Changing Education* 4.3 (Winter 1969–70): 15–21.

Hanfmann, Eugenia, and Gertrude Vakar. "Translator's Preface." Vygotsky, *Thought and Language* (1962). xi–xiii.

"Hard Work Pays Off: Open Enrollment Success Story." *Long Island Press* 12 June 1974.

Harris, Joseph. "Negotiating the Contact Zone." *Journal of Basic Writing* 14.1 (Spring 1995): 27–42.

———. "The Idea of Community in the Study of Writing." *College Composition and Communication* 40 (1989): 11–22.

———. "Three Metaphors for Basic Writing." Basic Writing Conference. St. Louis, Missouri, 30 Sept. 1989.

Harste, Jerome C., Virginia A. Woodward, and Carlyn L. Burke. *Language Stories & Literacy Lessons.* Portsmouth, NH: Heinemann, 1984.

Haswell, Richard H. "Dark Shadows: The Fate of Writers at the Bottom." *College Composition and Communication* 39 (1988): 303–15.

Hays, Janice N. "Socio-cognitive Development and Argumentative Writing: Issues and Implications from One Research Project." *Journal of Basic Writing* 7.2 (1988): 42–67.

———. "The Development of Discursive Maturity in College Writers." *The Writer's Mind: Writing as a Mode of Thinking.* Ed. Janice N. Hays, Phyllis A. Roth, Jon R. Ramsey, Robert D. Foulke. Urbana, IL: National Council of Teachers of English, 1983. 127–44.

Healy, Timothy S. "New Problems—New Hopes." *Change* Summer 1973: 24–29.

———. "Will Everyman Destroy the University?" *Saturday Review* 20 December 1969.

Heller, Louis G. *The Death of the American University: With Special Reference to the Collapse of City College of New York.* New Rochelle, NY: Arlington House, 1973.

Hicks, Emily. *Border Writing: The Multidimensional Text.* Minneapolis: U of Minnesota P, 1991.

Hill, Carolyn Ericksen. *Writing from the Margins: Power and Pedagogy for Teachers of Composition.* New York: Oxford UP, 1990.

Hirsch, E. D. Jr. *Cultural Literacy: What Every American Needs to Know.* Boston: Houghton Mifflin, 1987.

———. "Culture and Literacy." *Journal of Basic Writing* 3 (Fall/Winter 1980): 27–35.

———. "The Primal Scene of Education." *New York Review of Books* 26 Mar. 1989: 29–35.

Hoggart, Richard. *The Uses of Literacy: Changing Patterns in English Mass Culture.* Fair Lawn, NJ: Essential, 1957.

hooks, bell. "marginality as site of resistance." *Out There* 341–43.

hooks, bell, and Cornel West. *Breaking Bread: Insurgent Black Intellectual Life.* Boston: South End Press, 1991.

Horner, Bruce. "Difference, the Negotiation of Power, and Error." Conference on College Composition and Communication. Washington, DC. 25 March 1995.

———. "Discoursing Basic Writing." *College Composition and Communication* 47 (1996): 199–222.

———. "Mapping Errors and Expectations for Basic Writing: From the 'Frontier Field' to 'Border Country.'" *English Education* 26 (1994): 29–51.

———. "Rethinking the 'Sociality' of Error: Teaching Editing as Negotiation." *Rhetoric Review* 11 (1992): 172–99.

———. "Students, Authorship, and the Work of Composition." *College English* 59 (1997): 505–29.

Horning, Alice S. "The Connection of Writing to Reading: A Gloss on the Gospel of Mina Shaughnessy." *College English* 40 (1978): 264–68.

Howe, Irving. "A Foot in the Door." *New York Times* 27 June 1975: 35.

———. *A Margin of Hope: An Intellectual Autobiography.* San Diego: Harcourt Brace Jovanovich, 1982.

———. "Living with Kampf and Schlaff: Literary Tradition and Mass Education." *The American Scholar* 43 (1973–74): 107–12.

———. *Selected Writings 1950–1990.* San Diego: Harcourt Brace Jovanovich, 1990.

———. *World of Our Fathers.* San Diego: Harcourt Brace Jovanovich, 1976.

Hull, Glynda. "Acts of Wonderment: Fixing Mistakes and Correcting Errors." *Facts, Artifacts and Counterfacts: Theory and Method for a Reading and Writing Course.* David Bartholomae and Anthony R. Petrosky. Upper Montclair, NJ: Boynton/Cook, 1986. 199–226.

———. "Research on Error and Correction." *Perspectives on Research and Scholarship in Composition.* Ed. Ben W. McClelland and Timothy R. Donovan. New York: Modern Language Association, 1985. 162–84.

Hull, Glynda, and Mike Rose. "'This Wooden Shack Place': The Logic of an Unconventional Reading." *College Composition and Communication* 41 (1990): 287–98.

———. "Rethinking Remediation: Toward a Social-Cognitive Understanding of Problematic Reading and Writing." *Written Communication* 6 (1989): 139–54.

Hull, Glynda, Mike Rose, Kay Losey Fraser, and Marisa Castellano. "Remediation as Social Construct: Perspectives from an Analysis of Classroom Discourse." *College Composition and Communication* 42 (1991): 299–329.

Isaac, Jeffrey C. *Power and Marxist Theory: A Realist View.* Ithaca: Cornell UP, 1987.

Jameson, Fredric. *The Political Unconscious: Narrative as a Socially Symbolic Act.* Ithaca, NY: Cornell UP, 1981.

Jarratt, Susan C. "Feminism and Composition: The Case for Conflict." *Contending with Words* 105–23.

Journal of Basic Writing. New York: Instructional Resource Center, City University of New York, 1975– .

Kaplan, Barbara. "Open Admissions: A Critique." *Liberal Education* 58 (1972): 210–21.

Kapsis, Robert E., and James Murtha. "Victims of a Faculty Layoff." *Sociology and Social Research* 70 (October 1985): 20–32.

Karabel, Jerome. "Perspectives on Open Admissions." *Educational Record* 53.1 (Winter 1972): 30–44.

Kasden, Lawrence N. "An Introduction to Basic Writing." *Basic Writing: Essays for Teachers, Researchers, and Administrators.* Ed. Lawrence N. Kasden and Daniel R. Hoeber. Urbana, IL: National Council of Teachers of English, 1980. 1–9.

Katz, Michael B. *Reconstructing American Education.* Cambridge, MA: Harvard UP, 1987.

Kazin, Alfred. *On Native Grounds: An Interpretation of Modern American Prose Literature.* New York: Harcourt, 1942.

Keniston, Kenneth. "What's Bugging the Students?" *Educational Record* 51 (Spring 1970): 116–29.

Kibbee, Robert J. Testimony before the New York State Joint Legislative Committee on Higher Education. November 1971. Archives, City University of New York.

Kogen, Myra. "The Conventions of Expository Writing." *Journal of Basic Writing* 5.1 (Spring 1986): 24–37.

Krashen, Stephen D. *Principles and Practice in Second Language Acquisition.* Oxford: Pergamon, 1982.

Kriegel, Leonard. "Playing It Black." *Change* March/Apr. 1969: 7–11.

———. *Working Through: A Teacher's Journey in the Urban University.* New York: Saturday Review, 1972.

Kroll, Barry M. "Cognitive Egocentrism and the Problem of Audience Awareness in Written Discourse." *Research in the Teaching of English* 12 (1978): 267–81.

Kroll, Barry M., and John C. Schafer. "Error Analysis and the Teaching of Composition." *College Composition and Communication* 29 (1978): 242–48. Rpt. *Sourcebook* 208–15.

Labov, William. *The Study of Nonstandard English* (1969). Rev. ed. Urbana, IL: National Council of Teachers of English, 1981.

"Lad Finds Open Way to Degree." *Daily News* 5 June 1974.

Laurence, Patricia. "Error's Endless Train: Why Students Don't Perceive Errors." *Journal of Basic Writing* 1.1 (Spring 1975): 23–42.

———. "The Vanishing Site of Mina Shaughnessy's *Errors and Expectations.*" *Journal of Basic Writing* 12.2 (Fall 1993): 18–28.

Lawlor, William. "The Politics of Rouse." *College English* 42 (1980): 195–99.

Lees, Elaine O. "Proofreading as Reading, Errors as Embarrassments." *Sourcebook* 216–30.

———. "The Exceptable Way of the Society: Stanley Fish's Theory of Reading and the Task of the Teacher of Editing." *Reclaiming Pedagogy: The Rhetoric of the Classroom.* Ed. Patricia Donahue and Ellen Quandahl. Carbondale: Southern Illinois UP, 1989. 144–63.

Lentricchia, Frank. *Criticism and Social Change.* Chicago: U of Chicago P, 1983.

Lu, Min-Zhan. "Conflict and Struggle: The Enemies or Preconditions of Basic Writing?" *College English* 54 (1992): 887–913.

———. "From Silence to Words: Writing as Struggle." *College English* 49 (1987): 437–48.

———. "Reading and Writing Differences: The Problematic of 'Experience.'" *In Other Words: Feminism and Composition Studies.* Ed. Susan C. Jarratt and Lynn Worsham. New York: Modern Language Association, 1998. 239–51.

———. "Redefining the Legacy of Mina Shaughnessy: A Critique of the Politics of Linguistic Innocence." *Journal of Basic Writing* 10.1 (Spring 1991): 26–40.

———. "Representations of the 'Other': Theodore Dreiser and Basic Writers." Diss. University of Pittsburgh, 1989.

———. "Representing and Negotiating Differences in the Contact Zone." *Reflections on Multiculturalism.* Ed. Robert Eddy. Yarmouth, ME: Intercultural Press, 1996. 117–32.

———. "Writing as Repositioning." *Journal of Education* 172.1 (1990): 18–21.

Lu, Min-Zhan, and Bruce Horner. "The Problematic of Experience: Redefining Critical Work in Ethnography and Pedagogy." *College English* 60 (1998): 257–77.

Lunsford, Andrea A. "Cognitive Development and the Basic Writer." *College English* 41 (1979): 38–46. Rpt. *Sourcebook* 449–59.

———. "Politics and Practices in Basic Writing." *Sourcebook* 246–58.

Lunsford, Andrea A., Helene Moglen, and James Slevin, eds. *The Right to Literacy.* New York: Modern Language Association, 1990.

Lunsford, Andrea, and Patricia Sullivan. "Who Are Basic Writers?" *Research in Basic Writing* 17–30.

Lyons, Robert. "Mina Shaughnessy and the Teaching of Writing." *Journal of Basic Writing* 3.1 (1980): 3–12.

———. "Mina Shaughnessy." *Traditions of Inquiry.* Ed. John Brereton. New York: Oxford UP, 1985. 171–89.

Martinez, Joseph G. R., and Nancy C. Martinez. "Reconsidering Cognition and the Basic Writer: A Response to Myra Kogen." *Journal of Basic Writing* 6.2 (1987): 79–82.

———. "Who Is Alien in the Developmental Classroom? A Comparison of Some Student/Teacher Values." *Journal of Basic Writing* 8.2 (1989): 99–112.

Mayhew, Lewis B. "Student Activism and Protest." *Educational Administration Quarterly* 7.1 (Winter 1971): 91–94.

McLaren, Peter, and Peter Leonard, eds. *Paulo Freire: A Critical Encounter.* London and New York: Routledge, 1993.

McLaren, Peter, and Peter Leonard. "Editors' Introduction: Absent Discourses: Paulo Freire and the Dangerous Memories of Liberation." McLaren and Leonard 1–7.

McQuade, Donald. "Living in—and on—the Margins." *College Composition and Communication* 43 (1992): 11–22.

Mellix, Barbara. "From Outside, In." *The Georgia Review* 41 (1987): 258–67.

Mencken, H. L. "The Dreiser Bugaboo." *Seven Arts* 2 (1917): 507–17.

Miller, Susan. *Textual Carnivals: The Politics of Composition.* Carbondale: Southern Illinois UP, 1991.

Moffett, James. *Teaching the Universe of Discourse.* Boston: Houghton, 1968.

Moglen, Helene. "Allan Bloom and E. D. Hirsch: Educational Reform as Tragedy and Farce." *Profession* 88: 59–64.

Moran, Michael G., and Martin J. Jacobi. Introduction. *Research in Basic Writing* 1–13.

Murphy, Ann. "Transference and Resistance in the Basic Writing Classroom: Problematics and Praxis." *College Composition and Communication* 40 (1989): 175–87.

"New Era for CUNY." Editorial, *New York News* 21 September 1970.

"News from Hunter College." News and Publications Bureau, Hunter College. 20 May 1974.

"News: Open Admissions Freshman I." The City University of New York. Press Release. 18 September 1970.

"News: Open Admissions Freshman II." The City University of New York. Press Release. 18 September 1970.

"News: Open Admissions Freshman III." The City University of New York. Press Release. 18 September 1970.

"News: Open Admissions Freshman IV." The City University of New York. Press Release. 18 September 1970.

North, Stephen. *The Making of Knowledge in Composition: Portrait of an Emerging Field*. Upper Montclair, NJ: Boynton/Cook, 1987.

Nystrand, Martin. "An Analysis of Errors in Written Communication." *What Writers Know: The Language, Process, and Structure of Written Discourse*. Ed. Martin Nystrand. New York: Academic, 1982. 57–74.

O'Hare, Frank. *Sentence Combining: Improving Student Writing without Formal Grammar Instruction*. Urbana, IL: National Council of Teachers of English Research Report No. 15, 1973.

Ohmann, Richard. *English in America: A Radical View of the Profession*. New York: Oxford UP, 1976.

———. "In Lieu of a New Rhetoric." *College English* 26 (1964): 17–22.

———. "Literature as Sentences." *College English* 27 (1966): 261–67.

———. "Reflections on Class and Language." *College English* 44 (1982): 1–17.

———. "Speech, Action, and Style." *Literary Style: A Symposium*. Ed. Seymour Chatman. London: Oxford UP, 1971. 241–54.

———. "Teaching and Studying Literature at the End of Ideology." *The Politics of Literature: Dissenting Essays on the Teaching of English*. Ed. Louis Kampf and Paul Lauter. New York: Pantheon, 1970. 130–59.

———. "The Size and Structure of an Academic Field: Some Perplexities." *College English* 28 (1967): 359–67.

Ong, Walter J. "Literacy and Orality in Our Times." *ADE Bulletin* 58 (Sept. 1978): 1–7. Rpt. *Sourcebook* 45–55.

"Open Admission Found of Benefit to Whites, Too." *New York Times* 29 December 1978.

"Open Admissions." News Center 4, WNBC-TV, New York, NY. Transcript. 9 May 1974.

"Open Admissions: American Dream or Disaster?" *Time* 19 October 1970: 63–66.

"'Open Enrollment' Results Told." *Washington Post* 18 November 1971.

Out There: Marginalization and Contemporary Cultures. Ed. Russell Ferguson, Martha Gever, Trinh T. Minh-ha, and Cornel West. New York: New Museum of Contemporary Art; Cambridge, MA: MIT P, 1990.

Patterson, Orlando. "Language, Ethnicity, and Change." *Journal of Basic Writing* 3 (1980): 62–73. Rpt. *Sourcebook* 148–57.

Phelps, Louise Wetherbee. *Composition as a Human Science: Contributions to the Self-Understanding of a Discipline*. New York: Oxford UP, 1988.

Philip, Marlene Nourbese. *She Tries Her Tongue, Her Silence Softly Breaks*. Charlottetown, Prince Edward Island: Ragweed Press, 1989.

Piaget, Jean. "Comments on Vygotsky's Critical Remarks Concerning *The Language and Thought of the Child*, and *Judgment and Reasoning in the Child*." Pamphlet. Trans. and ed. E. Hanfmann and G. Vakar. Cambridge, MA: MIT P, 1962.

Polishook, Sheila Stern. "Collective Bargaining and the City University of New York." *Journal of Higher Education* 41 (1970): 377–86.

Pratt, Mary Louise. "Arts of the Contact Zone." *Profession 91*: 33–40.

———. "Daring to Dream: Re-Visioning Culture and Citizenship." *Critical Theory and the Teaching of Literature: Politics, Curriculum, Pedagogy.* Ed. James F. Slevin and Art Young. Urbana, IL: National Council of Teachers of English, 1996. 3–20.

———. "Linguistic Utopias." *The Linguistics of Writing: Arguments between Language and Literature.* Ed. Nigel Fabb, Derek Attridge, Alan Durant, and Colin MacCabe. New York: Methuen, 1987. 48–66.

Quinn, Edward. Letter to Dean Theodore L. Gross. 30 September 1975. Archives, City College of New York.

———. "The Case for Open Admissions: We're Holding Our Own." *Change* June 1973: 30–35.

Quinn, Edward, and Leonard Kriegel. "How the Dream Was Deferred." *Nation* 7 April 1984: 412–14.

Rapaport, Anatol. *Fights, Games, and Debates.* Ann Arbor: U of Michigan P, 1960.

"Record Budget Asked by City U." *New York Times* 30 October 1969.

"Report Card on Open Admissions: Remedial Work Recommended." Solomon Resnik and Barbara Kaplan. *New York Times Magazine* 9 May 1971: 26–28; 32–39; 42–46.

Rereading America: Cultural Contexts for Critical Thinking and Writing. 2nd ed. Ed. Gary Colombo, Robert Cullen, and Bonnie Lisle. Boston: Bedford, 1989.

Research in Basic Writing: A Bibliographic Sourcebook. Ed. Michael G. Moran and Martin J. Jacobi. New York: Greenwood, 1990.

Resnik, Soloman. Report to Dr. Timothy S. Healy on Open Admissions. 26 May 1971. Archives, City University of New York.

Richards, I. A. *Practical Criticism: A Study of Literary Judgment.* New York: Harcourt, Brace, World, 1929.

Right Versus Privilege: The Open-Admissions Experiment at the City University of New York. David E. Lavin, Richard D. Alba, and Richard A. Silberstein. New York: Free, 1981.

Ritchie, Joy S. "Beginning Writers: Diverse Voices and Individual Identity." *College Composition and Communication* 40 (1989): 152–74.

Robinson, Jay, and Patricia Stock. "The Politics of Literacy." *Conversations on the Written Word: Essays on Language and Literacy.* Jay Robinson. Portsmouth, NH: Boynton/Cook, 1990.

Rodby, Judith. "What's It Worth and What's It For? Revisions to Basic Writing Revisited." *College Composition and Communication* 47 (1996): 107–11.

Rodriguez, Richard. *Hunger of Memory: The Education of Richard Rodriguez.* New York: Bantam, 1982.

Rondinone, Peter. "Open Admissions and the Inward 'I'." *Change* May 1977: 43–47.

———. "Teacher Background and Student Needs." *Journal of Basic Writing* 10.1 (Spring 1991): 41–53.

Rose, Mike. *Lives on the Boundary.* New York: Penguin, 1989.

———. "Narrowing the Mind and Page: Remedial Writers and Cognitive Reductionism." *College Composition and Communication* 39 (1988): 267–302.

———. "The Language of Exclusion: Writing Instruction at the University." *College English* 47 (1985): 341–59.

Roskelly, Hephzibah, ed. "Survival of the Fittest: Ten Years in a Basic Writing Program." *Journal of Basic Writing* 7.1 (1988): 13–29.

Rouse, John. "The Politics of Composition." *College English* 41 (1979): 1–12.

Royster, Jacqueline Jones. "When the First Voice You Hear Is Not Your Own." *College Composition and Communication* 47 (1996): 29–40.

Salvatori, Mariolina, and Glynda Hull. "Literacy Theory and Basic Writing." *Research in Basic Writing* 49–76.

Schilb, John. "Composition and Poststructuralism: A Tale of Two Conferences." *College Composition and Communication* 40 (1989): 422–43.

Scholes, Robert. "Three Views of Education: Nostalgia, History, and Voodoo." *College English* 50 (1988): 323–32.

Schwalm, David E. "Degree of Difficulty in Basic Writing Courses: Insights from the Oral Proficiency Interview Testing Program." *College English* 47 (1985): 629–40.

Scribner, Sylvia. "Literacy in Three Metaphors." *American Journal of Education* 93 (1984): 6–21. Rpt. *Perspectives on Literacy.* Ed. Eugene R. Kintgen, Barry M. Kroll, and Mike Rose. Carbondale: Southern Illinois UP, 1988. 71–81.

Shaughnessy, Mina P. "A Second Report: Open Admissions." City College of New York Department of English Newsletter 2.1 (January 1972): 5–8. Archives, City College of New York.

———. "Basic Writing and Open Admissions." Intradepartmental Memorandum to Theodore Gross. 10 December 1970. Archives, City College of New York.

———. "Basic Writing." Tate 137–68.

———. "Diving In: An Introduction to Basic Writing." *College Composition and Communication* 27 (1976): 234–39.

———. *Errors and Expectations: A Guide for the Teacher of Basic Writing.* New York: Oxford UP, 1977.

———. Introduction. *Journal of Basic Writing* 1.1 (Spring 1975): 1–4.

———. "Some Needed Research on Writing." *College Composition and Communication* 28 (1977): 317–20. Rpt. *Journal of Basic Writing* 3.1 (Fall/Winter 1980): 98–103.

———. "The English Professor's Malady." *Journal of Basic Writing* 3.1 (Fall 1980): 91–97.

———. "The Miserable Truth." *Journal of Basic Writing* 3.1 (Fall/Winter 1980): 109–14.

Shor, Ira. *Critical Teaching and Everyday Life.* Boston: South End, 1980.

———. *Culture Wars: School and Society in the Conservative Restoration.* U of Chicago P, 1986.

Slattery, Patrick J. "Applying Intellectual Development Theory to Composition." *Journal of Basic Writing* 9.2 (Fall 1990): 54–65.

Sledd, Andrew, and James Sledd. "Hirsch's Use of His Sources in Cultural Literacy: A Critique." *Profession 88*: 33–39.

Slevin, James F. "Depoliticizing and Politicizing Composition Studies." *The Politics of Writing Instruction: Postsecondary.* Ed. Richard Bullock and John Trimbur. Portsmouth, NH: Heinemann, 1991. 1–21.

Sloan, Gary. "The Subversive Effects of an Oral Culture on Student Writing." *College Composition and Communication* 30 (1979): 156–60.

Soliday, Mary. "From the Margins to the Mainstream: Reconceiving Remediation." *College Composition and Communication* 47 (1996): 85–100.

———. "Translating Self and Difference through Literacy Narratives." *College English* 56 (1994): 511–26.

Sommers, Nancy. "Between the Drafts." *College Composition and Communication* 43 (1992): 23–31.

A Sourcebook for Basic Writing Teachers. Ed. Theresa Enos. New York: Random House, 1987.

Spellmeyer, Kurt. "Foucault and the Freshman Writer: Considering the Self in Discourse." *College English* 51 (1989): 715–29.

Stanley, Linda C. "'Misreading' Students' Journals for Their Views of Self and Society." *Journal of Basic Writing* 8.1 (Spring 1989): 21–31.

"Statement of Principles and Standards for the Postsecondary Teaching of Writing." Conference on College Composition and Communication. October, 1989. *College Composition and Communication* 40 (1989): 329–36.

Steele, Shelby. *The Content of Our Character: A New Vision of Race in America.* New York: St. Martin's, 1990.

Stein, Gertrude. *The Autobiography of Alice B. Toklas.* New York: Vintage, 1933.

Stoerker, C. Frederick. "Open Admissions: Emerging Concept in Higher Education: A Look at the Implications of a New Experiment in New York City." *Christian Century* 26 August 1970: 1013–17.

Stuckey, J. Elspeth. *The Violence of Literacy.* Portsmouth, NH: Boynton/Cook, 1991.

"Students' Right to Their Own Language." Committee on Conference on College Composition and Communication Language Statement. *College Composition and Communication* 25 (1974): 1–19.

Stygall, Gail. "Resisting Privilege: Basic Writing and Foucault's Author Function." *College Composition and Communication* 45 (1994): 320–41.

Tate, Gary, ed. *Teaching Composition: Ten Bibliographical Essays.* Fort Worth: Texas Christian UP, 1976.

Todorovich, Miro. "By Way of History." *The Idea of a Modern University.* Ed. Sidney Hook, Paul Kurtz, and Miro Todorovich. Buffalo, NY: Prometheus, 1974. xiii–xv.

Trask, Haunani-Kay. "From a Native Daughter." *The American Indian and the Problem of History.* Ed. Calvin Martin. Rpt. *Rereading America* 118–27.

Traub, James. "P.C. vs. English: Back to Basic." *The New Republic* 8 Feb. 1993: 18–19.

Tremblay, Paula Y. "Writing Assignments for Cognitive Development." *College Composition and Communication* 37 (1986): 342–43.

Tricomi, Elizabeth Taylor. "Krashen's Second-Language Acquisition Theory and the Teaching of Edited American English." *Journal of Basic Writing* 5.2 (Fall 1986): 59–69.

Trilling, Lionel. *Of This Time, Of That Place, and Other Stories.* Selected Diana Trilling. New York: Harcourt, 1979.

———. *The Last Decade: Essays and Reviews, 1965–75.* Ed. Diana Trilling. New York: Harcourt, 1979.

Trimbur, John. "Beyond Cognition: The Voices in Inner Speech." *Rhetoric Review* 4 (1987): 211–21.

———. "Cultural Studies and Teaching Writing." *Focuses* 1.2 (1988): 5–18.

———. Rev. of *English in America: A Radical Review of the Profession* and *The Politics of Letters*, by Richard Ohmann. *College Composition and Communication* 44 (1993): 389–91.

Troyka, Lynn Quitman. "Defining Basic Writing in Context." *Sourcebook* 2–15.

Vickers, G. *Freedom in a Rocking Boat.* Harmondsworth: Penguin, 1972.

Villanueva, Victor, Jr. *Bootstraps: From an American Academic of Color.* Urbana, IL: National Council of Teachers of English, 1993.

Volpe, Edmond L. "The Confession of a Fallen Man: Ascent to the DA." *College English* 33 (1972): 765–79.

Vygotsky, Lev. *Mind in Society: The Development of Higher Psychological Processes.* Ed. Michael Cole, Vera John-Steiner, Sylvia Scribner, and Ellen Souberman. Cambridge, MA: Harvard UP, 1978.

———. *Thought and Language* (1962). Trans. and ed. Eugenia Hanfmann and Gertrude Vakar. Cambridge, MA: MIT P.

———. *Thought and Language* (1986). Trans. and ed. Alex Kozulin. Cambridge, MA: MIT P.

Wagner, Geoffrey. *The End of Education.* South Brunswick: Barnes, 1976.

Wall, Susan V., and Glynda A. Hull. "The Semantics of Error: What Do Teachers Know?" *Writing and Response: Theory, Practice, and Research.* Ed. Chris M. Anson. Urbana, IL: National Council of Teachers of English, 1989. 261–92.

Walters, Frank D. "Writing Teachers Writing and the Politics of Dissent." *College English* 57 (1995): 822–39.

Ways of Reading: An Anthology for Writers. David Bartholomae and Anthony Petrosky. 2nd ed. Boston: Bedford, 1990.

Weiner, Howard R. "The Instructor and Open Admissions." *Urban Education* October 1970: 287–94.

Wertsch, James. "The Voice of Rationality in a Sociocultural Approach to Mind." *Vygotsky and Education: Instructional Implications and Applications of Sociohistorical Psychology.* Ed. Luis C. Moll. Cambridge UP, 1990. 111–26.

West, Cornel. "The New Cultural Politics of Difference." *Out There* 19–36.

Williams, Joseph M. "The Phenomenology of Error." *College Composition and Communication* 32 (1981): 152–68.

Williams, Raymond. *Keywords: A Vocabulary of Culture and Society.* New York: Oxford UP, 1976.

———. *Marxism and Literature.* Oxford: Oxford UP, 1977.

———. *Problems in Materialism and Culture: Selected Essays.* London: Verso, 1980.

Winchell, Donna Haisty. "Developmental Psychology and Basic Writers." *Research in Basic Writing* 31–48.

Yelin, Louise. "Deciphering the Academic Hieroglyph: Marxist Literary Theory and the Practice of Basic Writing." *Journal of Basic Writing* 2.1 (Fall/Winter 1978): 13–29.

"You Don't Need a Weatherman to Know Which Way the Wind Blows." *New Left Notes* 18 June 1969. Rpt. *University Crisis Reader, II: Confrontation and Counterattack.* Ed. Immanuel Wallerstein and Paul Starr. New York: Random, 1971. 260–93.

Young, Richard. "Invention: A Topographical Survey." Tate 1–44.

Young, Richard E., Alton L. Becker, and Kenneth L. Pike. *Rhetoric: Discovery and Change.* New York: Harcourt, Brace, World, 1970.

Index

227

Authors

Bruce Horner is associate professor of English at Drake University, where he teaches courses in writing, literacy studies, and song criticism. His essays on composition have appeared in *College English, College Composition and Communication, JAC: A Journal of Composition Theory, English Education, Writing on the Edge,* and *Rhetoric Review.* He is currently writing a book on the meaning of work in composition. He has also published in the field of music and song criticism, and is co-editor of *Popular Music and Culture: New Essays on Key Terms* (forthcoming).

Min-Zhan Lu is Endowment Professor of the Humanities at Drake University, where she teaches courses in writing, autobiography, fiction, and critical theory. She writes fiction and essays on the use of cultural dissonance in teaching and the politics of representing difference.

This book was typeset in Palatino by Electronic Imaging.
The typeface used on the cover was Walbaum.
The book was printed by Versa Press.